In memory of Dermot Lucking
A much missed and not forgotten cousin and friend
I know he would have approved

AN IRA
REVOLUTIONARY
AT WAR

AN IRA REVOLUTIONARY AT WAR

Sean Moylan

EAMONN DUGGAN

Pen & Sword
MILITARY
AN IMPRINT OF PEN & SWORD BOOKS LTD.
YORKSHIRE – PHILADELPHIA

First published in Great Britain in 2024 by
PEN AND SWORD MILITARY
An imprint of
Pen & Sword Books Limited
Yorkshire – Philadelphia

ISBN 978 1 03611 528 9

A CIP catalogue record for this book is available from the British Library.

Typeset in Times New Roman 11/14 by
SJmagic DESIGN SERVICES, India.
Printed and bound in the UK by CPI Group (UK) Ltd.

Pen & Sword Books Limited incorporates the imprints of Atlas, Archaeology, Aviation, Discovery, Family History, Fiction, History, Maritime, Military, Military Classics, Politics, Select, Transport, True Crime, Air World, Frontline Publishing, Leo Cooper, Remember When, Seaforth Publishing, The Praetorian Press, Wharncliffe Local History, Wharncliffe Transport, Wharncliffe True Crime and White Owl.

For a complete list of Pen & Sword titles please contact
PEN & SWORD BOOKS LIMITED
George House, Units 12 & 13, Beevor Street, Off Pontefract Road,
Barnsley, South Yorkshire, S71 1HN, England
E-mail: enquiries@pen-and-sword.co.uk
Website: www.pen-and-sword.co.uk

or

PEN AND SWORD BOOKS
1950 Lawrence Rd, Havertown, PA 19083, USA
E-mail: uspen-and-sword@casematepublishers.com
Website: www.penandswordbooks.com

FSC www.fsc.org MIX Paper | Supporting responsible forestry FSC® C013604

Contents

Introduction

Ireland at War
January 1919 to July 1921

From almost the beginning of 1919 Ireland was enveloped by a conflict that was destined to shape its future. Since that infamous day on 21 January when two Royal Irish Constabulary (RIC) men were killed by an IRA unit at Soloheadbeg in Co Tipperary, death and suffering became increasingly prevalent in the daily news cycle. During each passing month the level of violence increased as Crown forces and the Irish Republican Army stepped up their attacks on each other. By the end of the year, the die of revolution and violence had been well and truly cast and the people were resigned to the fact that the independence conflict was set to continue for much longer than they ever imagined.

That year also saw the emergence of a new political order, with the Sinn Fein party becoming the dominant political force at the expense of the Irish Parliamentary Party after sweeping the boards in the December 1918 general election. The republicans found their political voice in January with the establishment of the First Dail when twenty-seven of their elected number (the remaining successful candidates were in prison) turned up at Dublin's Mansion House to pledge their allegiance to the new republic. Those who made up the new political elite were young and enthusiastic and were determined to set the country on a new course towards independence. They also wished to see Ireland take her rightful place in the new community of nations that emerged after the conclusion of the Great War and the subsequent Paris Peace Conference. That first historic meeting of Dáil Éireann was highly significant because it marked the beginning of the end of British rule in Ireland. Cathal Brugha was elected as Ceann Comhairle (Chairman) in the absence of Eamon de Valera and the meeting adopted a declaration of independence that was rejected by the Unionist Party and the remnants of the Irish Parliamentary Party, both of whom still believed the country's future should be linked to that of Britain.

On the very day the First Dáil convened to establish the political agenda for Irish republicanism, the men of violence, who believed the only way to remove British influence from the country was by the use of the gun, sprang into action at Soloheadbeg. Dan Breen, Sean Treacy, Seamus Robinson and Sean Hogan took it upon themselves, as members of the 3rd Tipperary Brigade, to ambush a convoy escorting a consignment of gelignite to a local quarry and the consequences of their actions, culminating in the deaths of two RIC men, James McDonnell and Patrick O'Connell, reverberated around the country and beyond. The anger over the deaths of the policemen was palpable and the IRA men were condemned by the authorities in Dublin Castle and by the Catholic Church hierarchy. However, there was to be no turning back and the fight for independence was carried to the Crown forces by the IRA over the following two and half years.

* * *

During the early weeks of 1919 Eamon de Valera, the accepted leader of Irish republicanism, was still held in Lincoln Jail for his part in the so-called 'German Plot' of the previous year. With the help of a couple of inmates and the bravery and ingenuity of Michael Collins and Harry Boland, an escape plan was fashioned. De Valera's escape made the news across the globe and embarrassed the authorities in the jail itself as well as the government in London. The incident proved to be a huge morale boost for the republican movement and helped to garner increasing support across the country.

De Valera used his new-found freedom to expand the political agenda and he decided the cause of an Irish Republic should be brought to a wider audience. He despatched a delegation to the Paris Peace Conference led by Sean T. O'Kelly, to plead the cause of Ireland's right to self-determination but the mission essentially failed because of British skulduggery and interference. Undaunted, de Valera decided to visit America to promote Ireland's republican agenda in that country. It was supposed to be a short visit, having been smuggled across the Atlantic on an ocean liner in June but he ended up staying for eighteen months. Unfortunately, de Valera got caught up in an internal Irish-American political row but he did manage to raise impressive sums of money for the republican cause back home. In his absence, his colleagues in Dublin, led by Michael Collins and Arthur Griffith, continued to forge ahead with their policies and looked for every opportunity to agitate the British and their authorities in Dublin Castle.

Unrest manifested itself in an unusual manner in April 1919, when for twelve days the people of Limerick defied the British Army's decision to declare the city and parts of the county a 'Special Military Area' under the guise of the Defence of the Realm Act. That decision had been made after the IRA attempted, on 6 April, to rescue one of its members, Robert Byrne, from a local hospital where he was being treated for the effects of a hunger strike. In the rescue attempt, Constable Martin O'Brien was killed and another policeman was wounded. The army declaration forced anyone wishing to leave or enter the city to have a permit to do so and British troops and armoured cars were deployed on the streets. In response, a self-declared soviet ran the city from 15 to 27 April, during which it printed its own money, published its own newspaper and organised the food supply. The protest was brought to an end by discussions involving the Lord Mayor of the city and its Catholic bishop but the act of defiance underlined the growing sense of displeasure among the people over British involvement in Ireland.

In May, the IRA carried out the remarkable rescue of Sean Hogan at Knocklong railway station in Co Limerick. Hogan had been captured by Crown forces and was being transported to jail in Cork city. His comrades, Dan Breen, Seamus Robinson and Sean Treacy of the 3rd Tipperary Brigade, planned and carried out the rescue aided by members of the Galtee Battalion of the East Limerick Brigade. The ambush of the train resulted in the deaths of two RIC men who were escorting Hogan and a number of IRA men were wounded. The rescue was seen as a morale boost for the republican movement, though there was a sad postscript as two IRA Volunteers, Ed Foley and Patrick Maher, were arrested. Maher had played no part in the raid at Knocklong but both men were tried in civilian and military courts before being found guilty. They were hanged in Mountjoy Jail on 7 June 1921, despite many pleas for clemency.

* * *

During the month of June, the Dáil introduced radical changes to the country's justice system by establishing the National Arbitration Courts, which very notably allowed women to become judges. The new court system was designed to circumvent and sideline the British court system and was set up on the basis of parishes and districts. The new courts were to be arbitrated by local IRA commanders, Catholic clergy or Sinn Fein personnel. The 'Sinn Fein Courts', as they became known, worked surprisingly well over the course of the War of Independence and became the accepted courts of arbitration for the people.

The month of July was notable for the setting up of the infamous 'Squad' by Michael Collins, which was a group of Dublin Volunteers attached to his intelligence unit. This was a full-time assassination unit and its members were paid £4 10 shillings a week for their work. They targeted spies and other individuals suspected of working with the British authorities. Their first assassination took place on 30 July 1919 when they shot dead Detective Sergeant Pat Smith of the infamous 'G' Division based in Dublin Castle. The assassination was carried out under the authority of Dáil Éireann and in September another policeman, Sergeant Daniel Hoey, was assassinated outside Brunswick Street Police station. The killings were the first of many carried out by the Squad during the independence conflict.

The month of September also saw the first engagement of the independence conflict between the IRA and the British Army. It took place in Fermoy in Co Cork on the 7th of the month, a Sunday, when an armed party of soldiers marched to a service at the local Wesleyan church. They were ambushed by the IRA's Cork No. 2 Brigade led by Liam Lynch and the confrontation resulted in the death of one soldier and the wounding of three others. Rifles were captured by the IRA men and spirited out of the town to a safe place to be used at a later date. The following night the soldiers ransacked the town as an act of revenge, during which they smashed shop windows and looted the contents of many businesses.

On 19 December the IRA attempted to strike at the heart of British authority in Ireland when Lord French, the lord lieutenant, was targeted for assassination. It became known that he was due to leave a train at Ashtown in County Dublin and journey by car to his residence, the Vice-Regal Lodge in the Phoenix Park. The plans went awry and French escaped in one of the official cars, despite a road block being put in place. A gunfight did ensue between French's security detail and the IRA men, during which one Volunteer, Martin Savage, was killed and Dan Breen was severely wounded.

As the year ended the British forces in Ireland became more visible and the men of the IRA felt an increasing sense of insecurity. Sean Moylan recalled how he and his men were always under a nervous strain and constantly looking over their shoulders in case of an enemy attack. Christmas came and Moylan recalled the mist and fog that enveloped the country adding to a deepening sense of gloom among the people. Raids by the military and the RIC had been stepped up and it was clear that the War of Independence was set to become even more expansive and deadly. So, as one year ended and a new one dawned there was one obvious certainty for the people of Ireland. The country they loved seemed destined for an immediate future shrouded in the darkness of conflict.

* * *

As the Irish people welcomed in the New Year of 1920 many continued to hope for a cessation of the violence and that a political solution might be found to the question of independence, yet there was little to indicate their hopes would be fulfilled. Both sides of the independence divide were entrenched in their views and showed little inclination to compromise. As it turned out, the coming year was a pivotal one in the conflict and the country witnessed a huge increase in the level of violence as more lives were lost in attacks and ambushes. As it transpired, the worst of the violence and suffering was yet to come and as the year progressed there seemed to be no end in sight to the conflict.

The year started well for the political faction of the republican movement when it won control of Dublin, Cork and Limerick Urban councils in early January. On the other hand, the men of violence began the year with the first officially sanctioned attack on an RIC barracks in Carrigtwohill, Co Cork, carried out by the 1st Cork Brigade. Further attacks took place during the month at Drumlish, Co Longford and Ardmore, Co Waterford. On 20 January, Constable Luke Finnegan was shot dead in Thurles, Co Tipperary, leading to RIC reprisals in the town including the ransacking of properties belonging to local republicans. In Dublin, on the following day, the Squad assassinated District Inspector William Redmond of the RIC. The cycle of violence that was set to stalk the country for the whole year was well and truly under way.

The day 11 February 1920 saw the death of Seamus O'Brien, the commander of the Wicklow Brigade, in a shootout in Rathdrum, Co Wicklow. The following day, Sean Hales and his unit attacked the RIC barracks in Allihies, Co Cork. One constable was killed and the attack led to the abandonment of many small rural barracks deemed by the authorities to be vulnerable to attacks. Castlemartyr Barracks in Co Cork was also captured by an IRA unit led by Diarmuid Hurley on 14 February, and the following day Ernie O'Malley and Eoin O'Duffy led a unit that captured a barracks near Castleblaney, Co Monaghan. All this activity forced the authorities to proclaim the counties of Dublin, Wicklow, Louth, Longford, Westmeath, Sligo and Waterford, which was a clear indication they were worried about the escalation of IRA activity.

March saw little change in the violence and on the second day of the month, John Charles Byrne, a British intelligence agent, was shot dead by members of the Squad in Dublin. Over the following days, RIC men lost their lives in various attacks in counties Tipperary, Kilkenny, Limerick and Cork including one constable, John Martin Heanue, who was shot dead when he called at a local shop in the village of Bouladuff in Co Tipperary. On 20 March, the country was rocked by the murder of Tomas Mac Curtain, the lord mayor of Cork and commander of the 1st Cork Brigade. He was shot dead in front of his wife at his home by men with blackened faces, who were later seen entering a local police barracks.

Five days later one of the most momentous events of the conflict took place with the arrival of the Black and Tans into the country. Little did anyone realise the havoc this force of men would cause during their infamous stay and how hated they would become among the general public. The following day one of the more high-profile assassinations of the War of Independence took place in Dublin. Alan Bell, a resident magistrate, had been given the task of tracking down Sinn Fein finances and was having some success. By that stage he had confiscated some £70,000 from Sinn Fein headquarters' accounts and was on the trail of more funds across the country. Despite being warned to desist from his work he ignored the threat and was pulled from a tram by some Squad members and shot in broad daylight.

* * *

During the night of 3–4 April the IRA burned more than 300 abandoned RIC barracks in rural areas as well as 100 income tax offices, and on the night of 5–6 April another 150 barracks were destroyed. On 5 April, IRA prisoners in Mountjoy Jail went on a hunger strike and demanded to be treated as prisoners of war. A general strike on 14 April in support of the prisoners led to ninety of them being released. In Milltown Malbay, Co Clare, the RIC and British Army fired into a crowd celebrating the release of the prisoners, killing three people and wounding six others. On 27 April the Black and Tans went on the rampage in Limerick city as a reprisal for an IRA attack on the RIC barracks at nearby Ballylanders.

The month of May saw Dublin dock workers refuse to handle British military supplies and they were joined by members of the Irish Transport and General Workers Union. The railway drivers refused to drive trains carrying British troops and that action continued until December. During the early days of June, the RIC barracks in Blarney and in Carrigadrohid, both in Co Cork, Fenit in Co Kerry and Drangan in Co Tipperary were attacked. On the political scene, Sinn Fein won control of all but four of the county councils in elections as well as 172 of the 206 rural district councils, and all the republican-controlled councils gave their allegiance to the Irish Republic. The month of June also saw the collapse of the British courts system in Ireland as potential jurors refused to participate in trials.

In July, Alexander Will from Scotland became the first Black and Tan to lose his life in the conflict. He died in an IRA attack on Rathmore Barracks in Co Kerry, which took place on the 11th of the month. Two days later an RIC man was shot dead in Dingle, Co Kerry. Four days later Colonel Gerald Smyth of the British Army was assassinated in Cork city. He had previously urged RIC officers in the city to shoot civilians who disobeyed their orders. Railway workers refused to transport his body back to his native Banbridge in Co Down. On 19 July, an IRA ambush saw two RIC constables lose their lives near Tuam, Co Galway, and after an unsuccessful search to find the killers, the RIC ransacked the town. They burned down the town hall and another hall used by Sinn Fein before firing shots and throwing hand grenades at local people attempting to put the fires out. The last week of the month saw an escalation of violence across Munster with members of the RIC and the Crown forces dying in incidents in Bandon and Clonakilty in Co Cork as well as in Oola and Bruree in Co Limerick.

The violence continued through August when IRA ambushes and attacks caused the deaths of more Crown forces personnel. On the political front, the Restoration of Order in Ireland Act became law and the British government was given the power to govern Ireland by regulation. Courts martial could replace the criminal courts and coroner's inquests could be replaced with military courts of inquiry. On 12 August, one of the country's most well-known republicans, Terence MacSwiney, Lord Mayor of Cork, was arrested and he quickly began a hunger strike which would eventually take his life.

* * *

The first couple of weeks in September saw more Crown forces deaths at the hands of the IRA but civilians also suffered. There was one particularly sad incident in Kinlough, Co Leitrim, on the 14th of the month. A man called James Connolly was shot dead by the Black and Tans when they called at his house to arrest his son. Unfortunately, a deaf Connolly did not hear the order to put his hands up and was shot dead on the spot. On 20 September the conflict came to Dublin in a big way when the IRA ambushed British troops on Church Street. The attack claimed the lives of three soldiers, while others were wounded. One of the IRA men, eighteen-year-old Kevin Barry, was arrested at the scene and was subsequently charged with murder. He was later convicted of the crime and hanged despite international outrage. On the same day of the Church Street attack, RIC Head Constable Peter Burke and his colleague, Sergeant Michael Burke, were shot dead in Balbriggan, Co Dublin. Crown forces retaliated by burning and looting houses and businesses in the town. They killed two IRA suspects and there was widespread condemnation of the sacking of the town.

There seemed to be no end to the cycle of violence and two days later six RIC officers were killed in an IRA ambush at Rineen, Co Clare. The ambushers then successfully fended off an attack by British soldiers sent as reinforcements. Later that day the local resident magistrate, Alan Lendrum, was shot dead as IRA men attempted to take his car and in retaliation three local villages were ransacked by Crown forces. On 28 September, an IRA unit led by Liam Lynch and Ernie O'Malley attacked the British Army barracks in Mallow, Co Cork. They seized weapons and freed some republican prisoners, while a sergeant was killed during the gunfight. It turned out to be the only army barracks to be captured by the IRA in the War of Independence. Again, there was a price to pay as the enraged soldiers carried out a reprisal action by burning many houses in the town.

The month of October saw no respite from the violence, which in fact seemed to be increasing at an alarming rate. The 11th saw a shootout in Drumcondra in Dublin as Crown forces staked out an IRA safe house. Dan Breen was severely wounded making his escape, while two British intelligence officers, Major E. Smyth and Captain A.P. White, were killed. The following day, four RIC constables died in an ambush in Ballinderry, Co Roscommon. Also, that day, five IRA Volunteers died and nine others were wounded when they accidently detonated explosives in Saltmills, Co Wexford. On 18 October, two brothers, Ned and Frank O'Dwyer, were killed by Crown forces in Bansha, Co Tipperary. Two days later, Sean Treacy, one of the IRA's most wanted men and a participant in the Soloheadbeg ambush, was killed in a gunfight on Dublin's Talbot Street. On 22 October, two British soldiers lost their lives in an IRA ambush at Toureen on the Cork to Bandon road. Three days later, Terence MacSwiney succumbed to the hunger strike he started back in August and died in Brixton prison. Two of the ten men who joined him on the strike, Michael Fitzgerald and Joseph Murray, also lost their lives before Arthur Griffith ordered an end to the protest. The last day of the month was a dreadful day in Kerry as ten people died. Two RIC constables were killed in Abbeydorney, while two more died in Ballyduff. In retaliation the Black and Tans burned the creamery in Ballyduff and killed a local civilian. Two Black and Tans were shot dead in Killorglin and their comrades ransacked the town in retaliation and shot a local civilian. Also, that day, an RIC constable and a British Auxiliary were shot and killed in Tralee, which sparked days of terror and mayhem in the town.

* * *

If October was a dreadful month for violence then November matched and eventually surpassed it. Upwards of twenty people died in various ambushes and attacks around the country during the early days of the month. IRA Volunteers, members of the Crown forces and civilians lost their lives, and all before the most violent day of the entire conflict. One particular incident does stand out though, which revolved around the disappearance of Father Michael Griffin, who mysteriously left his residence in Galway on 14 November. His disappearance was reported to the authorities and it later emerged he had been abducted and killed by Loyalists. His body was found in a shallow grave near Barna some six days later.

The month will always be remembered for two of the most notable incidents of the conflict. The first was 'Bloody Sunday', which happened on the 21st when Michael Collins unleashed his Squad on the British intelligence community in Dublin known as the 'Cairo Gang'. Fifteen agents died across the city that morning at the hands of the assassins. The British retaliated in the afternoon by launching an attack on a football match at Croke Park where one player, Michael Hogan, was shot dead on the pitch and fourteen spectators died in the stands. Later that evening two IRA men, Peadar Clancy and Dick McKee, and, an innocent man, Conor Clune, were arrested and shot dead. The authorities claimed they were attempting to escape from Dublin Castle. In total, thirty-two people died that day in Dublin, marking the single worst day of violence of the conflict. The violence continued until the end of the month with further killings of individuals on both sides. On 28 November, Tom Barry led an ambush at Kilmichael, Co Cork, which resulted in the deaths of seventeen soldiers and three IRA Volunteers. The ambush has gone down in folklore as one of the iconic events of the conflict and it portrayed just how organised and ruthless the IRA flying columns around the country had become.

The escalating level of violence convinced the government to proclaim martial law at the beginning of December in counties Cork, Kerry, Limerick and Tipperary. On 11 December, the IRA ambushed an Auxiliaries patrol near Dillon's Cross in Cork city. That night the Crown forces retaliated by shooting dead two brothers, Cornelius and Jerimiah Delaney, in their home, both of whom were IRA Volunteers. They also proceeded to burn the commercial centre of the city as well as the Cork City Hall and the nearby Carnegie Library, causing many important documents to be lost.

The Government of Ireland Act became law on 23 December, which effectively set up the state of Northern Ireland but the requirement in the Act to establish a Dublin Home Rule parliament was ignored by republicans. During the rest of the month violence continued around the country, claiming more deaths and injuries. Even Christmas Day saw the killing of two suspected IRA Volunteers in Tralee, Co Kerry. Two days later, five IRA men and one Black and Tan were killed when Crown forces surrounded a disused mansion in rural Limerick that was being used by republicans for a fundraising dance. On 29 December, the government in London sanctioned an 'official reprisals' policy across the country and the following day martial law was extended to counties Clare, Kilkenny, Waterford and Wexford. The final act of violence of the year took place on 30 December when the IRA attacked an RIC patrol in Dundrum, Co Dublin.

It is clear 1920 was by far the most violent year of the War of Independence and the consequent suffering impacted communities all across the country. The arrival of the Black and Tans and the Auxiliaries exacerbated the tensions that had been in existence for more than a year. Their presence and the intransigence of the government in London and their authorities in Dublin Castle fuelled the increasing determination of republicans to rid the country of British influence.

* * *

The dawning of a new year in January 1921 brought new questions as to what was in store for the island of Ireland. The War of Independence was moving into its third year and ambushes and attacks were an everyday occurrence. The constant reports of deaths and injuries to those on both sides were more or less accepted as the price to be paid for the continuation of the conflict. The last six months or so of the independence conflict saw attacks and ambushes carried out across the country almost every day. IRA Volunteers, often in the guise of flying columns, took on the Crown forces determined to make life as difficult as possible for them. From the very outset of the year the IRA carried out attacks on RIC barracks and ambushed military patrols, often bringing about acts of reprisals against the IRA and the civilian population alike by the forces of the Crown. As the first half of the year progressed the pace of violence seemed to accelerate and every single day brought news of further death on both sides. Hardly any part of the country escaped the chaos and mayhem, and countless families on both sides of the conflict were impacted by the killing and suffering.

The war was also attracting attention outside of the country and it was becoming more obvious that serious efforts were needed to bring the conflict to an end. Even Pope Benedict XV felt compelled to make his views known and in May he issued a letter encouraging the 'English as well as the Irish to calmly consider some means of agreement'. By the last week of June, it was clear stalemate had set in and there was little chance of either side gaining the upper hand. Public and political opinion in Britain was pressurising the government, led by Lloyd George, to find a solution to the Irish problem, while Michael Collins and those around him in the IRA leadership were becoming increasingly concerned about their ability to continue the war.

By June 1921 the British government concluded it needed a new approach to the Irish crisis because there was every indication the independence conflict had reached a stalemate. Discreet overtures were initiated by the British to determine if the Sinn Fein leadership in Dublin was willing to engage in discussions to bring about an end to the fighting. After almost two and a half years the financial cost of prosecuting the war was putting a strain on the public purse. The situation was further complicated by the rising military casualties that the government found itself having to explain to an increasingly sceptical public. In early June the government, in a move of appeasement, decided to abandoned the policy of house burnings that the military were carrying out as reprisals. Cabinet ministers also took cognisance of the unhappiness of King George V over the conduct of the Black and Tans in Ireland. With pressure mounting by the day, Lloyd George felt he had little option but to write to the leader of Sinn Fein, Eamon de Valera, with a view to inviting him to talks in London. In response, de Valera held positive discussions with Southern Unionists and, on 8 July, he indicated to Lloyd George that he was ready to negotiate but only if there was a preliminary cessation of hostilities. The British were less than enthusiastic about that proviso but Lord Middleton intervened and persuaded Lloyd George to agree to de Valera's request. As it transpired, Jan Smuts, the South African military hero and Prime Minister, happened to be in Britain at that time and he offered to travel to Dublin to hold discussions with de Valera. He pointed out to the Irish leader that the best way forward for Ireland was to find a compromise, just as the British and Boers did in South Africa.

De Valera and Lloyd George met in London for initial talks and on 9 July the terms of a truce were agreed in Dublin's Mansion House between British and Irish representatives and the fighting officially ended two days later. Not everyone in Ireland was happy about the agreement and many IRA officers around the country were sceptical of the truce. They continued to recruit men into the Volunteers on the assumption hostilities might well resume at a future date. While some sporadic violence was reported in the days before and after the truce, in general, a peace, albeit an uneasy one, descended across the country.

* * *

Lloyd George and Eamon de Valera continued their dialogue and in a letter to de Valera dated 7 September, the Prime Minister seemed to indicate there would be a very big difficulty in persuading people living in Fermanagh and Tyrone to accept that their counties were part of Northern Ireland and not 'Southern Ireland'. The partition question had resurfaced and once again became the source of violence and disagreement among those living in Northern Ireland. On 24 September, Winston Churchill made his views known when, speaking in Dundee, he threatened a resumption of the war if Dáil Éireann refused to accept the British peace proposals.

On 9 October a plenipotentiary delegation chosen by Dáil Éireann arrived in London tasked with negotiating a permanent peace with the British based around the ideal of independence for Ireland. Under the leadership of Arthur Griffith and Michael Collins, the delegation included Eamon Duggan, Robert Barton and George Gavan Duffy. De Valera insisted on sending his confidant Erskine Childers to act as secretary to the delegation. His appointment was a controversial one as he was viewed with suspicion by the delegation members.

The fact that de Valera remained in Dublin during the negotiations proved to be one of the most controversial decisions ever made by an Irish political leader. He claimed at the time that by being detached from the highly charged atmosphere surrounding the negotiations he was in a better position to make a rational judgement on the eventual outcome of them. The intensive and protracted negotiations continued until 6 December

1922. The inexperienced Irish delegation found itself pitted against the best negotiating team in the world led by Lloyd George. From the outset the Irish delegation demanded a 'thirty-two county independent Ireland', but the British were only prepared to offer a 'twenty-six county dominion', which fell far short of what Irish republicans had fought for in the Easter Rising and the War of Independence.

While the delegation was doing its best to get an acceptable deal in London, de Valera travelled around Ireland in the company of Cathal Brugha making speeches and inspecting IRA units. He spent time in Galway, Clare and Limerick and, in a speech on 30 November in Clare, he reminded Volunteers they might still be required to defy the British and their 'savagery'. He was clearly hinting that preparations for further hostilities should continue to be made in case the negotiations broke down. In Northern Ireland, the Unionists continued to secure their position and on the same day as de Valera's speech in Clare there was no surprise when James Craig blamed Sinn Fein for the recent violence in the Province. He announced that 700 men were to be recruited into the police to be known as A-Specials, while a further 5,000 men would be enrolled as B-Specials. The Unionists were not inclined to believe the truce would hold and began to plan accordingly.

On 6 December news filtered back to the country that the Anglo-Irish Treaty had been signed in Downing Street between the British government and the Irish delegation. It failed to deliver the republic most Irishmen and women wished to see. Instead, Lloyd George got his way and a dominion of the Commonwealth based on the twenty-six counties outside of Ulster was agreed. It was clear from the public's reaction to the news that the Treaty was set to divide the country and be the source of further deaths and suffering. As part of the agreement the first contingent of Easter Rising IRA prisoners were released on 16 December and were welcomed home as heroes. The following day a meeting of the Irish Republican Brotherhood (IRB) Supreme Council in Belfast approved the Treaty, with eleven members voting for it and four against.

* * *

The delegation returned home to a bitterly divided Cabinet, Dáil and country. The Cabinet discussed the Treaty and, on a vote of four in favour and three against, it was decided that it should be sent to Dáil Éireann for debate. De Valera, Cathal Brugha and Austin Stack opposed sending the Treaty to Dáil Éireann and wanted to repudiate it there and then but Michael

Collins, Arthur Griffith and Robert Barton were in favour of further debate. W.T. Cosgrave broke the deadlock by voting in favour. The Treaty was debated in Dáil Éireann from 14 December up to the Christmas break but no agreement was reached. It is generally accepted that had a vote been taken on the Treaty prior to the Dáil's Christmas break it most probably would have been rejected.

However, once the deputies returned to their constituencies for the holiday, many had their views changed when they realised the majority of their constituents were in favour of accepting a treaty that they believed would bring about a peace they clearly wanted. The Treaty was eventually ratified by Dáil Éireann on 7 January 1922 on a vote of sixty-four to fifty-seven, and though the decision was welcomed by the majority of the people, a significant minority was determined never to accept such an outcome. The polarisation that then ensued had calamitous consequences later in 1922 when a bitter and brutal civil war wreaked havoc and chaos across the country.

This then is the background to Sean Moylan's extensive and enlightening witness statement, which he made to the Bureau of Military History in 1953 and is the basis of this book. The War of Independence raged across the country from January 1919 to July 1921 and it was a conflict Moylan willingly participated in. He, together with his loyal and committed band of brothers from the Duhallow region of mid-Cork, went on to play a significant role in bringing the British to the negotiating table for the first time ever to discuss the future of Ireland. Their bravery in the heat of battle and dedication to the quest for independence was nothing short of exemplary. Moylan's statement is a fine testament to all that he and his men achieved as well as the many sacrifices they endured in order to ensure future generations of Irishmen and women might have the opportunity to live freely and peacefully in a county devoid of British interference and subjugation.

CHAPTER 1

The Making of a Revolutionary

> Irishmen, they could not accept the view that they were a lesser breed, that their country was fated to remain a Province. Blindly, instinctively, they held to this refusal; out of it, because they were, intuitively right, came light and guidance and strength to achieve. Ireland would never again be quiescent under foreign rule.
>
> Sean Moylan

On 12 November 2007, the *Irish Examiner* reported on a commemoration held the previous day in Kiskeam, Co Cork, on the fiftieth anniversary of the death of the great IRA commandant and, later, national politician, Sean Moylan. The article pointed out that Moylan had a political vision that he shared with some of the major figures of the revolutionary era, such as Sean Lemass. According to Brian Lenihan, the then minister of justice, who gave the keynote speech at the commemoration, Moylan and Lemass went on to lay the foundations for what proved to be a remarkable transformation in Ireland's economic fortunes that took place throughout the 1960s. Lenihan, in his speech, rightly pointed out that Moylan was not only one of the outstanding military leaders of the War of Independence but also, in his capacity as a politician and statesman, he left a record of achievements in many areas of public policy that enriched the economic, educational and social fabric of the country. Lenihan went on to say that Moylan:

> left us with a set of personal qualities of integrity, honesty, nobility and forthrightness that provide an enduring standard for all holding high office. That is a measure of the contribution which this extraordinary republican made to the profession of politics in this country.[1]

Sean Moylan was born on 19 November 1888, at the home of his grandparents in Kilmallock, Co Limerick. His mother, Nora, (nee Raleigh), spent the last weeks of her pregnancy at the house as a precaution, having endured previous miscarriages. The infant was given the name John and went on to be called Jack by his family. While Nora returned to her home in Newmarket to be with her husband, Richard Moylan, the young Jack remained on in Kilmallock and was looked after by his aunts. According to Moylan's granddaughter, Aideen Carroll, in her exceptionally personal book, *Sean Moylan, Rebel Leader*, this meant that Jack Moylan was heavily influenced in his thinking by the Raleigh family and like-minded friends and neighbours in the area. In his extensive statement to the Bureau of Military History made in 1953, Moylan recalled his early upbringing among people who were dedicated to the republican ideal. He saw those who were around him during his formative years as hardworking people of integrity and honesty, all of whom longed for the day when their country would be free of British influence and oppression.

* * *

To illustrate that view of his own people, Moylan opened his statement with a personal recollection of a meeting he had as a small boy with a man called Patrick Pickett, who was his grandmother's brother. Pickett, a revered man among his people, had taken part in the Fenian Rising at Kilmallock on 6 March 1867, when he had been ordered to intercept a police despatch rider travelling between Bruff and Kilmallock. After disarming the rider and taking his horse and the despatches, he handed them over to his commanding officer at Kilmallock. For that action Pickett was sent to Limerick Jail. While in prison another man was convicted of the attack on the policeman and sent to Australia for five years as punishment. When an amnesty was introduced, Pickett was released from prison and, on hearing an innocent man had been convicted of the crime he had committed, he promptly presented himself at the local police barracks and confessed to it. The truth of Pickett's statement was eventually confirmed and the innocent man was brought back to Kilmallock and given £300 in compensation. In view of the amnesty, it was decided Pickett should not be tried for the crime and he was released. He subsequently emigrated to America. He was a man of integrity who, like his Fenian brethren, could be counted on to do the right thing and uphold the values of all those who lived in that community. It should come as no surprise then that Sean Moylan went on to live his life based on the same principles of his relative, Patrick Pickett.

The incident in Kilmallock also saw two other members of Moylan's family take on the RIC when they and a couple of hundred other attackers surrounded the local barracks. Ned Raleigh, Moylan's maternal grandfather and Batt Raleigh, his grand-uncle, were willing participants in the skirmish and when reinforcements arrived to aid the besieged policemen, they hotfooted it away to safety. Both men were shoemakers by trade and worked in the local workhouse; and while Ned Raleigh managed to stay under the radar of the authorities, his brother had to go on the run until an amnesty was announced that allowed him to return to Kilmallock. According to Aideen Carroll, Batt Raleigh lived long enough to witness another attack on the Kilmallock Barracks by the IRA in 1920.

It was no real surprise that the young Jack Moylan became immersed in the republican ethos. As well as being surrounded by people who gloried in Kilmallock's and Ireland's rebellious past, he was living in a town where physical reminders of altercations with the British abounded. Streets were named after past rebellion leaders and there was a monument commemorating an unknown Fenian. Parades were held annually to remember the rebellious past and old men often took the opportunity to talk of the bravery of men, local and national, who had struck out for Ireland's freedom. Moylan always maintained that the 1798 Centenary celebrations introduced him to Irish history. He recalled the fireside gatherings when he listened to the local schoolmaster read the history of the rebellion when it was published in weekly instalments in the newspaper. He was struck by the impassioned comments of the old men as they decried English justice that, of course, many of them had experienced during their lifetimes. Moylan, in later years, always claimed he began his hatred of British rule in Ireland during those heady days.

* * *

While Jack Moylan was living with his relatives in Kilmallock, his parents continued to live in Newmarket. His father was, by that time, running a successful building business in the town but tragedy struck in 1900 when he fell ill to pneumonia after a bad wetting and it eventually evolved into tuberculosis. Richard Moylan died after some months of being nursed by his wife, leaving behind five young children, of which Jack was the eldest. Of course, it was inevitable that the family's financial circumstances should change and Nora was forced to make ends meet by using her millinery skills and by setting up a grocery shop. Jack returned to Newmarket after his father's death to live permanently with his mother and his siblings, Ned, Joe, Mamie and Gret.

In contrast to Kilmallock, there was no tradition of Fenianism in Newmarket and the people were not really interested in the politics of the past or the nationalist future. In fact, the most prominent people in Newmarket were Unionist in their outlook. The local bank manager and his assistants were of that disposition, as were the local stationmaster, the petty sessions clerk and the postmaster. They all had, it seems, a definite loyalty to England and no loyalty to the ideal of Irish nationalism. There was a tradition in Newmarket of holding a concert once or twice a year to raise funds in support of the local Harriers and the evening invariably came to an end with the singing of 'God Save the King.' On one occasion, Moylan's younger brother, Joe, sang a rendition of 'God Save Ireland' in opposition to the anthem, leading to the hall descending into chaos and the nationalists in the audience milling out on to the street cheering and laughing. It turned out to be the last ever Foxhound concert and Moylan always claimed that he noticed the first signs of political change in the community that evening.

In 1904, Moylan joined the recently established Gaelic League branch in Newmarket and began a lifelong love affair with the Irish language. While attending classes he came into contact with people who discussed the merits of Sinn Fein and Arthur Griffith. Moylan had barely heard of Sinn Fein at the time and knew nothing about the party. He asked questions of those who were in the know and soon realised it was a political movement to which he could relate. The following year, he left his national school at Drominarigle and sat the Great Southern Railway Company entrance examination, which he passed with flying colours. However, no position was offered to him and his mother took the decision that he should begin an apprenticeship in carpentry, his father's trade, with a view to his resuming the family building business. Because of that decision, Jack Moylan returned to Kilmallock to take up the carpentry apprenticeship, with which he was not particularly enamoured. He persevered with the work more out of a sense of duty to his mother than of his love for the trade. In her book, Aideen Carroll provided us with a very enlightening description of the teenage Jack Moylan who, she said, was much more interested in taking up a book than a hammer. She wrote:

> Moylan was an energetic young man of average height and sturdy build. He had thick, dark, unruly hair, a strong Roman nose and a wide engaging smile. He appears to have been a thoughtful young man with conventional aspirations and was inclined to keep the company of adults. He read Charles Dickens, William Makepeace, Thackeray, George Eliot and

> Antony Trollope, as well as any newspapers he could lay his hands on, although his grandfather Ned had the annoying habit of sitting on the *Limerick Leader* while he read the *Freeman's Journal*.[2]

Moylan joined the Kilmallock branch of the Irish Volunteers in 1913, the final year of his apprenticeship, but was not impressed by those who joined with him. He believed many of his fellow recruits saw the organisation as just another arm of the Irish Parliamentary Party and he terminated his membership of the branch. With his apprenticeship complete, he moved back to Newmarket in April 1914 to run the Moylan family business, involving the sale of ironmongery and agricultural implements. His grandmother, Mary Noonan Moylan, who, seemingly, was a very astute business woman, had been acting as overseer. The wider Moylan family was much involved in business in the town, as his mother continued to run her grocery shop there while three of his aunts, Maud, Kate and Annri, ran refreshment rooms.

Moylan was a keen sportsman and he joined the Gaelic Athletic Association, playing hurling and football. He was, by all accounts, a better footballer than hurler, having been a member of the Kilmallock team that won the county championship in 1908 and 1909, playing in the half-forward line. In June 1914, a Volunteers Company was set up in Newmarket and initially attracted some two hundred recruits. According to Moylan, most of them had no idea about soldiering or the soldier's way of life. In fact, he described them as:

> a gay irresponsible crowd of young men attracted for the moment by the drilling, marching and shouted orders.[3]

However, he always held the view later in life that some of his early Volunteers comrades eventually became first-class material for military purposes and that they went on to prove themselves during the following years when they joined the IRA. The nightly drills before the outbreak of the First World War were attended by the more Unionist-minded members of the community, all of whom hoped the young men they were watching would eventually join the British Army to fight in the trenches of France and elsewhere. Unfortunately for the Volunteers organisation, the early enthusiasm soon dissipated and by the time war was declared in the first week of August 1914, only eight men remained in the company. Of that number, Moylan recalled, one was killed in action on IRA duty in 1921, while another was sentenced to death in the same year and two others died prematurely of wounds and disease while on active service.

Late in 1914, a Volunteers organiser, Tom McCarthy, arrived in the area and stayed around for a few months. He worked hard at the job but met with little enthusiasm and had a very difficult task convincing men that a fight was necessary to attain independence. The 1916 Easter Rising mostly passed the Newmarket community by and Moylan claimed the lack of interest and enthusiasm may well have been down to the absence of clear and explicit orders emanating from Dublin. Had there been clarity, he was sure there would have been attempts by some young men to fight in pockets around the country but probably not much more than that. As it was, he claimed, the lack of a coherent country-wide Volunteers organisation added to a distinct lack of arms as well as no general will to fight meant the rising remained essentially a Dublin-centric event.

* * *

Nevertheless, the twenty-seven-year-old Moylan, together with some other young men, did mobilise on Easter Sunday about a mile outside Newmarket at a place called Barley Hill. However, they went home somewhat dejected in the evening after waiting around all day for orders to arrive from Dublin. Despite the lack of enthusiasm in Newmarket for the nationalist ideal, Moylan and a few other Volunteers continued to meet and drill in secret, sometimes half-heartedly. The other problem, he maintained, was the fact that he and his comrades were living in an isolated rural district and their only contact with the outside world was via the daily newspaper, which was generally filled with news of the war rather than any information or comment on the Volunteers.

Yet, despite the fact that little happened in Newmarket during the rebellion, Moylan continued to believe many young men in Cork and elsewhere were willing to fight for their country's independence and had a firm allegiance to their own land. Though leaders had died and other men had been imprisoned, Moylan was convinced the Irish people continued to hold the ideal of an independent republic dear to their hearts and they were willing to fight for it on another day. In his witness statement, Moylan recalled that once the prisoners arrested after the Easter Rising had been released in December 1916, it did not take long for what had initially been an insurrection to quickly evolve into revolution and, as he admitted:

> Whether I intended it or not I became one of its organisers. I was never again to follow my humdrum occupation, to live my 'quiet uneventful life'. I was to travel many a weary mile, to make good friends and bitter enemies, to develop endless patience and tolerance, to know wounds and hunger and weariness of spirit, to learn how fear is conquered and to stand at last in the shadows of the gallows tree.[4]

By the middle of 1917 it was clear that Moylan's life was undergoing a major change. Even football took a back seat, despite him having won another county championship medal in 1916. His life as a humble carpenter was coming to an end and he was set to make a considerable name for himself, not only as a military leader but also as a very influential member of the republican leadership and elite.

The year 1917 was a pivotal one in Irish politics with the emergence of Sinn Fein as a credible political party with the ability to challenge the Irish Parliamentary Party. Count Plunkett's victory for Sinn Fein in the Roscommon by-election was the catalyst for a seismic political earthquake in Ireland and his success was followed during the year with victories for Joe McGuinness, Eamon de Valera and W.T. Cosgrave. In Cork, as in other counties, the Volunteers underwent a reorganisation and Moylan was present at the first meeting to set the campaign in motion. He was appointed to take over the Newmarket battalion, which represented his first real foray into the realms of military leadership. He recalled in his witness statement how life for him and his men in the battalion changed dramatically.

They began to engage in a physical training regime, which he believed played an important role in developing each man's character. They all enthusiastically took part in long-distance cycling on bad roads as well as punishing sessions of drilling, marching and training as they prepared for what essentially would be the fight of their lives. Their main problem though was the lack of arms and ammunition, which of course was not just a Newmarket one. The neighbouring battalions in Charleville and Millstreet also bemoaned the lack of arms and ammunition, though they probably had more than the few guns the Newmarket men had. During the last few months of 1917, Moylan and his men carried out some arms raids on the RIC, but to no avail, and it was only in March 1918 that he managed to secure a rifle for himself.

By the early months of 1918 the often-reluctant carpenter had fully immersed himself in Sinn Fein and in his role as a military leader. He was still living at home and his life was very different to that of his siblings. His brother, Joe, was studying for a degree, having secured a scholarship, while Ned had emigrated to America and joined the army there to fight on the Western Front. He attained the rank of captain and was awarded the French Croix de Guerre for bravery in the field. In Ireland the conscription controversy occupied many minds and the Volunteers experienced a surge in numbers. That brought with it an increased sense of uncontrolled enthusiasm, as outlined by Carroll in her book when she recalled how:

> Jerry Scannell, the Kiskeam company O/C, decided to attack Newmarket Barracks. About 150 men turned out. Dan Flynn recalled that the company was armed with all kinds of weapons: 'shotguns, slashers, pikes, pick handles'.
>
> They marched for some time, building up a head of steam as they bore down on Newmarket Barracks and 'when we got to Coolagh bridge, about a mile from Newmarket, we met Sean Moylan', standing arms folded, in the middle of the road. This stopped the men in their tracks and the march was aborted. Moylan was developing the habit of command and demonstrating the kind of hard-headed realism that would avoid combat except on ground of his choosing.[5]

Unfortunately, for Moylan and his comrades, many of the new recruits faded away as soon as the notion of conscription was shelved by the government in London. It wasn't long, however, before the RIC began to round up well-known members of the Sinn Fein leadership because of the infamous and ill-fated 'German Plot' conspiracy, which spuriously claimed Irish republicans were once again courting Germany for military assistance. While some seventy-three members of the party were arrested and interned in England, Moylan managed to evade arrest and detention, even though he came perilously close to being apprehended by the police on several occasions.

* * *

From May 1918 it was no longer feasible for Moylan to remain at home and, like so many other young men, he had to go on the run and depend on friends to provide him with food and shelter. He recalled that he needed nothing more than that. He did not smoke and only took a drink when, as he said:

> his wearied muscle had to be flogged to meet unexpected demands or as a remedy for complaints caught from soaking rain and chilling winds.[6]

He did though, as he often pointed out, welcome the delivery of a pound note and some underclothing from home.

Moylan often mused on the early development of the Irish Republican Army, which he maintained was reconstituted in 1917. He believed the organisation came to have widespread support and became effective to a remarkable degree in a short period of time. Lacking financial muscle and resources and somewhat devoid of equipment, it was created by men of selfless purpose and indomitable energy. He also believed the IRA did not emerge as a result of clearly conceived plans but was borne out of an uprising by the people that had its roots in a long tradition of resistance.

It was Moylan's firm belief that the IRA had been lucky to escape the control of professional soldiers and had, from the outset, veered towards the traditional guerrilla tactics based on locally organised clans. However, he was at pains to point out that some control and direction did emanate from the Dublin headquarters, but it was much more of a general nature rather than being specific. He pointed out that brigades and companies were really left to make their own decisions and to take opportunities that came their way to make life difficult for the Crown forces in their area. For him, the looseness of organisation was a major source of strength during the independence conflict with the British and any setback suffered by a company or a brigade in one area did not materially impact on the morale of men in another area. That, as far as he was concerned, was all important to the IRA's overall prosecution of the war.

Chapter 2

A New Life Begins

Arthur Griffith's June 1918 by-election victory for Sinn Fein in Cavan was roundly celebrated in Newmarket with a parade headed by the Kiskeam Brass Band. When the parade reached the local RIC barracks it was attacked by policemen and British soldiers and a violent fight broke out before order was restored. The following morning, Moylan was awoken from his sleep around 5 a.m. in the house he was staying in. The owner of the house informed him that it was surrounded by soldiers and he took the view there was no means of escape. Moylan dressed quickly and looked out the window to see soldiers swarming around the house. He escaped through a skylight on to the roof and dropped a considerable distance to the ground into the yard of a neighbour. He was forced to climb over walls and fences before reaching the open countryside. There was nothing for it but to run as fast as he could for about two miles without stopping and, eventually, he reached the farm of a man he knew well and just in time to partake in a hearty breakfast; thereby effecting a narrow escape. The following August he was spotted by the police in Newmarket near the local school. Standing on a wall, he was addressing a crowd of around thirty people encouraging them to give their support to the independence campaign. He escaped arrest that day but it was obvious he had become a marked man and a person of real interest to the authorities.

The autumn of 1918 saw the country impacted by the Spanish flu and it took, as its victims, some of the most promising men in the Volunteers movement. Indeed, Moylan himself was struck down by the disease and spent a long month fighting the illness and another month recuperating. Unfortunately, and like many others who survived it, the Spanish flu left a lasting legacy that always seemed to impact his general health. When he returned to his duties, his first task was to organise a convention for the selection of a candidate to stand in the December general election in his home area and he was actually nominated for the role but he refused it. He was of the opinion that he was better suited to the military aspect of the republican movement. He also believed that the candidate needed to be a man who had fought in the Easter Rising and his view was readily accepted by others in his area. All this resulted in Paidin O'Keeffe being given the nomination. O'Keeffe was elected unopposed to the First Dáil, which met on 21 January 1919. With no election taking place in his own area, Moylan went to Donegal in order to help get the Sinn Fein candidate, Joe Doherty, elected and, though the contest there was a keenly fought one, Doherty prevailed in the end.

The election campaign in Donegal was a bitter one and Moylan always believed the political experience he gained during his time there proved to be very valuable and stood him in good stead in his later political life. With the election over, Moylan returned to his native Cork, which he described in later years as 'the land of abandoned and destroyed police barracks'. Years later he mentioned in his witness statement how he recalled *The Times* of London describing the same barracks as 'Tombstones of British Supremacy in Ireland'. Once back home he resumed his work of rebuilding the Volunteers organisation in Cork and recalled it was a never-ending process. He and his comrades worked under difficult and harassing conditions as they were watched constantly by the authorities.

* * *

On 21 January 1919 the First Dáil met in Dublin, while on the same day the initial shots of the War of Independence were fired at Soloheadbeg in County Tipperary. Two RIC men, Constables James McDonnell and Patrick O'Connell, were shot dead when they were ambushed by members of the South Tipperary Volunteers. The episode and its impact reverberated across the country and it set in motion a campaign that eventually brought the British to the negotiating table and an end to their 700 years of rule and subjugation. Eventually the authorities caught up with Moylan and he was placed under arrest for sedition in mid-February 1919. He was taken to the Cork Male Prison to await his trial. He was placed in a cell on his own and was only allowed about four hours every day for recreation. In his witness statement he provided the reader with a very vivid account of how he was treated while awaiting his court martial:

> The cold, narrow, stone-floored cell was like a vault. The light from the small window, high on one wall, served only to emphasise the presence of the bars. On one corner stood a shelf, on which were a Bible, a small wooden box of salt and a

> comb, not over-clean. Against one wall was a narrow wooden platform standing on edge, on this neatly piled were several rough blankets. A slop pail completed the furnishings. At four p.m. supper was served. This consisted of a piece of soggy black bread and a tin of some kind of cocoa without milk or sugar, nauseous and bitter. With the delivery of this meal, business closed down for the night. Silence more profound descended on the prison … Breakfast came at eight. Half a pint of cold and lumpy porridge and a few ounces of black bread.[7]

A summary of evidence was prepared for the court martial by Lieutenant H.G. Jones of the Lancers and the preliminary hearing took place in the prison where Moylan continued to be held for some days until his trial, which commenced on 28 February. One of the main pieces of evidence brought against him came from Constable Patrick Rynne, who was stationed at Cullen, and in his statement to the court he said:

> On Sunday 2 February 1919, I was on duty with Sergeant Conlan in the village of Cullen in the County of Cork. On that morning we had noticed posters put up on the walls that there was a Sinn Fein meeting to be held there on that date.
>
> There was a meeting held at about twelve o'clock of about 300 people. Timothy Condon of Coalpits opened the proceedings and introduced to the meeting John Moylan, as Sinn Fein organiser and soldier of the Irish Republican Army.
>
> John Moylan, of Newmarket, the accused who I now identify, got up on the side of the car and delivered a few sentences which I believed to be in Irish but which I could not understand. He then commenced in English. He said, he saw a banner exhibited which demanded the release of the Irish prisoners and that they would never stop until they had them released. They had been slowly murdered in English prisons by the government in consequence of the so-called German Plot, he said. Do you believe such was the case or that Germans were such fools as to allow their agents to fall into the hands of the RIC. I see some of the RIC present. I advise ye to boycott them. Not even to speak to them. Treat them as Ishmaelites. There are some of them good Irishmen but they

> are paid English spies. I never hated anyone in my life … (He did not finish the sentence). We want to wipe England off the face of the earth and English rule from Ireland. He advised the old men to join the Sinn Fein club, especially the farmers, and get rid of English rule otherwise they should pay England's war debt. 'Bonar Law promised them that'. England is now promising land to soldiers. We know what the Irish soldiers got who fought for her. They got six feet by three. Any soldier who comes to Cullen will get a 'land' after.
>
> General Townsend surrendered with 10,000 men to the Turks, he afterwards stated they were treated as gentlemen. Was this the treatment the men of Easter week got from the government? When the men of Easter week surrendered what did England do? She put Tom Clarke, 75 years of age, up against the wall and shot him.
>
> A boy of 17 was brought out and treated likewise. James Connolly, who had only a few hours to live as he was suffering from gangrene leg, was brought out on a stretcher and the English lead affectionately poured into his heart. King George the Fifth of England would be 'the last' of Ireland.[8]

We cannot, of course, be certain the witness was accurate in what he reported as some of the language he used seemed very intemperate. We do know that Moylan was not totally against everything English and we can safely assume he did not want to see the English nation wiped off the face of the earth. Aideen Carroll in her book made a very important point by insisting Moylan was a man who loved English writers and poets and hoped one day a free and independent Ireland would see fit to 'replicate British political institutions'. While there is no official record of the court martial, Moylan referred to it in his witness statement when he said his abiding memory of the trial was that of a prosecuting British officer, a small Welshman. Moylan recalled how he argued with him over the precise meaning of certain words used by the witness, mainly, as he said, just for the fun of it and for the pleasure of seeing his adversary lose his temper. The records do show, however, that Moylan was sentenced to twelve months with hard labour.

Moylan's prison records show he was moved into Wing 10 after his trial, which was specifically set aside for political prisoners, and under the Defence of the Realm Act, he was entitled to certain privileges as long as he obeyed the prison rules. Prison though, was not where he wanted to be, though he did say in later years that being sentenced to time behind bars was viewed by many of his comrades as a badge of honour though he did not subscribe to that thought. As he settled into prison life, he was conscious the country was experiencing some real political unrest and a number of counties had been proclaimed, most especially in Munster. Notices were appearing in many areas setting out the powers of the police and the orders that had been made by the authorities. Some of these orders declared certain organisations as illegal, banned markets and imposed curfews as well as forbid transportation by car. Parades were also banned and police were given extended powers of arrest and detention.

It wasn't long before Moylan began a hunger strike and he recalled in his witness statement how he was tempted by the prison authorities with specially prepared delicacies as they tried to get him to eat. He refused to succumb to the temptations put before him and he was eventually taken to the prison hospital in a weak and an emaciated condition. While there he managed to formulate a plan to get himself out of the jail with the help of fellow inmates and, one in particular, Martin Beckett from Kilgarvan. He suggested that Moylan should simply pretend to be mad and his fellow prisoners agreed to play along with the ruse. They made it clear to the warders that Moylan came from a family noted for madness and that they were not prepared to share their cells with him because he was mentally unstable.

* * *

Initially, the warders did not buy into the notion of madness but Moylan played the role magnificently and very quickly the prison authorities decided to transfer him to a civilian hospital in Cork city. On 4 April he was certified by the prison medical staff as being insane and he was transferred to the Cork Lunatic Asylum. He recalled that day vividly in his witness statement:

> Early in the morning came the governor, the doctor and a mental specialist. I maintained my position and my silence. They departed, an hour passed and then came four warders. They dressed me while I lay passive on the bed, hauled me downstairs in their arms, put me in a cab and delivered me at a city hospital. Here I spent a day still speechless, still refusing

> food. Early the following day Tomas MacCurtain, the brigade O/C, came to see me, looked at me without speaking.
>
> There was no need for speech, we understood each other.[9]

A few days later the hospital had a number of visitors who took up positions quietly at doorways and on corridors. Within ten minutes, Moylan recalled, he was speeding to the mountains in the company of his comrades. However, it took some time for him to recover fully from his hunger strike, and he always claimed that, combined with the Spanish flu of a year earlier, it had taken a lot out of him physically. His health was, to all intents and purposes, broken and he spent the next few months recuperating at Ring College outside Dungarvan. He spent much of his time appraising himself with the many international events of that time and most especially in relation to all that was happening at the Paris Peace Conferences.

During Moylan's enforced absence from his home area, the Volunteers organisation there began to deteriorate alarmingly and, on his return, he had no option but to begin an endless round of meetings and trips designed to fire up the flame of independence among the young men of Cork. The added problem of having few serviceable arms did not help matters and he recalled there was, at that time, no possibility of staging attacks on existing RIC barracks. Attacks or ambushes on military patrols were also out of the question, and he recalled in his witness statement the frustrations of not being able to engage with the enemy, especially the RIC and military bicycle patrols, many of which, appeared at public functions such as race meetings, hurling matches and feiseannas. Though the Volunteers may not have been able to engage the enemy in a firefight, they did, however, endeavour to make life as difficult as they could for the police and the military. It was not uncommon for broken glass to be strewn across the road prior to the passing of a bicycle patrol, which of course caused no end of punctures and chaos. Another ploy was the strategic placing of wire across the road around dusk, which brought down many of the enemy as they passed by on their bicycles. There was, of course, an element of danger attached to these activities, which Moylan contended fired up the determination of his men to eventually carry out much more violent attacks on the enemy.

* * *

While many of these activities might have seemed somewhat harmless in light of what was to later unfold during the War of Independence, they did, in Moylan's opinion, create a sense of purpose among his men and contributed greatly to building up a background of popular support among the ordinary people in an area. He also maintained the gathering of intelligence, no matter how basic, proved to be very useful and no movement of the RIC or the military went unnoticed. Moylan recalled how the accumulation of intelligence made it possible for the IRA to stage what is generally accepted to be the first meaningful attack on British forces in Ireland.

In his witness statement he set out how the IRA intelligence officers in the Fermoy Company had observed for some time the Church Parade of British troops every Sunday morning. About twenty to thirty soldiers usually attended a service in the Wesleyan Chapel, having marched from their barracks. Liam Lynch, the company commandant, and Lar Conlon, who was later to become battalion commandant, formulated a plan of attack designed to capture the soldiers' rifles. Having gathered whatever small arms they could find, they selected a group of dependable men and accepted some assistance from the Mallow Company. On the chosen morning in early September, 1919, they confronted the soldiers outside the church and successfully captured two dozen rifles in an engagement that cost the life of a British soldier and resulted in the sacking of the town by his comrades the following night. Lynch and his men quickly dispersed despite the fact that thousands of soldiers and hundreds of policemen put in place many roadblocks and ruthlessly carried out raids, during which they destroyed property and assaulted civilians.

Moylan, because of his poor health at the time, was not part of the Fermoy attack but he later claimed the real test for his organisation was how to keep the cache and he was particularly pleased his comrades had managed to spirit the rifles across the county in a prearranged relay of men to very remote districts outside the immediate area of the military and police search. He later pointed out that hundreds of men were employed in the operation and it was also important to note, he said, that not one of the them revealed where the rifles were eventually stored or how they got to their final destinations. The impact on the IRA, he went on to claim, was profound in the sense that for the first time he and his comrades believed they had the capability to operate as a cohesive and formidable army. He pointed out that while the next opportunity to strike at the enemy did not come for some time, he and his comrades prepared for it assiduously by familiarising themselves with the rifles while, all the time, learning how to use them properly, often with the help of ex-British soldiers who had thrown in their lot with republicans. In his witness statement, Moylan reflected on how those particular rifles changed the mindset of many Volunteers and helped turn them into top-class soldiers ready to take on the forces of the Crown.

With no visible signs of an improvement in his physical health, Moylan decided to go to Dublin to seek treatment. He managed to get a job as a carpenter, which allowed him to pay for specialist medical care. While he was still weak in body, he made sure to continue educating himself at night by reading as many books as he could and perfecting his Irish language skills. He met Tomas Mac Curtain on one occasion in the capital, passing a pleasant day with him. Moylan attended lectures at Bolton Street and recalled Piaras Béaslaí making a dramatic appearance one night soon after his escape from Strangeways prison. During that time, Moylan had to contend with his debilitating and oftentimes painful illness.

* * *

While he was in Dublin, the authorities were determined to suppress the republican movement with the proclaiming of Dáil Éireann and the arrest of many of its members. Paidin O'Keeffe, whom Moylan stood aside for in the general election, was arrested for sedition and sentenced to two years in prison. Many other deputies suffered a similar fate in a wave of arrests and deportations to England. The month of December 1919 saw a real escalation in IRA activity and included an attempted assassination of the lord lieutenant for Ireland, Lord French, in the Phoenix Park. As it happened, Moylan was working in the area that day and he noticed frenzied activity at a nearby RIC depot where orders were being shouted and men were falling in. Instinctively, Moylan made a quick retreat from the park and, as he recalled, only narrowly avoided being caught up in the army cordon that very quickly surrounded the area. After that near miss, Moylan decided to leave Dublin and, on Christmas Eve, boarded a train destined for Millstreet. From there he walked to Newmarket, eventually arriving at his mother's house as darkness fell. By all accounts he was still in bad physical shape as the treatment he received in Dublin had failed to hasten a recovery from his illness. He remained at home, bedridden, until May 1920.

Chapter 3

A Gradual Return to Active Duty

The early months of 1920 saw the IRA ramping up its campaign against the RIC and the British Army across the country. It was determined that RIC barracks should become the main focus of attention for attacks in the hope they would yield a good supply of arms and ammunition. Attacks on the barracks usually took place at night, when trees were often felled to block any reinforcements entering the area under attack. Telephone lines were also cut to make any communication from the besieged barracks almost non-existent. More often than not, oil and petrol were used to douse the roof of the barracks in the hope of setting it alight and forcing the occupants inside to abandon their posts. The use of Mills bombs was not uncommon and they generally added to the mayhem and noise.

One of the main consequences of the IRA's emergence across the country during the early months of 1920 was the retreat of the RIC from the rural and often isolated barracks to the bigger and better-protected barracks in the towns. By April of that year, it was reported that some 300 evacuated barracks had been burned down by the IRA, the result of a general order issued by headquarters to brigades. The IRA campaign of destruction also extended to income tax offices, of which around 100 were attacked. This, according to Moylan, left the countryside open to a sense of lawlessness with age-old animosities over land, water rights and right of way showing their ugly heads once again.

While all of this was taking place, Moylan was watching intently from his sick bed and wishing he was out in the field commanding his men. It seems, however, his comrades were not confident of seeing their commander again in his position of leadership. In fact, many of them visited him at his home and, as Moylan recalled:

> No one expected me to recover and these were farewell visits … my mind was clear and eventually it became a habit with the local leaders to come and consult with me. Police barracks were being attacked in other districts. There had

> been no such attacks in ours. An attack was planned. It was discussed in all its details in my bedroom. It was carried out unsuccessfully. Again, another was planned and again without success, worse still, several Volunteers were wounded.[10]

A clearly frustrated Moylan decided to take matters into his own hands and defied his doctor, Algie Verling, a Great War veteran and a man who had extensive experience looking after victims of the Spanish flu. Despite Verling's protests, Moylan decided he would lead the next operation and recalled later:

> I struggled out of bed and into my clothes which hung woefully about me. I got outside … was driven to the point of mobilisation and when all was ready marched a further four miles to the point of attack. It was a weary march for me.
>
> A dozen times I lay flat on the road in sheer weariness, but I arrived.[11]

The raid he wanted to be involved in concerned the capture of a civilian gang of armed robbers whose activities had been wrongly attributed to the IRA. Most of the individuals were captured and the IRA ordered their deportations. The bulk of the money taken in the robbery was recovered and returned to the bank. Liam Lynch arrived after the raid and immediately reappointed Moylan to the post of Officer Commanding of the Newmarket battalion.

By the spring months of 1920 the numbers in the RIC had fallen dramatically and the IRA became even more emboldened. The strength of his own battalion increased considerably during the early months of the year and, as a result, an Active Service Unit was brought into being. Unsurprisingly, it did not take long for it to be moulded into a cohesive and determined fighting force. The commitment of the men in the unit was matched, according to Moylan, by the civilian population in the area. The railway men, for example, refused to handle trains carrying British troops and this often led to the dismissal of the drivers and the guards. Moylan recalled how he spoke one Sunday afternoon to the local Sinn Fein Constituency Committee and asked them to collect £1,000 for a fund in support of the railway men. Within a week, he said, the money was lodged with the officials of the men's union. Moylan pointed out that it was not a forced contribution but a spontaneous gift from the civilian population in the area.

In June, Moylan was elected to the county council and that same month he decided to organise a raid on a mail train in an effort to identify those who were supplying information to the RIC and the military. He was of the opinion a raid of that kind on the mails would yield prolific information but, as it turned out, his expectations were well and truly exceeded. The information gleaned resulted in a number of deportations and warnings and an almost complete drying up of enemy intelligence.

In his witness statement, Moylan recalled the raid took place on the night before the initial meeting of the newly elected county council. A dozen men under Moylan's direction skimmed through the letters and put aside, for his perusal, any of which they had a doubt about. He recalled it being a long night's work, which finished up around 6 a.m. when they all sat down for breakfast. Two of the group were, like Moylan, newly elected members of the county council and after breakfast they prepared to set off for their first meeting. They washed and shaved and one of the men drew the attention of the others to the condition of their shirts and collars, which were dirty and crumpled after the night's work. Moylan remembered seeing among the parcels one that carried the label of a well-known laundry in Cork. It was addressed to a police barracks in Portmagee in Kerry and when Moylan opened it he found it contained a number of pristine shirts and collars. He quickly kitted out his two comrades in the confiscated clothing and sent them on their way to the meeting, immaculately dressed thanks to some unknowing policemen in Kerry. Because the authorities soon took it upon themselves to raid the chamber when county council meetings were in progress, Moylan resigned his seat in order to make himself less conspicuous.

* * *

As a result of the raid, the British decided the mails needed to be protected and should be escorted every night to the railway station, with the soldiers remaining on the platform until the train had departed. Moylan and his men got to hear the soldiers were less than happy about carrying out that particular duty. With that in mind he and his men began to raid the mails and continued to do so for the best part of a month. This resulted in the British having to guard every movement of the mails, which placed a greater pressure on their forces. Moylan recalled the last raid of their campaign produced much in the way of laughter among his men. The mailbags arrived in Newmarket one morning accompanied by a number of troops on bicycles. The bags were delivered to the post office and soldiers waited outside for their own letters. In the meanwhile, two or three IRA men arrived in the post office via the back door, held up the staff and disappeared with the bags. The soldiers were less than enamoured when they discovered what had taken place and their 'sulphurous eloquence' remained a treasured memory, according to Moylan, for many people living in the district.

Moylan also recalled in his statement how he had cause to regret that many more laundered shirts and collars had not fallen into his hands or that he had not the means to provide them for his men. One of his first unseen difficulties came early in 1920 when there was an outbreak of scabies among his men. Improper hygiene, lack of underclothing, irregular hours and a deprivation of food and sleep were probably the causes of the problem, which, he said, affected his men in different ways. He maintained many strong, athletic young men were virtually incapacitated by the disease and he recalled Seamus Brislane being the first man to fall victim to it. Everywhere he went, it seems, he left a trail of infection behind him and when it was finally discovered that he was the carrier, the curses put on him by his comrades were, in Moylan's words, 'varied, eloquent and all inclusive'.

The early months of 1920 also saw the imposition of a curfew across the country and, in the garrison towns, curfew patrols were established to ensure the civilian population remained indoors. The curfew, according to Moylan, placed a real burden on the population and restricted life in general. Those working indoors, he maintained, had no opportunity for outdoor recreation, the children had less time to play outdoors and the ordinary and friendly conversations that often took place on the streets of towns and villages became less frequent. Moylan recalled how, in Newmarket, the military patrols appeared in single file, often coming by a roundabout way in an attempt to catch unsuspecting civilians not obeying the order. They were watched, of course, by the IRA in the hope they could mount an attack on them. However, as Moylan recalled, they never got the chance to do so and he put it down to the probability of informers at work within the local community. Moylan did point out, however, that the Active Service Unit in the area was 'pitifully armed' and could only have hoped to be successful against well-armed patrols by way of a sudden rush and swift surprise. But, as he maintained, the attempted ambushes that were laid for the patrols had a positive impact in the sense they set the British nerves on edge and ensured both the police and military remained inside a very confined area of control.

* * *

Though the Active Service Unit attached to Moylan's battalion did not manage to engage the enemy to any great extent during the early weeks of the curfew, there was, according to Moylan, a belief that he and his men were developing their self-confidence and were taking their first steps towards creating an effective fighting force. He provided an example of that growing confidence by recalling an order from headquarters in July 1920 directing him and his unit to cut the police and military telephone wires in their area without damaging the ordinary telephone communication system. Two of his men, interpreting the order in its most rigid form, climbed a padded ladder, in their bare feet, to the roof of the police barracks in Newmarket and cut the telephone wires at the chimney before making a clean getaway.

The continued destruction of the RIC barracks in rural areas meant the traditional British courts could not rely on the police to freely gather evidence to make arrests or to serve a summons. By the spring of 1920, republican courts had replaced the old British Petty Sessions court system and Moylan, together with his battalion men, provided services that allowed these courts to flourish. The courts were operating all over the country by the summer of that year and it was no different in Moylan's area of responsibility. The republican courts quickly became the accepted vehicles for the dispensing of justice and even solicitors who had no real affinity to Sinn Fein found it necessary to accept them if they wished to retain business. Many different disputes were settled in the courts, some of which revolved around disagreements over land. Public order offences as well disputes over money were also settled in the republican or Sinn Fein Courts as they were sometimes called.

Moylan often found himself sitting in judgement at these courts, while on other days he ensured they were conducted in an orderly and civil manner and that fairness was seen to be the basis of all decisions. Parish judges were usually elected by local organisations including Sinn Fein, the IRA and the republican women's organisation, Cumann na mBan. Local trades councils and farmer groups also cast their votes and it wasn't unusual to find the local parish priest presiding over the court. Moylan, in later years, indicated how he welcomed the emergence of the republican court system because at that time the country was plagued by bullying, burglary and riotous behaviour. He always maintained the antisocial behaviour was fuelled by easy access to alcohol. However, most people, he said, took real notice of the republican courts because behind them was the spectre of the gun as well as the severe justice often imposed upon those found guilty of an offence. He also recalled how the Arbitration Courts, as they were sometimes referred to, had no set procedures and evidence was often accepted that no traditional court would ever have allowed.

* * *

In his witness statement, Moylan alluded to a number of cases to illustrate how the republican courts operated. The first case concerned the wife of a British soldier who was forced to leave a rented home by her landlord in order that he could avail of the higher rents that were available in the rental market. Previous to the outbreak of the War of Independence, married quarters attached to the various barracks around the country were sufficient to provide housing for the families of married members of a garrison. However, with the increase in violence in the countryside, more and more soldier's wives were forced to seek housing in the safer larger garrison towns. As a result, landlords attempted to evict existing tenants on lower rents in order to let their properties out at higher rents. The woman in question heard about the Sinn Fein Arbitration Court and brought her case before it. It was of course a problematic one for those involved in the court having to defend the wife of a British soldier against an abuse of her rights. They discussed the possibility that the episode was a ruse and the British military intended to turn up on the day of the court hearing. Nevertheless, it was decided to go ahead with the case but, as a precaution, scouts were posted all over the area the previous night ready to raise the alarm if any military activity was spotted.

When the court was called into session, the irate landlord pointed out the case had already been heard by a law court and a decision in his favour had been passed down. Moylan recalled the landlord making it clear that, in his view, it wasn't the business of Irish republicans to interfere on behalf of a British soldier's wife and the property was his and he could do as he liked with it. According to Moylan, the landlord attempted to pander to the court by expressing his anti-British feeling. Yet, the English woman was allowed to make her case before the court and Moylan remembered her as middle aged, rotund and good humoured, and had the attention of all those present though at times they failed to understand her strong Lancashire accent. She related her sorry tale of how she had a fruitless search for another house, how she had to rear a number of children and keep the household going on a soldier's pay and allowances. Moylan pointed out that though she was an English woman and was a stranger she was, like many other women in Ireland, poor and in difficulties. In effect, the crowd could identify with her and when the court handed down a verdict in her favour it proved to be a popular one. Moylan recalled the woman offering to pay the cost of the proceedings and he informed her that there was no cost. Beaming and obviously pleased with the decision she said:

> Young man, when you need a midwife, you know my address.[12]

In order to show the fairness of the Sinn Fein Arbitration Court system, Moylan recalled another incident involving a dispute between two gangs of poachers over a salmon net. The river Blackwater, noted for the abundance of salmon, passed through his area, though the fishing was reasonably well protected by bailiffs and the RIC. Moylan recalled in this instance two groups of men were indulging in the illegal and antisocial activity of poaching and he and his comrades took a dim view of it and the men were brought before the Arbitration Court. The case was heard and a verdict handed down. All the men were fined and the net was confiscated. Moylan interestingly pointed out that another illusion was shattered by the verdict. While republicans refused to recognise British authority in Ireland, they were willing to uphold the law to maintain order across the country and that stance, he claimed, had the backing of the majority of the people.

* * *

Moylan also maintained that the Arbitration Courts helped to rid many districts of the eternal litigant, an individual who took every opportunity to go to court to lay claim to a farm occupied by another man. He recalled one such individual in his area who hauled another man through all the British courts in an effort to dispossess him of his rightful holding. His efforts resulted in a complete failure but he viewed the forthcoming Sinn Fein Court as another opportunity to make his claim. When he failed in that court he rose in front of the judges and vowed to have the case tried once again in the British court. The case was discussed by Moylan and his battalion officers, all of whom decided the man in question needed to be taught a very important lesson. He was arrested, a mock court martial was arranged and he was sentenced to death. According to Moylan, the man was still defiant but when he faced the firing squad his nerves gave way, and he begged for mercy while promising to refrain from any litigation in the future.

In his witness statement, Moylan also discussed how the IRA dealt with and combatted the existence of bad and unsociable behaviour in its own way and without recourse to the Arbitration Courts. They managed to implement a very robust intelligence structure that was perfected to the point where those who carried out crimes or disturbed the peace were quickly identified and apprehended. Moylan maintained that in most cases it was sufficient just to issue a warning to the culprits and many of them were settled by the handing over of money to those who were wronged. There were, he claimed, the odd few cases that were settled with the forced deportation of those who committed the crimes. He was adamant that all of the above remedies were successful and resulted in a significant drop in crime across the country. In essence, the increasingly dominant Sinn Fein party took the matter of law and order into its own hands and dispensed with the long discredited and hated British justice system in Ireland. The Arbitration Courts operated by Moylan and his republican colleagues quickly proved to be very successful and were readily accepted and embraced by a majority of the populace.

Chapter 4

The Capture of General Lucas and an Escalation of the Conflict

On 26 June 1920 three English officers, Brigadier General C.H.T Lucas and Colonels Tyrell and Danford, all stationed in the mid-Cork town of Fermoy, left for a weekend fishing trip on the river Blackwater. A party of Volunteers including Moylan took the opportunity to stage an ambush of the men and set in train a series of events that developed into something of a soap opera lasting for quite some time. In his witness statement, Moylan made it clear that the initial ambush was staged with a view to obtaining much-needed guns and ammunition. Acting on information received, Moylan and his comrades became aware of the three fishermen's penchant for taking time out and retiring to a fishing lodge near Fermoy. In his statement, Moylan recalled the reasoning behind the capture of the three men:

> These officers were of the class that created and controlled an empire. Why not pull them down and see what made them tick. Why not prove to the Volunteers that they were not endowed with any qualities denied to the rest of the human race?[13]

It was also believed that the commandant of the Cork No. 2 Brigade, Liam Lynch, approved the capture of the officers in the hope that they could be swapped for IRA prisoners being held by the British, most notably, Michael Fitzgerald from Fermoy, who was being held in Cork Jail at that time. Lynch was so committed to the operation that he led it himself in tandem with Moylan and, among others, Paddy Clancy and George Power. They had the logistical support of Laurence Condon and some local members of the Volunteers. They borrowed a car from a local man called John B. Curtin and, in his statement, Moylan recalled the operation in great detail, saying:

> The centre of the immediate operation was a small fishing lodge surrounded by a low stone wall and occupied, we were informed

> by the scouts, by a number of British soldiers, the officers' escort. The Brigade commandant decided that the first step should be to capture this escort and Clancy and I were detailed to lead the charge on the house. My men and I crept through shrubbery and to cover outside the boundary wall at the front. My comrade with his section carried out the same manoeuvre at the back.[14]

Moylan blew on his whistle and the attack on the lodge began and, in his statement, he recalled what happened next:

> At the whistle both sections charged for the front and back doors, burst them in and swept through the house. There was nobody in possession but an old lady, the cook and housekeeper and a young girl. We searched the house for arms but found nothing.
>
> We reported back to the Brigade Commandant, who instructed us to take cover and await developments. We lay in the shrubbery for about an hour and then three men approached the house coming from the river. Two were tall, athletic men, one smaller and lighter. The bigger men disappeared from my sight round an angle of the house. The smaller man came in my direction and I took him in charge. He proved to be a batman. Driving him before me, I came to where the others were. Here those others had been held up by the Brigade Commandant and those with him. The first part of the operation was over.[15]

General Lucas was picked up by George Power on the river bank shortly after. It was all very formal at first as Lynch introduced himself and his officers by name and rank and Lucas reciprocated in a similar vein. Continuing the good manners, the batman was allowed to prepare a meal for his superior officers. Once the meal was taken, the next stage of the operation commenced. Moylan recalled:

> We had two cars, the car I had brought out and that of the British officers. It was decided that the assistant brigade commandant, George Power, would sit beside the driver of the leading car. He was familiar with the area and knew all the bye-roads we had to travel. I sat in the back with one of the prisoners. The brigade commandant sat with the driver of the next car and Clancy sat between the remaining prisoners at the back. We started. George

> Power kept an eye not merely on the road we were travelling but backwards to assure himself that the second car was following. Having travelled several miles, we rounded a bend. Power looked back but the car that was to follow did not appear. We turned at once and a quarter of a mile from our turning point, we came upon a dogfight in the road. The second car was ditched. The driver had just extricated himself from behind the wheel and there was a life and death struggle between two pairs of men on the roadway. I could not help in the struggle. I drove my prisoner out of the car and kept him covered. The little driver dived like a terrier on to the back of the big British officer who was on top of Clancy on the road, both struggling for possession of a gun. At that moment, a shot rang out, and the struggle between the brigade commandant and his opponent (Danford) was over. The British officer lay wounded on the road. The second combatant, seeing the game was up, threw in his hand.[16]

It transpired that Colonel Danford sustained a graze to his forearm as well to his head and was rendered unconscious for a number of hours. Colonel Tyrell was released so that he could look after his comrade at the side of the road but not before the British car was put out of action. General Lucas was handcuffed and bundled into the other car together with Moylan and his comrades. They then drove to the nearest village to find a doctor and directed him back to Danford and Tyrell.

It was some time that evening before the British Army in Fermoy realised that something was amiss and the garrison was readied to go out and search for Lucas. Mounted soldiers and groups of others in motor vehicles scoured the countryside overnight and during the following day looking for him but with no success. Lucas's captors managed to slip the cordon and arrived at O'Connell's farm in Glantane near Mallow at around 3 a.m. on Sunday morning. Being the gentleman, he was, Moylan arranged for his sister Mamie to go out and buy pyjamas and a toothbrush for the hapless Lucas. With the British stepping up their search across the area, arrangements were made with the West Limerick Brigade to move Lucas on. Soon news came through that the British were ransacking Fermoy, where around four hundred soldiers broke plate glass and other windows in their search for Lucas. It was also reported that General Sir Nevil Macready at British Army Headquarters in Dublin wanted to take hostages to swap for Lucas but he was denied by the government ministers in London, who were anxious not to inflame the situation. Macready was, however, permitted to flood Cork and Limerick with thousands of troops in an effort to find Lucas but it was, embarrassingly, to no avail.

As the search for Lucas continued, the unfortunate general, who had become the butt of many a joke in England, was treated very well by his captors and on 1 July a letter he wrote appeared in *The Irish Times* in which he said:

> I am being well and considerately treated. Letters will be delivered to me after being censored, provided they are done up and delivered at … in Fermoy. If you try to follow up the letters they will not be delivered … I have nothing to complain about as to the consideration shown to me. They are doing all they can to provide me with everything I want. I want some money, about £10. I am very glad to know that Colonel Danford is not dead.[17]

During July, Lucas was passed on to the East Clare Brigade under the command of Michael Brennan. He was kept at a number of places including Corbett's in Cratloe and Brennan's in Clonmoney as well as in houses in Tullyvarraga and in Doonass. His incarceration was becoming an expensive exercise for the IRA in terms of supplying men to guard him as well as keeping him supplied in whiskey and food. Lucas was a tennis enthusiast and his captors went out of their way to arrange a match for him and he played bridge nearly every night until 2 a.m. with some educated young Volunteers, including Moylan's younger brother Joe, who were drafted in to keep him company. To his credit, Lucas did volunteer to work in the fields when the weather permitted. He also went salmon fishing one night and, though he was concerned he might be arrested for poaching, his mind was put at ease when it was revealed to him that the head bailiff was one of his captors.

As the week passed the British stepped up their campaign of terror in the rural heartland but there was still no sign of Lucas. There was no indication the British were prepared to swap prisoners for him, and in fact, as time passed it seemed they were less and less concerned about him and his safety. Lucas, however, was always on the lookout a for a chance to slip the net and on 4 August, *The Times* of London reported that he had escaped. The report claimed he was left unattended by his captors while they were organising an attack on a mail train at Oola. Lucas, it seems, removed the bars from a window and got clean away. He then walked through the night and made his way to Pallas Green RIC Barracks, from where he was transported in a tender and guarded by men of the Oxford and Bucks Light Infantry.

However, it wasn't long before Lucas and his comrades ran into an ambush at Oola and *The Times* reported:

> During the fight at Oola he was as busy as the privates of the military with a rifle, and in his efforts to counter the attack of the raiding party he received two, slight wounds, one under the nose and the other in the forehead.[18]

The fact that Lucas managed to evade the IRA as he made his way to Pallas Green suggests his captors may well have been very glad to see the back of him. With no sign of the British agreeing to swap him for republican prisoners, Lucas's incarceration had become an expensive imposition for Brennan and his men. Lucas returned to England just after his wife gave birth to their child. He did make a report on his experience for his superiors and maintained the Volunteers were a formidable force and had to be taken seriously. He did also admit that he had been treated as a gentleman by gentlemen during his incarceration.

By the middle of the summer in 1920 the intelligence war took a turn for the worse and the violence increased markedly. British intelligence officers became targets for the IRA across the country and most especially in Cork and other Munster counties. Members of the IRA had to be particularly vigilant and constantly had to look over their shoulders for fear of being captured. In July, Tom Hales and Pat Harte of the West Cork Brigade were captured by soldiers under the command of the infamous Major Percival, the intelligence officer of the Essex Regiment. They were both tortured at the military barracks in Bandon and were later brought to hospital. Hales made a full recovery but the unfortunate Harte never recovered from the brain damage he suffered and died insane. The stepping up of military activity on both sides necessitated a renewed campaign by the IRA for the acquisition of arms and ammunition and Moylan was determined to do all that he could to arm the men he commanded.

* * *

In July Moylan fortuitously obtained some money from personal friends as well as unexpectedly benefitting from an American relative's (most likely his brother, Ned) bequest. He quickly decided to utilise the cash to purchase some arms and ammunition for his battalion and made a trip to Dublin after consulting with Liam Lynch, his brigade commandant. He travelled to Dublin and booked into a hotel, and the following day he called at another hotel where an appointment had been arranged for him to meet three members of the headquarters staff. When he arrived, he found Liam Tobin, Tom Cullen and Fintan Murphy sitting down to lunch as if, as he said, 'they hadn't a care in the world'.

Moylan was amazed by their apparent indifference to the fact that they were being watched constantly by British agents in the dining room. They sat there, he said:

> unabashed in a gathering of which one half at least were sworn enemies.[19]

Moylan discussed his requirements with the three men, all of whom pointed out that it would not be easy to come by what he wanted. Eventually they agreed to supply him with six 'Peter the Painter' Mauser pistols (called after the Latvian anarchist Peter Piaktow, who used the pistols in the famous Sidney Street siege in London in 1911), two parabellums, with ten rounds of ammunition for each, one dozen percussion bombs, a rifle and 50 rounds of .303 ammunition.

The whole consignment was delivered to Moylan's hotel by a man called Chris Harding and the total cost was £120. Moylan was of the opinion that he had actually paid through the nose for the guns and he eventually discovered that it was a worse bargain than he initially imagined. The bombs proved to be useless and, while the pistols were good, the few rounds of ammunition meant they had to be used sparingly. The rifle was the best of the lot and the best value for money. Despite his misgivings about the guns, Moylan recognised the psychological value of having them around his men. They all displayed a great deal of interest in the guns and eagerly took instructions as to how to take them apart and reassemble them.

In August, Moylan attended a Brigade Council meeting and one item on the agenda was the distribution of a small quantity of revolvers among battalion commandants. To Moylan's amazement, he was not allocated any of the guns on the basis that it was known he had secured a cache of arms and ammunition by his own volition in Dublin. He protested but his words fell on deaf ears even though, as he recalled in his witness statement:

> I pointed out that I had taken the risk of going to Dublin and of bringing home the guns, that I had with my own money paid for them, that the revolvers now being distributed were the property of the Brigade and, therefore, that my quota was included.[20]

Unfortunately, all Moylan's protests came to nothing but he was still determined to have his share of the guns, which had been parcelled up and put into another room as the business of the meeting continued. After a while, Moylan excused himself from the meeting and went outside the house. With the help of a table knife, he slipped the catch off the window of the room where the parcelled guns were being stored and grabbed one parcel. He opened it and removed two revolvers, leaving one and substituting wood and stones for the guns he had taken. He then returned to the meeting and on the way home with his great friend and comrade Paddy Clancy he told him what he had done. Clancy, it seemed was very impressed and laughed uproariously as he quickly saw the funny side of the matter. Unfortunately, the guns he took were almost useless and Moylan deduced they had come from some European port where they were for sale to revolutionaries. He was by then convinced more than ever that their British opponents were the best source of effective guns and ammunition.

Moylan and Clancy shared an unbreakable bond as comrades in arms but more importantly as friends. One week after the Council meeting and the taking of the parcel of guns, Clancy was dead and his passing had a most profound impact on Moylan. In many ways he lost a soulmate and a sounding board for all of his ideas and dreams for an independent Ireland. Clancy was a creamery manager at the Allensbridge Co-operative near Newmarket at that time and was due to take up the post as commander of the newly formed brigade flying column. On returning to their home area, they both attended Sunday Mass in Kanturk and listened to Father Bowler deliver a homily that, according to Moylan, was tinged with a sense of rebelliousness that would not have found favour with most of his superiors. During the following week, Moylan travelled to another brigade area for discussions on a proposed joint operation. He recalled being delayed over the weekend and when he opened the newspaper on the Monday morning he learned of Clancy's death.

On the previous Saturday, 14 August, a British aeroplane made a forced landing at Drominagh, near Clonbanin, some 4 miles south of Kanturk. A company of British soldiers was detailed to protect it until repairs were made. Around dawn on the Sunday, a poorly armed group of local Volunteers led by Jack O'Connell, the battalion commanding officer, launched an attack on the British soldiers. However, as they approached them, they were surprised by a sentry, who was then shot dead. The shots alerted the main body of soldiers, who opened fire on the Volunteers and these were repelled after several hours of fighting. The fighting, according to Moylan, brought the British military into the area in force and they began a search to track down those responsible for the attack. Clancy and O'Connell retired to O'Connell's home at Derrygallon, 3 miles outside Kanturk, in the hope of evading the British. Unfortunately, they had been seen by an informer, who passed on the information to the police in Kanturk. Both men were sleeping when it was surrounded by soldiers and police. They attempted to fight their way to safety but were eventually shot dead some distance from the house. According to Moylan, both men defended themselves heroically until they had expended all their ammunition.

Moylan was clearly distraught at the death of his comrades and in his witness statement he recalled:

> They were both shot dead; one a good courageous officer, the other outstanding in courage, character and capacity, the possessor of all those manly graces which endeared him to all who knew him and which keep his memory still fragrant in their hearts.[21]

He went on to poignantly recall how he:

> carried his (Clancy's) body over hill and dale and murmuring stream to bury him beneath the haunted mountain on which his eyes first opened.[22]

He also recalled how he returned from Clancy's funeral by way of unfrequented roads. The general body of those who attended the funeral drove back along the main roads and most of them were held up, searched and questioned by British military personnel and all the young men were beaten savagely. Moylan was convinced the impact of that action intensified more than ever the support for the IRA and also served to add to that organisation's numbers. The following day Moylan met with Liam Lynch to discuss not only the difficulty created by Clancy's death, but also the operational methods employed by the IRA in general. By that time the view being held by many officers was that there could be no real success for the IRA if it continued to depend on ordinary Volunteers, poorly armed, hurriedly mobilised, not sufficiently trained and disciplined, to act as a coherent unit under a responsible leader.

The British were, by then, moving around the country in much greater strength and if they were to be attacked successfully it could not possibly be done by men who were suddenly called away from their ordinary work and expected to use a gun for a few hours before returning again to their daily chores and employment. Moylan then proposed that the most suitable men in the brigade should be called together, given the best arms available and trained to act as regular soldiers. Lynch and other officers agreed to go down that route and a call went out to battalions for volunteers. A quota for each battalion and a date for mobilisation was agreed upon. According to Moylan, the number of men who volunteered for duty in what would eventually be a flying column was overwhelming. Lynch decided that Moylan should take charge of the new Active Service Unit, a position that would have gone to his lost and much-missed friend, Paddy Clancy.

With his new position confirmed, Moylan attended a Sinn Fein Constituency Convention and appealed for financial support, which came the following day in the form of a substantial sum paid to him in cash. He passed the money on to the brigade leadership and it was used to buy arms and step up the training of the men recruited to the flying column. This allowed Moylan to set up a training camp that continued to operate until the cessation of hostilities in July 1921. The camp was moved around regularly to avoid burdening any one area too much in terms of billeting the men. He recalled most of the recruits in training responded intelligently and energetically to the demands made of them. He also maintained that an esprit de corps was created and each company sought to outshine the others in soldierly flair and effort.

The training was in every sense very intense and it started with close order drill and went on to the proper handling of a rifle. Physical training was a major element of the programme and included jerks, running, jumping, wrestling, route marches on roads, where possible, and cross-country marching. There was a course in the care and mechanism of a rifle and revolver and the recruits were trained in the making and deployment of bombs. Sentry and outpost duties were learned, as was the art of signalling. There was also an emphasis on engineering as well as first aid, and within weeks a course in street fighting and silent movement at night had been developed successfully. By the late summer of 1920 a cohesive unit of fighting men had emerged under Moylan's command and was ready and willing to engage the enemy at any time.

Chapter 5

Ready for the Fight

In September 1920 the War of Independence was beginning to escalate at a rapid pace and Auxiliaries were being recruited by the British authorities to bolster the Crown forces in Ireland. By that time the Restoration of Order in Ireland Act, which was designed to crack down on any dissidence across the country, was beginning to have an impact. Under the act the authorities could intern anyone considered to be a threat for indefinite periods and it also gave the British Army the power to try capital offences as well as public order offences. Elected local authorities who were deemed not to be loyal to the Crown were liable to have their funding curtailed or even cut off. Coroner courts were replaced by military courts in cases where the deceased died at the hands of Crown forces. There was an increase in public displays of unrest and protests over British rule in Ireland, with hunger strikes by Terence MacSwiney and other republicans beginning to make the headlines.

Moylan and his comrades were, by this stage, constantly watching the movements of the Crown forces and it became apparent there was a regular schedule of movement in certain areas. For example, they realised two lorries of Black and Tans travelled weekly between Cork and Mallow, though their hours of travel did tend to vary. Taking that information on board, it was decided at brigade level that Moylan and his Active Service Unit should make their first assignment an attack on that particular patrol. A meeting of the Brigade Council was held one Sunday to make final arrangements for the attack, which was expected to take place on the following Tuesday. As it transpired, Moylan was a little late for the meeting because he had to take a detour around a party of British soldiers who were searching houses along his route as well as holding up traffic. When he arrived at the house in which the meeting was to be held, he discovered it had been burned to the ground. He then found a young Volunteer crouching behind a fence ready to redirect him to the new meeting place, which was around 300 yards away.

Moylan eventually joined the reassembled Council members, who were continuing their work despite the enemy scouring the surrounding countryside in search of them. The group was in a solemn mood, which was unusual as it was being questioned by a stranger sitting beside the brigade commandant. The young man, Moylan recalled, had red hair and blue eyes, with a scar across his face. He was clad in guns and fountain pens and surrounded by maps and notebooks. He was, as it turned out, a staff captain from headquarters in Dublin on a tour of inspection and the type of individual Moylan readily admitted to having an aversion to. He was, as he said:

> Prepared to dislike the fellow even before he barked a reference to unpunctuality to me.[23]

However, Moylan did, there and then, recognise that his comrades sitting around the table had accepted him and he seemed to have the authority and approval of the brigade commandant. Moylan recalled he had a robust and lively interaction with the young man, whom he felt was a very serious individual with a sense of his own importance. Moylan admitted to being antagonised by his adversary and he answered his questions with complete inaccuracy. Both the brigade commandant and adjutant were aware of Moylan's approach and they both maintained a straight face but with a definite glint of approval in their eyes. However, appearances, as often is the case, can be deceptive and over the course of the following few days that the young man spent in the presence of the Council members their attitude towards him visibly changed. It became obvious to all of them that he was a young man of courage and ability and that he had, in fact, seen a great deal in the way of fighting. Over time the members of the Brigade Council developed a great deal of respect for the young man and came to recognise him as a comrade of high character. That young man went on to make a name for himself throughout the independence conflict. His name was Ernie O'Malley.

With O'Malley's questioning completed, the attention of the meeting turned to the proposed attack on the Black and Tans convoy scheduled for the following Tuesday. Much to the disappointment of Moylan and his comrades the, brigade commandant informed them that it would not take place. He proposed, instead, an entirely different activity as new information, he said, had been brought to him by a young Volunteer, Dick Willis, which greatly interested him. Willis, was at the time, working on a building contract in the British military barracks in Mallow and the information he brought suggested there was a distinct possibility the building could be captured. Willis had carefully noted the movements of the guard and sentries and the manner in which visitors to the barracks were received.

Willis proposed that he and another Volunteer, Jack Bolster, should be given revolvers and that they should introduce a third man, also armed, posing as a foreman, who would turn up to check on the work being done. On a given signal they would hold up the guard and sentries and allow the Active Service Unit (ASU) an opportunity of rushing the gates from outside. The question of getting the gate open, according to Moylan, was a tricky one and a proposal was made that a member of the Active Service Unit should at first approach the guard with a letter for the officer in charge of the garrison. Once the guard had been engaged in conversation, the members of the ASU would then charge the gate. Moylan recalled there was no lack of volunteers for the operation and O'Malley more or less nominated himself to carry the letter. Moylan put himself forward to act as the foreman but he was overruled by the brigade commandant, who said he was not prepared to risk losing a valuable officer on an operation where, in his view, the chances of success were entirely out of proportion to the risk involved.

* * *

Paddy McCarthy, a great personal friend of Moylan, was chosen to pose as the site foreman, even though he knew next to nothing of the building trade. Moylan tutored him in building trade jargon and produced a draft repair specification for him. By the time Moylan had finished his tutoring, McCarthy was reasonably well informed of what he might expect to encounter on a building site. Moylan then turned his attention to being part of the storming party but again he was to be disappointed by his superior officer, who ordered him to proceed to a district some twenty miles away to undertake another activity or engagement. He was, as he recalled, bitterly disappointed, as were the men from his Active Service Unit he had brought with him, ostensibly to give them some experience in close combat with the enemy. He had, as he said:

> hoped to give them the opportunity of being shot over; to utilise the ambush as the finishing touch to the training they had undergone.[24]

Their disappointment was compounded when the brigade commandant ordered all of them to hand over their rifles before they left the area. They were all very disconsolate on the journey home and there was little in the way of conversation. Before dawn, Moylan reached the safe house he was staying in, which was the home of Dan Galvin. Soon Galvin and his wife joined Moylan in the kitchen anxious for any news he might have brought with him and fearful that something had gone wrong for him and his unit. The embers in the fire were gathered together and Moylan recalled how he turned the wheel of the bellows and soon the kettle was singing over a glowing fire. Galvin, a local schoolteacher, and his wife were completely in Moylan's confidence and he often put great store in their advice and wisdom. That morning, Galvin advised him to put his disappointment to one side and look to the future. Moylan slept well into the afternoon and spent that evening attempting to placate the men in his Active Service Unit, many of whom felt undermined and undervalued by being excluded from the attack on the Mallow Barracks.

The following day, Moylan and his men proceeded to an unoccupied house, where they began to experiment in the making of explosives and land mines. They knew nothing of chemicals but Moylan had set a local chemist's apprentice the task of studying the subject and, from his notes, they carried out their first tentative trials. From that day onwards the unoccupied farmhouse became a well-equipped factory with a staff of skilled craftsmen. While they worked during the day, they all speculated as to what might be happening in Mallow. The attack was timed for the morning and news of it did not arrive until night had had fallen in the form of a brief note from the brigade commanding officer. The note confirmed the attack was a complete success with no IRA casualties, although one British Army sergeant had been shot dead. The arms haul included fifty rifles, two machine guns and lots of ammunition, and the news was greeted by Moylan's comrades with a tremendous roar of triumph. However, there was a downside as the town of Mallow was burned and sacked by the British some hours after the raid. The flames of the many fires were very intense and people living some miles from the town watched in horror as the night sky turned gold and red.

* * *

Moylan recalled he later received an account of the raid from some of those who had taken part in it. The plan had been discussed on the Monday and a large map of Mallow was procured before the final arrangements were agreed upon. Dick Willis confirmed the British officer in charge of the barracks in Mallow was concerned about the inadequacy of the water supply and had spoken to him about it. Willis assured him that he would speak to the town clerk and arrange for a water inspector to call to the barracks on the Tuesday morning to see if a better supply could be tapped into the barracks. The arrangement fitted perfectly with the attack plans and it was decided that Ernie O'Malley should play the role of the Council's water inspector.

On the morning of the attack, Paddy McCarthy, posing as a foreman, arrived at the barracks and had a discussion with Willis about the work being done. Bolster, in the meantime, was working outside the window of a room where off-duty soldiers were taking their ease. Ernie O'Malley, posing as a Council official, appeared at the gate brandishing a letter for the barracks commandant. He was admitted on to the premises and, as soon as he was, he grabbed the sentry's rifle, which was the signal for the others to move. Bolster then threw open the window where he was working, drew his revolver and yelled at the troops to stay where they were. Willis and McCarthy then rushed to the guardroom door with their guns drawn and jumped between the soldiers and the rack where the rifles were stored. A British sergeant charged at Willis, who had no option but to shoot him dead. Simultaneously, a number of IRA men poured into the barracks but encountered no resistance. The raiding party managed to acquire every weapon and every round of ammunition in the barracks before leaving.

Moylan recognised his comrades had carried out an excellent job and their planning had paid off admirably. No one, however, envisaged the act of reprisal carried out by the British military in Mallow hours after the attack on the barracks. Some sporadic outbursts by unruly troops were expected in the town but what occurred went far beyond that, and it did so with official approval. For Moylan and his comrades, the reprisal carried out by regular soldiers on a civilian population was totally unacceptable and outside the rules of engagement. It served to make them even more determined to continue the struggle for independence in the months that followed.

The arms capture at Mallow allowed for the Active Service Unit to become a well-equipped one and less dependent on rifles from the local battalions in the area. By October and, after several weeks of intensive training, the Active Service Unit was more than ready to take on the forces of the Crown. Men were deployed to various proposed ambush sites on local roads, over which, British troops were expected to travel. However, no opportunity arose to enable the unit to carry out an attack on the enemy. Around that time, according to Moylan, the 3rd Charleville Battalion carried out two successful engagements with the British. During one of the skirmishes, Commandant Paddy O'Brien from Liscarroll was shot in the face. He lost some teeth and his jaw was fractured but he was miraculously back in action within weeks. Moylan believed O'Brien's courage was indicative of so many Volunteers, all of whom were determined to see the independence struggle through to a successful conclusion.

* * *

It is generally accepted that the second six months of 1920 was a period of real chaos and mayhem in many parts of the country. By that stage the Black and Tans were well established across the country and, according to one observer:

> They had neither religion nor morals, they used foul language, they had the old soldier's talent for dodging and scrounging, they spoke in strange accents, called the Irish 'natives', associated with low company, stole from one and another, sneered at the customs of the country, drank to excess and put sugar on the porridge.[25]

To complement the Black and Tans, some 2,000 Auxiliaries were also recruited. They were ex-British Army officers, many of whom, had been decorated in the Great War. Because they were not placed under the control of the army or the police, they became a law unto themselves during their tenure in the country and contributed to the general mayhem and chaos of that time. Moylan later claimed, however, his worst experiences with the enemy often came when the British Army was involved. He found the soldiers were more likely to act in an unbecoming manner than either the police or the Black and Tans, though, he was at pains to stress many other republicans probably had the opposite experiences.

He gave one example of despicable behaviour by the army when he recalled an incident that took place at Liscarroll. There the farmers had to contend with the army burning their hay and one farmer in the district, by the name of Noonan, was particularly singled out for harsh treatment. Mr Noonan had two sons, Paddy and John, who were active Volunteers and the army called at their farmhouse one day. Mr Noonan and Paddy were inside the house while John happened to be in the farmyard with another local Volunteer. When they saw the soldiers arrive, they slipped out of sight and watched them enter the farmhouse. The father and son inside the house were questioned and beaten and Paddy, who was just nineteen years of age, was brought outside and shot. As he lay on the ground an officer put a bullet through the boy's face, severing his tongue as well as fracturing his jaw and teeth before leaving him for dead. By some miracle, Paddy Noonan survived the attack, despite having taken ten bullets to his body. According to Moylan, he went on to have a full life, fathering ten children in the process. Moylan believed the British, even then, had not accepted one basic fact; that they would never subdue Irishmen and women by the use of what they manufactured in their munitions factories.

Moylan spent the early weeks of October 1920 scrutinising intelligence reports in an attempt to familiarise himself with the movement of British troops in his area. This resulted in a successful ambush of the enemy at Ballydracane near Kanturk, when soldiers were detained for a while before being released but not before they were relieved of their arms and ammunition. Jack O'Connor from Newmarket was the local intelligence officer and his reports were always accurate and reliable. He reported that two lorries carrying military personnel passed between Kanturk and Newmarket at least twice a week and were very susceptible to an ambush. Taking on board that information, Moylan decided to put a proposal to Liam Lynch, the brigade commanding officer, who happened, at that time, to be with an Active Service Unit training camp near the village of Freemount. Moylan visited the camp, discussed O'Connor's report with Lynch and convinced him that an ambush was worth a try. Lynch undertook to cast an eye over the proposed ambush site the following day in the company of Moylan and Ernie O'Malley.

That evening there was a circus in Freemount and the villagers mingled freely with the Active Service Unit members, all of whom were billeted in the village and the surrounding hinterland. After the circus, the villagers returned home and the IRA men returned to their billets. It was a peaceful night when Moylan retired to bed. He was awoken from his sleep sometime later by a scout, who said the village was being surrounded by British troops on horseback. Moylan dressed quickly and went outside to join his comrades as they emerged from other houses. He made his way to a fence overlooking a road and lay on top of it, where he was joined by Paddy McGrath from Meelin. They heard the noise of horses hoofs below but soon another scout arrived to tell them it was a false alarm. The horses did not belong to the British Army but in fact belonged to the circus, which was leaving Freemount and moving on to their next engagement. Moylan recalled McGrath swearing with magnificent eloquence and threatening retribution against the scouts. The reason for his ire soon became clear. In his haste leaving his billet he could not find his clothes in the dark and had no option but to join his comrades outside in the freezing cold clad only in a shirt and cartridge belt.

The following afternoon, Moylan, Lynch and O'Malley visited the proposed ambush site in a pony and trap and travelled the last mile across farmland on foot. On the journey they discussed the general situation in the country and during their conversation O'Malley was full of praise for the rural Volunteers and the improvements they were showing in the ways of soldiering. At the site they discussed the merits of it as well as its faults, eventually agreeing it would be a suitable place to ambush the enemy. Moylan was questioned as to the accuracy of Jack O'Connor's intelligence reports and he assured his superiors that they had nothing to worry about; O'Connor was good at his job and his reports could always be relied upon. As it happened, he had confidently informed Moylan some days earlier that a convoy would pass on the road that afternoon. Moylan suggested they wait around for a while and see if O'Connor was correct and test his accuracy. They took up a position out of sight of the road and it wasn't long before two lorries approached carrying around twenty-four soldiers. There and then it was decided an ambush should be attempted the following week. Lynch and O'Malley returned to the Active Service Unit camp, while Moylan returned to his own headquarters to begin preparations for the ambush.

The night before the ambush the Active Service Unit arrived unexpectedly early at Moylan's headquarters in Drominarigle. He had been expecting the men to arrive the following morning. Hasty arrangements were made to accommodate them in billets and also to feed them in addition to the thirty men or so from his own battalion. He recalled the local community came to his aid with a generosity that, he said, knew no bounds. The various families in the locality put the men up and the women cooked meals that evening for everyone and again in the morning before the men travelled to the ambush site. The local men stood guard all night just so the fighting men could snatch some hours of sleep. Moylan was at pains to point out that the struggle against the British, while a demanding and often cruel one, had the full support of the civilian population and nowhere was it more evident than in rural Ireland.

The operation began at 3 a.m. when, in bitterly cold air, the men began their trudge across very sodden fields. Some ninety minutes later they were in place and settled down to wait for the enemy. It was a long and boring wait lying in cold and damp ditches. Moylan recalled how:

> The early morning workers passed on their way unsuspectingly, later came the children on their way to school. At eleven

> o'clock we were still crouching beneath the fence. Suddenly we heard the sound of a lorry.[26]

What happened next was described in great detail by Paddy O'Brien, who later commanded the Charleville Battalion, in his witness statement:

> A single lorry approaching from Kanturk was signalled by the column. This lorry moved directly into the ambush position. A milk cart taking milk to the creamery at Allensbridge was within the ambush position at this time. Fire was opened on the lorry, the driver was shot dead and the lorry collided with the milk cart, coming to a halt in the middle of the ambush position. The enemy returned fire and some of them jumped from the lorry and took cover underneath it.
>
> The fight lasted only about a minute, when the military intimated by shouting they would surrender. A few members of the column immediately jumped over the fence and the military underneath the lorry again fired at them: none of whom were wounded. A return blast was then given by the remainder of the column, inflicting slight wounds on the majority of the military.[27]

Moylan was fulsome in his praise for the valour of the English boys, all of whom, he said, showed grit even though they were outnumbered and trapped. All were wounded when they surrendered but their young driver was dead. Their rifles, ammunition and equipment were collected and taken away. Moylan looked at the young driver and recalled saying to himself; 'God help his mother.' He and his men retreated and once back in Drominarigle the battalion men dispersed to their own districts. Cognisant of a possible reprisal, the Active Service Unit took possession of Kanturk and creameries in surrounding areas. However, no reprisal came and the unit marched back to Freemount a few days later. The fact that there was no reprisal was unusual because during that autumn there were numerous of them across the country and they inflicted much in the way of suffering on many communities.

* * *

The latter months of 1920 saw many ambushes carried out by the IRA and the number of RIC casualties, in particular, continued to rise. Some notable republicans also lost their lives. Michael Fitzgerald died in late October as a result of his hunger strike. Terence MacSwiney and Joseph Murphy died some days later, also as a result of hunger strikes. The month of November saw the young Kevin Barry hanged and a number of civilians lost their lives across the country at the hands of the Crown forces. The month, of course, was defined by two major events, the first being Bloody Sunday in Dublin, when Collins's Squad eliminated British intelligence officers across the city that morning and the British retaliated in the afternoon by attacking Croke Park during a football match between Dublin and Tipperary, shooting dead one player, Michael Hogan, and opening fire on those in attendance. Thirteen spectators died that afternoon and, later that evening, two prominent IRA men, Dick McKee and Peadar Clancy as well as an innocent civilian, Conor Clune, were murdered in Dublin Castle. The end of the month saw one of the bloodiest incidents of the War of Independence when a Tom Barry-led flying column ambushed a convoy of British Auxiliaries at Kilmichael in Cork, killing sixteen of them. Two Volunteers were killed in the incident, which became one of the most controversial military engagements of the war. December saw a major act of reprisal carried out by the Crown forces when they burned Cork city and left a trail of devastation in their wake. While the British might have derived some great satisfaction from their endeavours, the incident only served to convince Moylan and all of his comrades in Cork that the cause they were fighting for was a just and righteous one.

During autumn 1920, Moylan remained in the background and concentrated on organising and training his men while moving from one billet to another. His battalion provided logistical backup to the brigade column through intelligence gathering, transportation, signalling and storage. They also engaged in road blocks and tree felling as well as carrying out scouting sorties. Near the end of October, the brigade column was broken up and each battalion was required to form its own column. This allowed the smaller columns to become more flexible and elusive and, of course, they were easier to billet and feed. Moylan set up a training camp at Toureen where, over a period of ten days, the men were given instruction in the use of arms as well as in signalling, first aid and scouting. Cross-country marches were also part of the regime, many of which took place at night time. Moylan also set up an engineering section in a well-hidden workshop and some of his men with engineering inclinations set to work using equipment he either bought or borrowed, and in some cases stole, to make bombs and landmines as well as repairing guns. With so much going on Moylan felt it was also a good time to move his headquarters and he chose Kiskeam, from where he planned to carry out further ambushes and attacks on the enemy.

Chapter 6

The Art of Being a Leader

In his statement to the Bureau of Military History, Moylan discussed the enormity of the task he had in his capacity as a battalion commander. He had readily agreed to do the job but there were times when he doubted his own ability to see it through to the end. He recalled that he found himself in charge of an ever-developing regional section of a national organisation. The Active Service Unit he had campaigned for in his region was, by October 1920, strong in numbers, armed effectively and, in his view, led properly by good officers. He was anxious to join the unit himself had he been given permission to do so by the brigade commanding officer. However, for the time being his superiors believed it would be better if he created a background against which the unit could operate.

Accepting that decision, Moylan concentrated on providing intelligence information to the unit as well as organising the billeting and feeding of the men. He also organised transport for them as well as the provision of arms and ammunition, and generally made sure the unit was not inhibited in any way as it carried out its orders. His task, he said, of maintaining the battalion as an efficient fighting unit was made easier by the quality of the character of the men he worked with and also by the generosity of the civilian population in his area. Despite his success, he often doubted if he was doing enough for those he commanded. He also worried, at the end of any given day, that he had not accomplished all that he had planned to do. He took to writing a nightly diary in an effort to reassure himself that he had in fact accomplished something of note during the day. He also insisted on every company captain doing the same and compiling a report from it to be presented at every Battalion Council meeting. After each meeting those reports were destroyed.

Moylan lost one of his best men, Paddy McCarthy, the battalion's quartermaster, to the Active Service Unit and he was forced to find a replacement of comparable ability. He chose a man called Sean Nunan who, though different in style to McCarthy, turned out to have outstanding qualities. Nunan was a man possessed of energy and initiative and he immediately carried out an assessment of all the companies in the battalion.

Arms and ammunition were checked and he was not shy to sharply reprimand men who were showing a certain laxity. He set about having each company build a well-concealed and waterproofed arms dump, overseeing each one personally. Nunan was a man who had the ability to smarten up any Volunteer he came into contact with. He managed to accumulate a knowledge of every man in the battalion and that, combined with his acumen for business in civilian life, marked him out as a top-quality leader of men. In fact, Moylan admitted that he had to increase his own efforts just to keep pace with him. He saw Nunan as an inspiration and a real driving force, wholly sincere and not interested in personal gain. He made allowances for folly but not for carelessness or neglect and, according to Moylan, he was the very essence of a loyal and generous friend.

Nunan, though a fine soldier, actually hated soldiering, according to Moylan. He saw it as his duty to involve himself in the independence conflict and once a member of the IRA he dismissed all thoughts of home and any ambitions for personal gain. He was a strict disciplinarian with no tolerance for slackness, yet he managed to develop a fine esprit de corps among the men. No day was too long for Sean Nunan and no task was too arduous, while no hardship was too great to be borne. His love and admiration for his comrades knew no bounds and he always sought to improve their conditions. Moylan believed that Nunan's self-discipline was the basis of his success. Like Moylan, he also looked to develop the political wing of republicanism through the Sinn Fein party and was a keen advocate of the fledgling republican court system. Moylan recalled him saying one day:

> the people and all their needs and concerns must always be matters for keen consideration by us. If they know that their real interests are ours, if they appreciate the fact that in each area where we are in power strict and absolute justice will be done, we shall have the goodwill and co-operation essential to success.[28]

Nunan insisted on the republican courts meeting the needs of the people and he maintained they should always be subservient to the people. He was adamant that a scheduled court session in an area should continue to sit until all cases on the list were heard, even if it meant judges presiding in relays. Moylan recalled one particular case that Nunan involved himself in and when he delivered his verdict in a dramatic fashion it left those involved in no doubt that he was a man of real and meaningful authority in the republican movement.

The incident in question took place around May or June 1920 when there was a row at a fair day in an outlying district in the battalion area. It all started with some good-natured horseplay that began to get a little out of hand. Had there been a functioning RIC presence there that day the antics of those involved would have been curtailed very quickly. However, that was not to be and inevitably the action on the street developed into more serious fighting. After it subsided both parties demanded retribution and decided to bring their cases to a republican court. The justices chosen to hear the case were overwhelmed on the day in question by the presence of two truculent and hostile groups mainly made up of muscular young men, all of whom were convinced of the righteousness of their respective cases.

A big crowd, mainly made up of relatives and friends of both litigants, arrived at the small courthouse. In Moylan's view the scene was set for another magnificent and unholy row and he recalled seeing the justices breathing a collective sigh of relief when they spied Nunan moving silently through the crowd before taking his place as chairman of the court. There were charges and counter-charges as well as long protestations, mainly from the female witnesses, while fierce and wild accusations were levelled by the men folk. All of which was followed by a hot and angry exchange between two of the litigants and, according to Moylan, a fierce and uncontrollable row looked inevitable. Suddenly, a crashing sound reverberated around the room that silenced the crowd. It was the sound of the barrel and cylinder of a Webley 45 making contact with the justice's table. Sean Nunan had, in an instant, brought the court to order.

Moylan recalled you could hear a pin drop in the courtroom and all eyes turned towards the justice's table, where Nunan sat quietly as he held the gun loosely in his hand. He then addressed the court, saying:

> Let it be clearly understood now by everyone here that whatever fighting is to be done in this locality in future the I.R.A. will do it, and maybe you'll all have quite enough before they're finished. I have listened carefully to all the accusations and arguments today. I believe there are faults on both sides, faults for which each offender here will now have a penalty imposed upon him. I fine each man concerned in this trouble one pound and bind him to the peace for one year. The money will be paid now. The fines will now be paid to the Clerk of the Court.[29]

Everyone in the courtroom knew that a voice of authority had spoken and that the decision he handed down would be adhered to. All present realised this was not the voice of a farmer's son, the creamery manager whom they all knew, but the voice of the people. Moylan pointed out that Nunan represented the authority of Dáil Éireann and the arms of the state were ready to enforce its dictates. With Nunan's authority assured, a few men in the room smiled and the smiles then developed into laughter and very soon peace and good humour reigned in the room.

The important point to note here is that the people's repudiation of the traditional British courts system created a law and order vacuum. That void was filled by the republican courts system, which was essentially an Irish authority stepping in and speaking with certainty. Moylan recalled the prestige of the republican court system was quickly established in his area and none of its decisions were questioned. The republican courts system, he believed, became a source of comfort and assurance among the civilian population, all of whom knew that the decisions handed down by justices of Sean Nunan's ilk would be fair and equitable.

Some six months after the court case, the Active Service Unit, together with two local companies, took part in a planned ambush of some Black and Tans and a high-ranking officer who were in the vicinity collecting evidence against prisoners being held in a military detention barracks. Moylan determined they should be ambushed and from his intelligence concluded the enemy could return to their headquarters by three possible routes. The likelihood was, he believed, that they would travel through his area as it was the shortest way back to their headquarters and he laid an ambush at a particular point on the route. He and his men lay in wait for two days in the damp and cold air for the arrival of the Black and Tans before their cars came into view. Moylan barked out his orders and settled down in the long grass to await the arrival of the convoy.

As he readied himself for the fight, he was disturbed by someone moving towards him under cover. It was one of the litigants of the court case, Con Finucane of Glounalougha. With a mocking grin, he looked at Moylan and said, 'What will I do Sir? Sure, I am bound to the peace.' Moylan spat a vile word, and turned with a grim smile to face the road thinking to himself that men who could joke in the face of battle and possible death were, in fact, unbeatable. The man may have been disciplined by a republican court but what took place in that court house six months earlier had been superseded by a far more important disagreement. Finucane, like many others, willingly put a personal and a small local difficulty to one side and joined with all his republican comrades to launch another attack on their common enemy in the pursuance of Ireland's independence.

During the course of his witness statement Moylan discussed the importance of the intelligence system that had been put into place in order to further prosecute the war against the British. It was deemed essential that every unit commander keep in contact with all the others and one of the main ways it was achieved was by the use of despatch riders. They were generally young men who used bicycles or horses in their endeavours and they were all very familiar with the topography of their local districts. They were, according to Moylan, courageous and prepared to take great risks as they carried out their orders. Moylan often went out of his way to acknowledge the work of the despatch riders, and to illustrate his admiration of them, he went into detail in his witness statement about his own particular association with one of that number whom he said, because of the work he engaged in, would always have to remain nameless.

Moylan woke up one morning at the beginning of September 1920 to the sound of an unfamiliar boyish voice outside his window. Looking out, he saw a boy of about seventeen helping a couple of men to construct a rick from turf that had been delivered. After dressing and shaving, Moylan went out into the yard and as he approached the men the newcomer stood smartly to attention and saluted him. The young lad then approached Moylan and produced a letter from his pocket before handing it to him. It was a despatch from the brigade's commanding officer informing him that the young man standing before him had been assigned to him as his despatch rider. Moylan admitted to being very disappointed because he had hoped an experienced man attached to the brigade staff would have been assigned. The letter assured Moylan that the young man selected for the job was totally trustworthy and was unknown to the RIC. The first impression Moylan had of him was that he seemed very affable and confident despite his young age.

Moylan soon realised the young man had an inexhaustible energy and an imperturbable temper, as well as an abundance of courage and daring. During their first conversation, Moylan questioned the young man and learned he had been a Volunteer for a year, having worked on the family farm beforehand. He had his father's blessing to leave the farm and join the IRA. He had three months' experience as a company despatch rider and had filled in for brigade riders. He had not, as yet, fired a gun but his ambition was to eventually join an Active Service Unit. Moylan had some misgivings, mainly because of his young age, but there was something about the lad that led him to believe he would be useful.

As it happened, the day eventually came when Moylan vehemently objected to a proposal that the young man should be transferred from his staff to the brigade staff. In essence, according to Moylan, their relationship was to be cemented over time as one based on trust and integrity. From that day on the young man became Moylan's constant companion as well as a general favourite with everyone else. He tackled all jobs from milking cows to rocking cradles in many of the safe houses Moylan stayed in. He had a fine gift for lying, which he put into practise many a time. He had a vivid imagination and could embellish any story, much to the delight of his many listeners, who never once disbelieved him. He idolised his commanding officer and built his character up to a point where, in his view, Moylan was the very embodiment of a superman, a charge Moylan made clear he could never hope to live up to.

When the young man came to Moylan, he was unknown to the RIC even though he had been questioned a few times by them. He had, up to then, managed to answer their questions in a satisfactory manner but it was inevitable that he would run into the police before long and find himself in a difficult situation. Moylan recalled the young despatch rider was delayed one evening at brigade headquarters by the presence of a British search party in the locality. It was late when he began his long journey home of about twenty-five miles. All was well until around midnight when, cycling on a byroad around a town, he rounded a bend and cycled into the vicinity of two policemen, who called on him to stop. Declining their invitation, he increased his speed and managed to evade them but, unfortunately, he encountered two more policemen further up the road, one of whom managed to insert his walking stick into the spokes of the front wheel of the bicycle, thereby upending our brave young man on the road. He rolled over into a ditch of briars and high grass where, probably somewhat dazed, he lay still until he was hauled out by a policeman, although not before he managed to thrust the despatches into the briars.

The policemen questioned him very stringently for a while and he acted as if he was very disorientated before unleashing a barrage of expletives and becoming highly indignant that he should be accosted while he was out on legitimate business. This is where his renowned imagination kicked in and he told the policemen that he was out looking for a stray bull that he greatly feared would cause untold damage if not quickly caught. Though they were doubtful of his story, they failed to find any real fault in it and when they searched him they found no documents or any other incriminating evidence. They dismissed him with a warning to stop when called upon to do so in the future and not to be venturing out at night time. When taking his leave, he still had the problem of how to retrieve the despatches and further up the road he left his bicycle in a ditch and made his way back through the fields to the spot where he was brought down by the policemen. The smell of tobacco confirmed he was in the right place and he waited until the policemen had moved off before retrieving the despatches. He then collected his bicycle, which was not in the best condition, but he managed to continue his journey and arrived home at 3.a.m. exhausted but happy in the knowledge that he had another wonder story to relate to his ever-growing band of admirers.

Moylan recalled the young despatch rider did eventually come a cropper and fell into the hands of the enemy. The brigade commanding officer was in an adjoining county attending a conference when a message came through for him from Michael Collins. The message was given to Moylan by the brigade adjutant with the instruction that it should be delivered immediately. Moylan passed it to the young despatch rider, stressing the importance of it and the necessity of having it delivered quickly. The young man took the despatch and sped off on his bicycle and Moylan did not expect to see him back for at least a couple of days. Much to his surprise, he returned that evening very crestfallen and devoid of his usual cheerful demeanour. He had a tale of woe to relate to Moylan and was feeling very sorry for himself. It seems he ran into a column of British troops and Black and Tans, who took him into a barracks in a garrison town. There they stripped him naked and questioned him. Somehow, he managed to throw the despatch under the plank bed in the cell without being seen. His clothes were searched and the lining stripped out but nothing was found. He was allowed to dress under supervision and released. He cycled back home by a different route and, according to Moylan, when he arrived, he was nothing more than 'a deflated self-condemnatory object'.

The problem Moylan had was how to retrieve the despatch. The young man was devoid of ideas as to how it might be managed but Moylan quickly put a plan into action. He instructed the man of the house he was billeted in to go into town and get in touch with a mutual friend. He was to find out the name of the woman who cooked and cleaned in the barracks and pass it on to a trusted local tobacconist. Moylan then left the house and cycled three miles to another safe house where he knew there was a British Army officer's uniform. He donned the uniform and made his way to the town, arriving around dusk. He left his bicycle in a safe place and made his way into the back of some houses on Main Street. He knocked on one back door and it was opened by a woman who, though surprised, never uttered a word. Moylan walked through the house and out the front door on to Main Street and made his way to the tobacconist shop. He even encountered some British soldiers on his journey but they just stood and saluted a man they believed to be a superior officer. At the tobacconist he asked for a packet of cigarettes and when he opened the packet he found, overlaid on the cigarettes, a note with the name of the woman who worked in the barracks scribbled on it. Moylan was pleasantly surprised because he knew the woman well, having helped her when her husband died in the Great War. He then made his way to her home and instructed her in what he needed to be done. He slept overnight in a local safe house and the following evening the despatch was delivered to him. The woman had fished it out from under the bed with her broom and placed it in her blouse before taking it home.

Moylan arrived home the following morning with the despatch intact and gave it to his young comrade with instructions to deliver it immediately and, for once, the young man was speechless as he departed on his journey. The moral of the tales related here is that men like Moylan and his trusted despatch rider were always required to be alert when it came to prosecuting the struggle against the British. Situations inevitably arose where they had to call on their abundant courage as well as their ingenuity to extricate themselves from precarious situations. Time and again they rose to the challenge while achieving extraordinary successes, all of which went a very long way to eventually convincing the British that the best way to end an increasingly difficult and protracted independence conflict was by engaging with republicans around the negotiating table.

* * *

In October 1920 Moylan was in consultation with his battalion quartermaster, Sean Nunan, about the state of the battalion's arms and ammunition supply and the progress of their attempts at making land mines and bombs. He recalled they had been experimenting for some time but their knowledge of explosives was meagre and it was only by the grace of God that they had all escaped with their lives on a number of occasions. They also agreed that the greater number of the shotguns in their possession were defective and in need of repair. At the end of their review of the arms situation they decided on the need for somebody familiar with gun repair to overhaul the dangerously defective weapons.

The work could not be carried out in a farmhouse, so it was decided to set up a workshop somewhere out of sight of the authorities. They also agreed to continue with their bomb-making efforts but they would require a supply of iron and other metals. Moylan sent a note to all the companies under his command ordering them to collect as much scrap metal as they could. He also arranged for a raid on the home of a British official where he knew there was a lighting system that had an engine and a dynamo. He then decided on the site for the workshop and asked Con Flynn from Newmarket to oversee the delivery of the materials to it.

During October and November 1920, there was anger in Millstreet among the townspeople concerning the behaviour and attitude of the Black and Tans stationed there. According to Moylan, they were behaving in a more and more obnoxious manner and something had to be done about them. It was decided that the local Active Service Unit should move into the town to tackle the problem. The unit happened to have a number of Millstreet men in its ranks, so there was a natural enthusiasm to rid the town of the hated enemy. At the time Moylan's young cousin, Liam Moylan, was his constant companion and he carried out day-to-day tasks for him. Young Moylan was keen to join an Active Service Unit but Sean was reluctant to let him do so because of his age. He was just seventeen and had no real experience of battle but he badgered Sean to let him do more than just running errands.

When the Active Service Unit arrived in Millstreet, Liam asked if he could join them and Sean had to decide if it was time for him to get some experience in the field. Moylan recalled that Paddy McCarthy, who was a good friend and a leading member of the flying column attached to the Cork No. 2 Brigade, arrived to obtain some revolver ammunition. McCarthy revealed he and his Active Service Unit comrades were about to go into Millstreet that evening to shoot it out with the Black and Tans. Liam Moylan happened to be in Sean's company that day and for some reason he and McCarthy famously hit it off. Liam demanded he be allowed go to Millstreet and play some role in the operation. Sean relented and decided to let him go and off he went in high spirits with McCarthy determined to take on the enemy.

That same night Moylan was occupied elsewhere and during his time away he had misgivings about letting his young cousin join the Millstreet operation. When he arrived back at his headquarters in the early hours of the morning, he heard the sad news that Paddy McCarthy had been killed in the confrontation and that Liam had been beside him when he died in the close fighting that had ensued. When he saw Liam, it was plain the young lad was in a terrible state of shock. Though he was personally devastated at the death of McCarthy, Moylan took the view that he had to maintain an apparently cold exterior in order to impress upon Liam the magnitude of the situation he had chosen to be part of. He reminded his young charge that the loss of young men in war was inevitable and, no matter how close the comradeship was, the grim shadow of death was there all the time. Moylan maintained that his young cousin had, that morning, attained the status of a fully fledged soldier.

Moylan had a coffin made for his friend and comrade, McCarthy, in Kiskeam and travelled to Millstreet to collect his body and bring him home for burial. He recalled McCarthy as:

> A man of much dare-deviltry, was so infectiously gay and good humoured that he was an all-round favourite.[30]

His death, according to Moylan, was:

> the sorest blow that could be given to his comrades.[31]

He recalled that it was:

> an eerie experience, following a coffin at midnight along lonely byroads from Millstreet to Kilcorcoran. In spite of the secrecy attached to the funeral and burial, the cortege reached immense proportions.[32]

Men, he said, came from everywhere to pay their respects to their fallen comrade. Loyal friend Father Leonard made his way from the village of Freemount to recite the prayers at the graveside. At the funeral, Moylan met Charlie O'Reilly, who had acted as battalion commandant during Moylan's own 'Spanish flu' illness. O'Reilly had been badly injured when a petrol can exploded during an attack on an RIC barracks earlier in the year. He maintained he was fully recovered from his injuries and asked to take McCarthy's place in the Active Service Unit. Moylan agreed to the request but, unfortunately, like many of his comrades, O'Reilly was soon to follow McCarthy to a violent and premature death.

Two days after the funeral, Moylan sent some men to collect the engine and dynamo in order to get the bomb-making workshop up and running. He put Con Moylan, brother of Liam, in charge of the workshop because he was a fine mechanic and a forceful individual. The engine and dynamo were delivered and stored before the sun rose one morning. Con Moylan was, at the time, under the radar of the police and military and was still living at home, though Sean was at a loss to know how he managed to do that. All his nights were occupied by his IRA work but he had the knack of evading the enemy. He oversaw the building of the workshop and its fitting out while all the time keeping his cousin up to date with all matters relating to the military and police in Newmarket. The scrap iron collection, it seems, was a great success, so much so that there was a major difficulty in storing and concealing it.

* * *

The last two months of 1920 saw an increasing campaign of destruction and mayhem carried out by the Black and Tans. Munster was placed under martial law and Cork city was burned at a time when Moylan's Active Service Unit was harried from pillar to post. They had little opportunity to strike at the enemy and were constantly aware the 'safe houses' they were staying in were very vulnerable to enemy raids. Moylan made the point that the spirit of the people came to the fore during those months. The capture of an IRA man in any house meant imprisonment or worse for all male members of that household and it also meant the destruction of the home and property. Moylan memorably described that type of intimidation by the enemy as: 'the unbridled licence of undisciplined gangsterdom'. Yet, in every household where he and his colleagues stayed, they were welcomed with open arms and without any preconditions. Moylan gave just one example of how he was treated when he talked of Mrs Nora Galvin of Glashakinleen. On one occasion he apologised to the woman for his all too frequent visits to her home. 'This,' she said, 'is my country as well as yours.' Both she and her husband were teachers and they had a lot to lose by harbouring members of an IRA Active Service Unit, yet unassumingly, and with a quiet determination, they took that risk. Moylan mused that there were various kinds of courage, but theirs, it seemed to him, could be counted among its highest forms.

In November 1920, the brigade Active Service Unit was divided and the British were forced to deal with two smaller forces that were much more elusive and capable of swifter action. Moylan recalled the eastern-based column had almost immediate success when they ambushed the British on 10 December at Leary's Cross and on 19 December at Glencurrane. Training camps were set up in every company area and from those camps the best men were chosen to attend two battalion camps at Ballinguilla and Tureen for special training covering a two-week period. The men were given intensive training in rifle, revolver and machine gun use as well as engineering, signalling, first aid and intelligence.

When the course was finished, the men went back to their respective districts on Christmas Eve much fitter and with a higher morale and soldierly spirit. As they paraded before their departure, a scout arrived to inform Moylan that the British were approaching the area. The men formed into their allotted sections and took cover armed with just shotguns. Moylan scouted the area, picked up the British through his field glasses and watched the six lorries move slowly along the road to a nearby crossroads before moving off in a different direction towards Killarney. Moylan later heard the British had taken an old man by the name of Moynihan prisoner and shot him at the roadside before leaving him to die.

On Christmas Eve night, Moylan met with Con Moylan and Con Flynn in Newmarket concerning the bomb-making workshop. He was accompanied by Liam Moylan as the meeting was held in his parents' house. When they arrived in Newmarket the town was in darkness with no Christmas candles lighting in the windows and not a soul on the streets. The meeting was held in near darkness with only the light of a single candle and all doors and windows carefully shrouded to comply with curfew regulations. Liam's mother put together a bundle of clean clothes for him and recounted local news and gossip while his father produced a bottle of whiskey and they drank to their usual toast 'Success'. The conversation turned to the state of Moylan's clothes and he recalled they were so worn and dishevelled that he had the appearance of a scarecrow. Moylan, embarrassed by the way he looked, just laughed it off before they departed the house.

That night in Newmarket an old man, John Murphy, took his Christmas candle from his kitchen to his bedroom where there were no curtains. A military patrol in the streets, seeing the light, knocked on his door and called to the old man. He came to the window and the officer in charge shot him through the throat. It was just another example of the British version of law enforcement in Ireland at that time. Two days later, Con Flynn sent Moylan a new suit of Irish tweed, which helped him face into the last six months of the independence conflict in a much better mood.

Chapter 7

Taking the Fight to the British

Moylan, in his witness statement, reflected on how difficult it had become to maintain communications with other officers near the end of 1920. He recalled how, during the year, several Brigade Council meetings had to be abandoned because of British Army raids. He was always reluctant to put in writing to his fellow officers any proposals he had and much preferred to speak with his comrades directly. During Christmas he reflected on the past year and took comfort in the fact that he and his men had inflicted some severe punishment on the forces of the Crown, though a price had been paid for their success. Taking on the enemy had been difficult, and made even more so by the fact that there seemed to be an increasing number of them in and around his area of operation. As a consequence, Moylan and his men were forced to traverse the countryside on little-known roads and across fields, glens and mountainsides. Yet, they did so with enthusiasm and dedication to the cause of independence, foregoing many of the comforts of home and accepting the often harsh realities of the Irish weather and terrain.

Around Christmas time, Moylan decided to visit Seamus Brislane in Dromina who at the time commanded the 3rd Battalion. Moylan and Brislane were friends and worked well together, and both men were always keen to co-operate and kick around ideas. Believing a visit was overdue, Moylan set out on the thirty-mile hike to visit his esteemed comrade. He recalled that no sooner had he stepped on to the road in the early afternoon the rain started to fall and it continued to do so incessantly throughout his journey. When he arrived at his destination it was almost midnight and he was not only soaked to the skin but also tired, hungry and chilled to the bone. Brislane was more than pleased to see his comrade and hauled him directly to sit before a blazing and comforting fire. He then rushed across to the kitchen cupboard and fetched a bottle of whiskey. Moylan was so cold he became impatient to get his hands on the whiskey but, as Brislane reached out for a glass, he let the bottle fall and it smashed to pieces on the flagstones. Moylan groaned in anguish and recalled he swore profusely at Brislane, who could do nothing but apologise. Moylan recalled:

> I was gazing at the fragments of the bottle on the flagstone at my feet. I put my left hand towards him and said 'Don't move.' I bent down, carefully removed some of the broken pieces of glass. There was a depression in the flagstone worn by the feet of many generations who had lived in the house. It was now full of whiskey. Hygienists and teetotallers may raise their hands in holy horror, I was no Philip Sidney, and my need was greater than theirs is ever likely to be. I went on my knees on the flagstone and drained the depression dry.[33]

Moylan remembered January 1921 as a month of incessant rain, intensifying sometimes into sleet and snow. He recalled there was hardly a day when he wore dry clothes and, on a few occasions, he slept under a fence, often waking up covered in snow. Yet, he never caught a cold or a chill and began to accept the conditions under which he was living as normal. On New Year's Eve, he was staying at John O'Leary's house in Killoseragh where, he recalled, he always got a warm welcome. He was visited that night by Mick Sullivan, who was an intensely serious man deeply committed to the independence cause. He was a brilliant leader of his Active Service Unit and earned a reputation among his comrades as a fearless warrior. During the conversation that night both Moylan and Sullivan felt that a sufficient number of men had been trained as far it was possible to train them without bringing them under fire from the enemy. The time had come, they agreed, to put them into the field even if it was just to have the experience of confronting the enemy in a face-to-face combat situation.

Moylan and Sullivan decided to target the British soldiers stationed in Newmarket, where they were living inside barbed wire and sandbag emplacements. In order to get some exercise, the soldiers tended to march out of Newmarket a few evenings during the week. It was noticed that they sometimes used the Meelin road to exercise and Moylan decided on organising some of his men to wait for the soldiers on that road. He arrived in Meelin on New Year's Day before leaving for Tullylease and Freemount on the following day to select men for the operation. He arrived back in Meelin on 3 January and early the following morning he and his men got into position one mile south of the village. He recalled:

> We had a dozen rifles, the rest of the men were armed with shotguns, it was therefore necessary that the fight should be at close quarters. Scouts were stationed in position where an early view of the approach of the British could be obtained. There was nothing to do but wait well into the afternoon without result. We then got word of their approach, not from the south as expected but from the west, not a marching patrol but a strong raiding party in lorries. They had, in fact, already that day raided the houses of some of the Volunteers who were members of our party. The position we occupied was exposed, without any real cover by way of retreat and quite unsuitable to this new problem. I decided that if we had time to get to the turn of the road at Meenkerragh that we'd reach a position that would be reasonably satisfactory.
>
> On our way we got a further message that they were coming too swiftly towards us to enable us to reach the desired position. We had perforce to turn off the road when we had passed through the village and take the cover that immediately offered itself.
>
> Scarcely had we done this when the lorries arrived. Our position was, from the point of view of success, rather hopeless. Nevertheless, we opened fire with the rifles and succeeded in stopping the lorries. The British dismounted quickly and there began a duel that lasted till dusk and then the arrival of British reinforcements.[34]

Unluckily, Moylan had chosen a day when the garrison at Newmarket was being relieved, which meant there was a greater number of reinforcements available. There was nothing for him to do but withdraw his men and they did so very unhurriedly. Moylan's spirits were very downcast but his men did not share his emotions, most likely, he believed, because the adrenalin was still flowing after the excitement of the battle.

A communique issued the following day by General Macready's headquarters in Dublin stated:

> Two military lorries each containing five soldiers and one policeman were ambushed on Tuesday afternoon near Newmarket, County Cork, martial law area. Machine gun fire and rifle fire was opened on them by a large party of civilians and

> after an exchange of fire lasting a considerable time the attackers made off leaving a quantity of ammunition behind them.[35]

The report went on to claim that the reinforcements made their way to the rebel position at the crest of a hill, where:

> They found blood and other evidence that the attacking party had suffered injuries.[36]

Moylan later made it clear that neither he or any of his men suffered any casualties or injuries. He later took time to reflect on the decisions he made on the day and concluded he should not have carried out an abrupt change of plan when he was confronted by a new situation brought about by the enemy. He was aware that he just about avoided a disaster and had put his men in real danger. It was something he was never to do again. He also concluded that his unit on the day was far too big and many of his men were clearly unsuitable for that type of operation. The following day a party of British troops arrived in Meelin, looted and burned half a dozen houses. They rounded up all the men they could find and generally behaved in a brutal and bullying manner. The day was made even worse for the people of Meelin when a local youth by the name of Morgan Sweeney was shot and killed in the raid.

The day after the raid an official bulletin from the British Army headquarters maintained the governor of the martial law area ordered the destruction of four houses in Meelin. The action by the British Army was officially recorded as the second ever reprisal carried out by them during the War of Independence and it caused Maud Gonne MacBride and Charlotte Despard to travel from Dublin to witness for themselves the destruction that was laid upon the village. Moylan and his men were elsewhere during the raid thawing out gelignite, which they had brought from Sixmilebridge some months earlier. The work had a negative effect on all of them as the chemicals made them very ill for several days. The need to use gelignite became a necessity because the RIC barracks were, by that time, very heavily fortified. Gelignite had been acquired by some brigades, including Moylan's, but they all lacked the expertise to use it properly. During January 1921, Tom Barry led three assaults on RIC barracks in West Cork but they were all repelled because the explosive charges failed to detonate.

* * *

The intelligence reports in the days after Meelin, mainly supplied by Jack O'Connell, indicated there were no regular movements of troops or RIC, but when they did move, their numbers were much larger than previously. Moylan did notice how the British visited a few villages in the area and posted up proclamations. He attempted to second guess the military in the hope that he and his men might lie in wait for them between Newmarket and unvisited villages but nothing came of their endeavours. At the time, established fairs and markets were banned by the authorities but to circumvent that order they were held in remote areas. The British, having got wind of these fairs and markets, went out in force to prevent them being held and one was due to take place at Rockchapel on 15 January. Moylan calculated the British would visit Rockchapel on the day in question and made plans to ambush them. He recalled:

> I got together a specially selected group and collected every rifle. I secured about twenty and proceeded to select a spot for the ambush.[37]

One of Moylan's main difficulties when it came to carrying out ambushes was how to get the lorries to stop in the correct location on the road. This time the problem was solved for him in an unusual way when someone abandoned a car on the road after an accident about two miles west of Newmarket. The car remained in the same place for a number of days without anyone coming to reclaim it. Moylan felt sure the British patrol would stop to examine the car and so he arranged the ambush around it. He left Kiskeam after dark on 14 January, the day before the ambush, and made a number of calls along the way before arriving at the ambush site around 4 a.m. It had been raining heavily and it was a bitterly cold night. Moylan crept under a hedge and slept for a few hours. When he awoke, he was covered with snow. He recalled:

> It was not yet daylight and the boys had begun to gather. Inside the hour we were all in position. During the next few hours nobody would suspect that a group of men of deadly purpose were concealed behind the bare hedge that lined the road.
>
> A messenger cycling furiously from Newmarket brought the news that four lorries of soldiers had arrived in the town. They were at the military barracks as he left. This was the number we had expected and prepared for so there was no need

to make any alteration to the arranged position. The wait had been tedious but everybody was satisfied now at the prospect of action and each man, ready and alert, settled himself into his position. Then another breathless cyclist arrived with a hurriedly written note from Con Moylan. The British had a number of hostages in their lorries and were then engaged in gathering a number of others in Newmarket. Among those already seated in a lorry was our most prominent and effective supporter, Denis D. Curtin. I was in a quandary. I had made every effort and taken all care to make a success of this fight. Now if I fought, it meant certain death for a number of non-combatants. It certainly meant 'lights out' for Denis Curtin, my very good friend and a man we could ill spare. I still hoped against hope that an opportunity would present itself for attack which would at the same time embody a sporting chance for the hostages. I explained the position to my comrades and ordered that except my whistle went there was to be no attack. I got back to my own position beside the fence outside which the car lay.

We soon heard the sound of approaching lorries immediately they were in sight. They were crowded with men in civilian dress and these seemed to outnumber the soldiers they carried. My anticipation was sound. When the British sighted the car they slowed, their rifles were pointed outward. The lorries moved past it. One pulled up in line with it. The last lorry twenty yards to the rear of this. Had there been no hostages there would have been slaughter. Each lorry was in perfect position for our purpose. An officer and some men dismounted to examine the car. The others remained in the lorries with the hostages, all of whom were handcuffed. Where I lay half a dozen British Tommies were five yards away, no member of the group more than fifty yards from an IRA rifle.

Yet I could not blow my whistle. I could not condemn those unarmed, handcuffed men to take death that would surely be theirs if the fight started. The British remounted their lorries and drove away, never suspecting how close they had been to death. We waited all day in the hope that on their return the position might have altered. But their return through the ambush position was a repeat performance. They again halted,

> some dismounted and again, examined the car while the majority stood guard over their prisoners. Had these prisoners been young I might have taken a chance, but some of them were old and most were middle aged, breadwinners, with dependent families. I couldn't do it. And so again we marched away disgruntled. We had worked hard for success but success evaded us.[38]

The practice of carrying hostages had become part of the British operations when, during the previous month, Brigadier General Higginson, based in Cork city, announced that captured Volunteers would be carried on lorries as protection for his soldiers. It is difficult to say how this measure prevented other ambushes from being carried out but the new policy presented just another difficulty for Moylan and other officers.

* * *

While success evaded Moylan and his men that day, the same could not be said of some men in the 3rd Battalion later that same night. Around midnight they lay in ambush at Shinnagh, having discovered that a number of British military cars passed weekly in the early hours of the morning between Limerick and Buttevant. The Volunteers dug a deep trench across the road at a selected position earlier during the night but it had not been completed when the British came on the scene in a car a few hours before the expected arrival time. Seamus Brislane, who was in charge, ordered his men to open fire. The driver of the car, despite being under fire, accelerated in an attempt to get the car over the trench but it was too heavily laden and its back wheels struck the face of the trench on the far side and it toppled back into it almost on top of the men who had been digging and who had no time to get out. The driver shut off the car lights and a short firefight ensued.

The British managed to escape to their barracks just a few miles away but they left the car and some guns and ammunition behind together with a bag containing files and despatches sent by British intelligence officers in Limerick to their counterparts in Buttevant. Before morning the documents were in the hands of the brigade commanding officer and, as the mail train left Mallow that evening, the guard carried a bulky package onwards to Dublin, where it was eagerly received by Michael Collins.

For Moylan and his men, it was a case of one disappointment after another over the following weeks as well-laid plans failed to come to fruition. However, all was not lost on him as he continued to develop a tactical appreciation of the continuing war while at the same time the men under his command were gradually becoming a very cohesive and disciplined fighting unit.

By January 1921 it had become very difficult to attack a police barracks by the methods used during the previous year. Garrisons had been strongly reinforced by the arrival of the Black and Tans while sandbag emplacements were put in place. Steel shutters were installed over windows and barbed wire and machine guns were mounted around the barracks. In the area where the police still remained, military posts were set up, garrisoned by any number from sixty to one hundred men. Moylan recalled he and his men were able to keep both the military and police closely confined within a narrow circle but they had no equipment with which to drive the enemy from the positions they occupied.

Moylan attempted to get around the increased security by coming up with a novel way of doing so when he considered the use of an old seventeenth-century cannon that he and his comrades sourced from Ross Castle in Killarney. He recalled:

> We cleaned it up, built a frame for it and one night Dan Vaughan, Tom McNamara and I went into Newmarket railway station and collected two wheels from a railway truck which we attached to the frame. We tried it early one morning. We set it up one hundred yards from a disused limekiln, loaded it with a quantity of black powder and a ten-pound sash weight, set off the charge with a short piece of fuse. It worked perfectly. We hit the face of the kiln dead centre and burst a hole through it. We were elated. When the British travelled over our district they were sheltered behind a screen of hostages. Now we could attack them in their own barracks. We made preparations for such an attack.[39]

Moylan and his comrades found themselves spending many days hiding in ditches waiting for the enemy to appear along the roads but they saw very little signs of them. The weather in January 1921 was foul and the endless waiting on the roadside entailed much in the way of hardship. Moylan allowed the men who lived in country districts a few days off to visit their homes and families and retained the men for whom it was too dangerous to make such a visit. One afternoon, near the end of January,

Moylan and Dan Vaughan left their safe house, Jones's of Glencollins, to visit Con Murphy, the Kiskeam company captain. The rain poured down as they made their journey and Vaughan pointed to the road surface and fresh tyre tracks, which they concluded were most likely from a military vehicle. Moylan recalled:

> We decided that the British had gone to Kingwilliamstown to post their latest proclamation and we both cursed the decision that had dispersed our group.
>
> We proceeded to Kiskeam to make enquiries about the matter. The rain came down in sheets. Kiskeam was a deserted village. Con Murphy had no knowledge of the passing of any cars, nor could we elicit any information anywhere in regard to such an occurrence. We returned to Glencollins. On our way we met a man loading rushes into a cart. As a last hope we questioned him. Yes, he had seen the cars, two of them, loaded with Black and Tans, they had a cannon. He described the cannon. I diagnosed a Lewis gun. We proceeded to Kingwilliamstown and made inquiries. A few people had seen the cars passing, they had gone through the village toward Castleisland. It was natural for us to think that they had gone to Tralee, which was the British headquarters in Kerry, and we considered that owing to the lateness of the hour they were unlikely to return, particularly in view of their experience at Shinnagh a few days before.[40]

Knowing that they would eventually return at some point, Moylan returned to Jones's at Glencollins and while there decided on a plan to ambush the British at Tureengarriffe. He sent a note to the commandant of the Kanturk Battalion, explaining his plans and suggested that as there was a possibility the British might return via Killarney and Rathmore he should make plans to lay an ambush at Clonbanin. He also sent a despatch to the commanding officer of the Kerry Brigade.

* * *

Moylan recalled that Jones's kitchen was a scene of tremendous activity that night as men came and went and the attacking party was selected. Guns and ammunition were examined before everyone got to bed. Around 5 a.m.

they were awake and up again and ready to march off at 6 a.m. When they reached the ambush site the men began to dig a trench across the road. It was a vile day with a fog so thick that one could see only a few yards, and so wet that it seemed to penetrate to the bone. They waited all day and well into the night but there was no sign of the British. Moylan left a number of men on guard while the majority of the unit snatched an hour or two of sleep. By six o'clock the following morning everyone was back in position again. The fog had disappeared and it was a clear dry day. Around noon, Moylan decided to let some of the men go off to have a cup of tea at a nearby house but before he issued the order, he focussed his field glasses on the road and the schoolhouse at Scartag, which was painted a bright yellow colour and easily identifiable. Just as his glasses rested on the patch of road, two cars swung in. He shouted to the others and told them what he had seen. In his own mind, Moylan had determined that nothing was going to stop their ambush of the enemy.

He recalled they had ten rifles ready for the fight and he and his men took up positions that approximated to a semicircle with the road cutting it in half. Tom McNamara, Dan Vaughan and Johnny Jones were on its northern end. Denis Galvin, Sean Healy, Liam Moylan, Con Morely, Tom Herlihy, David McAuliffe and Con Finucane on the south side. Moylan lay in the middle armed with a parabellum. He remembered their position was, from the viewpoint of observation, perfect but from the viewpoint of protection it left a lot to be desired. The fight, however, had to be fought to the finish and Moylan was adamant that there was to be no retreat for the Black and Tans. If they did try to do so they would have to face the men of the local companies, who were armed with shotguns.

James Cashman, a lieutenant with the Kiskeam company, was crouched in an exposed position behind rocks and stones on the south side of the road. In his later witness statement to the Bureau of Military History he described what took place:

> The convoy, consisting of two cars, was allowed to drive into our position, where it was greeted by a burst of machine-gun fire and a call to surrender. The driver of the leading car accelerated out of the straight stretch round the bend at the eastern end where he was held up by the trench. The second car halted and the occupants of both cars dashed for cover behind the roadside fences. As the enemy did not surrender at the opening burst all sections of the IRA party opened fire.[41]

The first burst of the machine gun fire was directed above the heads of the RIC men, which gave them a chance to find cover, and the fighting continued for about twenty-five minutes, during which time the enemy were called on a number of times to surrender. Moylan then signalled to his men to cease firing by a blast of his whistle and called again on the enemy to surrender. This time they heeded his request and threw down their weapons. When Moylan and the rest of the ambush party came down from their positions, they found Divisional Commissioner Holmes had been badly wounded. There were seven other RIC men, mostly wounded and one of their number, Constable Moyles, who was just twenty years old, was dead.

* * *

As it transpired, Holmes was very seriously wounded as his right leg was broken and he had sustained bullet wounds to his left leg, left shoulder and above an eye. A cigarette was lit for him and a coat was placed over him. Soon the sound of an approaching car was heard and Moylan and his men believed it to be another one containing police or military. When it came into view the driver was identified as being the school inspector, Tim Cronin, who was instructed to take the wounded to Castleisland for medical attention. Holmes was brought to hospital as requested and two surgeons came by special train from Dublin to attend to him at the Central Military Hospital at Victoria Barracks, where he died the following day. A veteran of the Great War, Holmes was buried with full military honours in Glasnevin Cemetery.

Moylan, who sustained a slight leg wound, recalled the enemy fought gallantly and when the fight was over he and his comrades found they had secured a fine haul of armaments, including rifles, automatic shotguns, grenades, revolvers and ammunition. The enemy were searched and their personal property was returned to them. One of the cars was set aside to allow them carry off their wounded. The second car was loaded up with the captured armaments and a bush, heavily weighted with stones tied into bags, was attached to it to wipe away the tyre tracks as it was driven to a designated hiding place by a couple of Moylan's men. He and the rest of his men marched away to a designated meeting place about one mile from the ambush site. As it happened, the car was never traced by the huge search party that the British launched. The arms and ammunition were distributed and some placed in reserve. Among the captured items was a number of waterproof overcoats and they were shared out according to need and suitability of size. Moylan and his men marched away from Tureengarriffe tired and hungry but in great spirits. For some of the men in the local companies this was their first time under fire and the experience was to stand them in good stead over the following months.

That evening they all arrived in the district they had intended to stay in for a few hours and were welcomed by the farming community. Though the people living there had little enough for themselves, it did not stop them from preparing hot meals and places to rest for the fighting men. Moylan was later full of praise for their hosts, all whom, he said, were eking out an existence on a bleak, cold, bare and often unfruitful land and yet they were generous to a fault. Under the cover of darkness, some of them went back with Moylan to retrieve the hidden car, and by secret and devious ways, guided him, his men and the vehicle across seemingly trackless and impassable country to a safe place outside the ring of the enemy search parties.

Moylan and his Active Service Unit parted from the courageous civilians, all of whom were prepared to face the inevitable wrath of the military and police the following day. They were fully aware that an inadvertent word, the slightest accident, might bring disaster upon their community, resulting in a blazing homestead, cattle destroyed, prison or perhaps even a bullet for, in Moylan's words:

> Some of these Black and Tans were maniacal and sadistic.[42]

The ambush at Tureengarriffe was to all intents and purposes a major success and a fine testament to Moylan's meticulous planning as well as the courage and determination of his men. It raised their morale and indeed that of the civilian population in the area and across the country. The arms and ammunition captured in the ambush proved to be valuable assets during the last months of the conflict. The expected reprisal did come the following day. Thirty lorries of troops arrived at Ballydesmond. Officers demanded to know the identities of those responsible for the ambush, but no information was proffered. A house and grocery shop belonging to Tim Vaughan were burned, together with William McAuliffe's home and drapery store. Despite all of the incriminations and threats, the resolve of the people remained steadfast.

Chapter 8

The Struggle Continues

On 4 January 1921 the British arrested Con Murphy of the Cork No. 2 Brigade on a charge of gun possession and he was eventually executed at Victoria Barracks on 1 February. He was the first man in the country to be executed after the declaration of martial law. Some days later, eight of the ten men captured by the British during the Dripsey ambush on 28 January were brought before a court martial at Victoria Barracks. Five were found guilty of 'levying war against His Majesty' but the sentence of death was put on hold because of legal challenges led by the former Irish Parliamentary Party MP Tim Healy. However, the challenge failed and the men, Daniel O'Callaghan, Patrick O'Mahony, John Lyons, Timothy McCarthy, Thomas O'Brien and Captain John Allen, captured in Tipperary, were eventually executed on 28 February. Yet, despite these setbacks the IRA, during the early months of 1921, continued to pursue its policy of ambushes and attacks on the forces of the Crown.

On 1 February, the Drimoleague Company ambushed four RIC men, killing Constable O'Connor and wounding Constable Griffin. Four days later, at Tullybeg, a four-man RIC bicycle patrol was ambushed and two constables, Edward Carter and William Taylor, lost their lives while another man was wounded. On 4 February, Patrick Crowley of Kilbrittain was shot dead by Auxiliaries in a shootout and some days later members of the Cork No. 3 Brigade launched an attack on the barracks in Skibbereen. They captured two soldiers of the King's (Liverpool) Regiment but freed them some hours later. On 11 February, there was an attack by the flying column of Cork No. 3 Brigade on the Drimoleague RIC Barracks. On the same day, the Millstreet flying column of Cork No. 2 Brigade attacked a train carrying troops near Rathcoole. It was reported that one British soldier was killed while his comrades surrendered. They were released after they handed over their guns and ammunition.

Moylan had to decide what to do with the captured Crossley car from the Tureengarriffe ambush and one night soon after the event he and some of his men brought it to Caherbarnagh. They stayed at Horan's and in the morning hid the car among the rocks at the foot of a mountain before moving back to Cullen. When they arrived in Cullen, they heard that Kingwilliamstown had been burned in a reprisal for IRA ambushes. There was little they could do about it so they all remained in Cullen overnight, sleeping at Casey's of Ardnageeha. Moylan recalled he sat up for some hours talking with their host, William Casey, who was a Justice of the Peace and a long-time supporter of the Irish Parliamentary Party. Their conversation was convivial and at the end of it Moylan realised there was little to separate the two men politically. As he left the house the following morning, he was convinced that Irishmen could indeed differ in their political views and still be good Irishmen. He genuinely believed, there and then, that the most unfair charge that had ever been levelled against the men of his generation who took up arms against the British was that they had no realisation of that fact. When he left William Casey that morning, Moylan had a much clearer understanding of his host's view of the world and Ireland and he felt sure Casey had a acquired a good understanding of his views and opinions.

* * *

That same morning the British were raiding into the Millstreet Battalion area but were not looking for Moylan. They passed the house in a dozen lorries to join another party on the main road a mile away. Soon after, Moylan met with Donal McSweeney, the most prominent member of Sinn Fein in the area, to discuss republican court's business and to arrange a meeting of the Sinn Fein Executive. Once that business was concluded, Moylan and his men left for Kiskeam, arriving at dusk only to be met by a Volunteer who had been looking for him. He relayed the news that the Black and Tans had burned a house in Newmarket and Moylan took the view that Kiskeam was probably next on their list. They had six rifles and half a dozen bombs that they had acquired at Tureengarriffe. They took up a position on the cliff over the bridge leading into Kiskeam from Kingwilliamstown and Moylan deemed it a perfect position from a bomber's point of view. He calculated they could at least get two lorries before any real fight started. They waited for a number of hours and only left the area when four Volunteers, Liam Nolan, David McAuliffe, Johnny Jones and Con Morley, arrived from Kingwilliamstown to confirm the Black and Tans had departed towards Kerry.

All four Volunteers had been at Jones's in Glencollins when they heard the Black and Tans were burning houses. They rushed down to the village with their guns to find the houses burning and the enemy departed. On the way back they heard that Moylan and his men were lying in ambush at Kiskeam and went on to join them. In his witness statement, Moylan somewhat fondly remembered some of the men who were with him that night and it was clear he had regard for all of them. He recalled how Johnny Jones was quiet and dependable, blessed with a sense of responsibility and no little courage. Davy McAuliffe was a mere boy who was small, thin and delicate but his spirit overcame his physical deficiencies. He had an inexhaustible energy and Moylan recalled how he possessed a cool courage. Tim McNamara was not unlike the other two men in character and he was quiet, cool and imperturbable and very easy to handle. However, Moylan also recalled four others who he said were different and were often a problem. These he said were Con Morley, Denis Galvin, Sean Healy and Liam Moylan. He went on to say:

> I called them the 'Three Musketeers', not that they had anything in common with the characters created by Dumas other than their daring and the fact that they were four in number. Liam had been recognised as a front-line soldier since the night he accompanied Paddy McCarthy to Millstreet. The others were a hard-bitten trio; experienced and capable fighting men who believed that soldiering should have its due accompaniment of relaxation and that pubs should not be out of bounds, nor pockets patriotically empty. They had fallen into disfavour with officers who had taken to heart too literally the phrase, 'Ireland sober is Ireland free' and had graduated with many others of their like into a sort of Foreign Legion under my command.[43]

Moylan claimed the four young men had a lively contempt for staff officers. He maintained two of them, Morley and Galvin, were infantry men, pure and simple, while the third, Healy, was a natural mechanic and was put in charge of the first machine gun captured by Moylan and his men. Liam Moylan was drawn into the other three's company by a youthful admiration of their exploits and by their devil-may-care attitude to life. The young Moylan was also mechanically minded and the second captured machine gun fell into his care, so the four men together became the core of the machine gun section. All four of them, according to Moylan, had a nose for a fight and they always turned up on the morning of a military operation. They were invariably ready and willing to accept the brunt of an attack and to hold the last line of defence when a column had to retreat.

A few weeks after the Tureengarriffe ambush, Moylan became aware of a general interest among the civilian population in the car he and his men had hidden in Caherbarnagh. In fact, the vehicle had become something of a tourist attraction in its own right. At one stage a party arrived from Rathmore just to look at it and Moylan came to the conclusion that it was only a matter of time before the British or the RIC got to know of its whereabouts. One afternoon he sent his Musketeers, two of whom could drive, to fetch the car and take it to another safe hiding place that he had decided upon. During a busy day, Moylan forgot about the car and it was only later that night the thought struck him that the police in Rathmore might well have been lying in wait for his men to arrive to take the car away. Worried that they were in danger, he got on his bicycle around 1 a.m. and started off for Caherbarnagh. He got a puncture on the way and ended up pushing the bicycle for most of the journey to Cullen.

At Cullen he roused a man known as the Bard who was usually familiar with everything that happened in the area. He confirmed to Moylan that his Musketeers had indeed called to him around 9 p.m. the previous evening. After an hour's delay and the acquisition of another bicycle, Moylan was on his way from Cullen at about 3.a.m. The going became even tougher and more punctures ensued on a very bad road and he reached Caherbarnagh around 6 a.m. He knocked on the door of Andy Horan, who was up and fully dressed and had the kettle boiling on the fire. Moylan enquired if he had seen his men and he replied in the affirmative. He then informed Moylan that they had taken the car off to a wedding in Killarney. Moylan recalled he swore to 'high heaven', thinking that:

> Here was a car, the description of which was in every barracks, a car in size, power and colour standing out from the ruck of cars like a sore thumb. And these lunatics had driven it into Killarney. 'Do you mean to tell me, I said, that they drove the car to a wedding at the Cathedral?' 'They did,' he said, 'and what's more, they took the bride and the bridesmaid with them. The car that was to take them broke down on the road and the boys, sooner than disappoint the girl, drove her to town.'[44]

A livid Moylan swore they would hear from him and feel the wrath of his tongue. Despite his annoyance, he was somewhat pleased his errant men had demonstrated that the age of chivalry was not dead and, privately, he had a sneaking admiration for them. As it transpired, they drove the car through Killarney, which was thronged with British soldiers, Tans and RIC men. They then parked it at the cathedral gate and before long headed the wedding party back through the town again. Moylan concluded that it was best not see the four of them again until his temper had eased and he avoided contact with them for several days.

In the meantime, Con O'Leary came to see Moylan with an ambush proposal to be carried out by the Kerry No. 2 Brigade and, after going over the plans, it was decided that a machine gun would be required for the operation. Moylan sent for his Musketeers and they arrived proffering apologies as well as making their case as to why they drove the car into Killarney. After a bit of a dressing down, the four miscreants left very disgruntled but returned an hour later ready to go into action armed with their machine gun and revolvers. A newspaper report some days later confirmed the ambush had been a success. A few days later, a Volunteer from the Kerry Brigade area arrived at Moylan's door looking for his revolver. A perplexed Moylan failed to understand what he was talking about. The man informed Moylan that he had seen the Musketeers equipped with two revolvers each, and he did not see the need for them to be so armed. He then bought one of the revolvers from them for £5 with the arrangement being that the gun was to be delivered when the ambush had taken place. However, when the man in question looked for the Musketeers, they had departed the area, taking the gun and the money with them. Moylan recalled:

> I sent for the Musketeers. They came and I questioned them. They denied point blank that they had sold the gun. Getting on my right side they asked, 'Did I believe for a moment that they would sell a gun?' I roughly ordered the unfortunate man out of my sight. He left disconsolate. Years after I heard the truth of the matter. They were dead broke after the wedding and ensuing celebrations. My attitude towards them was such that they dared not ask me for any money. They planned, therefore to sell the gun believing that in the excitement and division of the spoils, to which they had no claim, after the fight that they could slip away unnoticed. They managed to do so and did not cry halt until well inside their own Brigade area. Four hours later they had changed the fiver in Kingwilliamstown and, as they said, had four pints by the throat in Klondike's pub drinking to the health of the farmer who provided the cash.[45]

Moylan had given some of his men time off to return to their homes and families and they were not involved in the Tureengarriffe ambush. When they returned, they expressed their disappointment at not being involved in the operation but were appeased when they heard Moylan was planning an attack on the Newmarket Military Post. It was a plan he had been thinking about for some time and he had asked Con Moylan and Jack O'Connell to make regular trips into the town to observe the regular comings and goings of the military. One night, Moylan went into Newmarket with Davy McAuliffe and Liam Moylan and, leaving the others to keep watch on the police and the military barracks, he walked up New Street in the darkness. As he reached Denis Murphy's house, he spotted a military patrol approaching him. He contemplated turning back but instead pushed Murphy's front door and it opened. He stepped through it and into his shop, which was in darkness. The patrol stopped outside the shop upon hearing the Murphy children making a bit of a racket upstairs but then moved on. Moylan watched them through the window and waited for them to return, all the time noting their numbers and disposition. Once they had left the street, he joined McAuliffe and Liam Moylan and moved out of the town.

After a few days of observation, Moylan felt he had accumulated enough information about the movement of the police and troop patrols in the town to make concrete plans in relation to an attack. Before doing so, however, he decided to call into the town again one evening to see his mother and sisters, all of whom had been subjected to a good deal of harassment from the military. The doors of the family home had been kicked in numerous times and it had also been ransacked. He asked his mother if there had been any recent raids on the house and she confirmed all had been quiet for some weeks except for the day after the Tureengarriffe ambush when Auxiliaries had taken over the town. As they were speaking, they heard the sound of footsteps on the road outside and since the curfew was being strictly enforced, Moylan knew to whom they belonged. He recalled:

> I suggested she should go upstairs and ascertain if all was clear as I intended departing. My real reason was that I didn't want her present when the fight which I believed to be imminent started. I moved to the back of the shop and looked through the glass door leading to the room behind. There were two soldiers in the room. One an officer, whose head was within a foot of my revolver, was talking to my sister. The other, a Sergeant, was near the outer door engaged in animated

> laughing conversation with a Miss Baby O'Mahony who was that night staying in the house. I stood still as a statue until, after a few minutes, they both left. The door was shut and both girls collapsed into the nearest chairs. They both knew where I was, they expected shooting and yet they smiled and calmly talked themselves and me out of a most difficult situation. I stood without movement outside the house for five minutes and then reasonably assured that the coast was clear headed for the West.[46]

Moylan recalled the British were very active that week in Kerry just across the Blackwater river. They had chosen Buttevant as their headquarters for some reason and raids were conducted by troops moving from Killarney or Tralee to Buttevant or vice versa. Moylan and his men concluded fairly quickly that the troops did not return to their particular base for several days after each raid and Sunday seemed to be a favoured day for any return. He decided to stage an ambush on Sunday, 6 February. The previous day he made a reconnaissance trip along the road he expected the British to travel and selected a position about three miles east of Kingwilliamstown. That night he crossed the fields to the house he intended to stay in prior to the ambush. His journey there meant he had to traverse a pathway used by children on their way to school. As he was readying for bed, Moylan realised he had lost a Mills bomb that had been attached to his belt. Concerned that he may have lost the bomb along the pathway used by the children, he retraced his journey to the house and eventually found it in the early hours of the morning.

That Sunday was, according to Moylan, a beautiful day weather wise and he and his men got into position beside the road. They waited all day for the troops to pass by and around 3.30 p.m. they received a message from Kingwilliamstown that the military had passed through the village but instead of travelling directly from Buttevant through Newmarket they continued south to Knocknagree. Unbeknownst to Moylan and his men, a tragic event was played out at Knocknagree and they only got to hear about it later that evening. He recalled in his witness statement the events of that tragic afternoon:

> In a field beside Knocknagree village a hurling match was in progress between a number of small boys. These little lads had no anticipation of danger and stood in groups to watch the

> approaching lorries. Two bursts of machine gun fire directed towards them was the first indication they had of any danger. Some of the boys rushed southwards, the others lay on the fields and beside the fences.
>
> The British soldiers advanced, pouring volley after volley on the fleeing boys and on the playing pitch. When the firing ceased the boys on the playing pitch were rounded up. It was then found that Michael J. Kelleher, aged seventeen, had been shot through the head; Michael Herlihy, aged thirteen, was shot through the thigh and Donal Herlihy, his brother was shot through the lung. The Herlihy boys both recovered.[47]

In later life both Herlihy boys went on to become noted clergymen, with Donal eventually taking up the position as Bishop of Ferns. The body of Michael Kelleher was taken to Rathmore RIC Barracks, where the sergeant refused to be associated with the crimes of the military. The soldiers then returned to Knocknagree and handed over the body to the young man's grief-stricken father. The military did not deny the boys had been shot but asserted they had been caught in the crossfire. The official report as published in the *Irish Independent* on 8 February stated:

> A military patrol saw a body of armed civilians in a field near Knocknagree. Fire was opened and replied to, resulting in the death of one youth and the wounding of two others.[48]

Of course, the report was rejected by the local people and there was no evidence that any of the young lads were carrying weapons or had any connections with the IRA. There was also no IRA activity in or around Knocknagree that day and no record of any ambush can be found in the British Army records. Unfortunately, the Knocknagree incident was not an isolated one at that time as there were many other reports of women and children dying all across the country at the hands of the Crown forces.

Around that time Moylan and his men noticed an increasing use of the railways by British forces. A watch was kept and a report came back that the soldiers seemed to be mostly unarmed during the train journey. It was decided to lay an ambush one mile east of Millstreet Station at a point where a high embankment made it possible for riflemen lying on each side of the track to have a clear field of fire without endangering each other. The plan saw a number of armed men placed on the station at Millstreet and they were to watch for a train carrying British military. When that train left the station, they were to jump on the footplate and force the driver to bring the train to a stop where their comrades were waiting. The waiting went on for a week and the signal for action eventually came on 11 February. The train came to a standstill at the ambush point and, as it was night time, lit oil torches were thrown into the cutting beside the train, thereby illuminating the carriages containing the British soldiers. They were called on to surrender but they instead opened fire. The column replied with fire of their own and the soldiers all tumbled out of the carriages. After ten minutes of continuous firing from the column, some fourteen soldiers surrendered and one other lay dead. The column had started the attack with eight rifles and marched away with twenty-three and their ammunition reserve was increased by around a thousand rounds.

One soldier did attempt to escape and rushed up the embankment, eventually running into the rifle muzzle of one column member, Jer Long. Luckily, Long was an experienced and exceptionally cool Volunteer who contented himself with pushing the soldier back down the embankment. It transpired that the man was a Munster Fusilier who later, after being de-mobbed, joined an IRA column in Kerry. One of Moylan's comrades that night was a man called Michael O'Riordan from Millstreet, the eldest of three brothers who served with the Active Service Unit from its inception to the end of hostilities. The story goes that some years later O'Riordan was on holiday in Ballybunion and he went for a swim. Seemingly he got into difficulties having swum out too far and was unable to get back to the beach. Two strong swimmers came to his rescue and after a struggle they managed to get him back to the shore. One of O'Riordan's rescuers that fateful day turned out to be the same Munster Fusilier who had climbed the embankment and found himself looking into the muzzle of Jer Long's rifle.

* * *

February continued to be cold, wet and miserable and Moylan and his men moved from one billet to another. The people of his area never relented in their willingness to provide for the men despite the dangers associated with giving them refuge in their homes. By that time Moylan was three years on the run and must surely have been weary and missing the comforts of home. In his witness statement he spoke little of his lack of home comforts but he did allude to the fact that all he really owned at that time were his books. Throughout the statement one can find various refences to Dickens, Hugo,

Burns and Shakespeare, indicating that at some point in his life literature and the classics became an important factor in it. However, during the early months of 1921 his life was one of isolation though his sacrifice, he would have admitted, was no greater than that of his men. However, the arduous and uncomfortable life Moylan and his comrades led often meant their health was compromised. Many of them were confined to bed for weeks on end laid low by exposure and chills, poor diet and a lack of clean dry clothes. As the month of February 1921 came to a close, there was every indication the campaign against the British was about to intensify and Moylan and his men were going to be called upon to redouble their efforts for the cause of independence.

Chapter 9

The Ambush at Clonbanin

According to Aideen Carroll, there are many versions of what happened at Clonbanin in March 1921 when Moylan led an ambush against the forces of the Crown. There is even some argument over the exact date of the incident but what we cannot argue about is that the ambush did occur and it now occupies a revered place in the War of Independence folklore. The ambush was to be the highpoint of Moylan's military activities during the revolutionary era and the outcome enhanced his already high standing among not only his own men but also with the public in general. Over the course of the past century much has been written about the Clonbanin ambush but, of course, the most authentic account came from Moylan himself in his witness statement.

The story of the ambush starts near the end of February 1921 when Con O'Leary, the adjutant attached to the Kerry No. 2 Brigade, came to see Moylan. It was no secret that Moylan rated O'Leary very highly, believing him to be a man of soldierly thrust and determination. O'Leary had information about the regular movement of the British between Killarney and Rathmore. After the attack on Rathmore Barracks during 1920, the RIC in the village had been reinforced by Black and Tans and lorries travelling from Killarney brought them supplies and pay. O'Leary told Moylan that he was anxious to launch an attack on one of the sorties coming out from Killarney but as they varied in numbers, he was anxious to recruit Moylan's help and co-operation to ensure the success of his plan. He also said there was a possibility that General Strickland, commander-in-chief of the 6th Division, who was on an inspection tour of Munster, might well be part of one of the patrols. Though Moylan was, at the time, putting his own plans in place to attack the barracks in Newmarket, he willingly set them aside in order to help O'Leary.

Moylan and his men set out for Kerry on the last day of February and on 1 March settled themselves into position at a place called the Bower, which is about halfway between Killarney and Rathmore. Moylan recalled it as a cold place, a somewhat bare and windswept glen. It was desolate and contained none of the panoramic scenery so often associated with the Kingdom county. On arrival they found an abundance of Kerry men, all of whom were enthusiastic but possessed little in the way of guns and ammunition. Their best offerings were some shotguns but most of them were unarmed. Everyone lay in position for most of the day but there was no sign of the enemy. The same scenario played out on the following day. It was early on the third morning that Moylan and O'Leary reluctantly accepted that General Strickland was probably not going to come their way that day.

Later that morning Moylan was told a British patrol was approaching the area along a byroad to their rear. He quickly amended the positions of his men and, just as he finished doing so, a motor car coming from the east drove into the glen. Moylan's first thought was that the car might be the lead car in a British patrol. He ordered that the car not be fired upon and then, with some of his men, moved out on to the road to stop it. The driver stopped the car very quickly and Moylan and his men, rifles at the ready, moved towards it. They discovered the car contained four men, two of them American journalists, accompanied by a photographer and a fourth man who was the hired driver. After a discussion, Moylan asked the men to give him their word that they would not mention the meeting to anybody. They assured him they were neutral in the matter of the war and had no intention of disclosing the meeting. According to Moylan, they were true to their word and it was only on 7 March that the *New York Times* carried the story of the ambush, claiming it took place on 5 March.

* * *

Moylan, his men and the Kerry men waited for four days at the Bower without seeing anything of the enemy and by Friday evening there was every likelihood their position would soon become known to the British. Moylan spoke to Denis Galvin and asked him to take three men with him and return across the border into Cork and select an ambush site on the main road west of Banteer. He informed Galvin of the expected movements of the Active Service Unit and asked him to organise billets for the men. He also requested Galvin to get in touch with the Millstreet Battalion so that they might have the co-operation of their riflemen and of the companies whose areas adjoined the selected position. Con Meaney, who was commandant of the Cork No. 7 Millstreet Battalion, received a request from Moylan in the early hours of 5 March to prepare men, horses and traps to be sent as reinforcements to Clonbanin. In his own witness statement he later recalled:

> The message arrived at about 5.30 to 6.30 a.m. Horses and traps were immediately procured, and still under cover of darkness, the column, consisting of about twenty men, was drawn to within three miles of Clonbanin.[49]

After Galvin and his party had moved out for Cork, there was nothing left for Moylan and his men to do but move on, as darkness fell, to Ummeraboy near Knocknagree. Moylan recalled:

> Jack Mahony was the keyman here. He was an earnest and capable worker and I knew that the billets would be ready and that horses in good condition would be available to us for transport on the following morning. At midnight Galvin reported back to me at Ummeraboy. The position chosen was at Clonbanin and all other arrangements had been made. We left at 3 a.m. for Clonbanin and the latest comers were in position before 6 a.m. It was a beautiful calm morning, we had an usually strong force, riflemen from Charleville, Newmarket and Millstreet, as well as the riflemen from Kerry who had come with us. We also had one of the Hotchkiss guns captured at Mallow and half a dozen road mines. Commandant P. O'Brien had put the troops into position while I arranged for the laying of the mines. When I had finished he took me round to each section. In our tour we had the leader of the section with us so that each man should have a clear idea of the plan of attack.
>
> We made it quite clear that General Strickland and his party were the objects of our attack and we intended to ignore every other opportunity for attack offered no matter how tempting the offer proved to be. It was well that we were so insistent on this matter as later events proved.[50]

Moylan's decision to move the ambush site proved to be the correct one. Records of the 6th Division later showed the British had reasonable intelligence in relation to the first ambush site. It also transpired that the army convoy travelling from Killarney to Buttevant that afternoon carried General Hanway R. Cumming and not the much sought-after General Strickland. After Moylan and his men had moved out, the troops escorting Cumming actually carried out a search of the abandoned ambush site before escorting the general onwards.

The scene was then set for what promised to be a fairly large-scale confrontation and one that neither Moylan or his men had ever before experienced. Aideen Carrol, in her book, made some salient points about the men when she said:

> None of the IRA party had experience as professional soldiers. Moylan had been a carpenter, most of the others were farmers or labourers. It is fair to describe them as men with a conservative outlook in which family life, Catholicism and a strong work ethic were the defining elements. It was a momentous step for such men to set upon a course of action that involved the taking of human life. To engage in an armed conflict with the largest empire in the world was an ambitious enterprise and to attack a heavily armed convoy carrying the commander-in-chief of all armed forces in the southern Ireland region illustrated their breath-taking determination.[51]

While on his tour of the positions taken up by his men, a brigade despatch rider arrived to inform Moylan that the brigade commanding officer, Liam Lynch, was looking for him. It seemed a meeting of the Brigade Council had been called while Moylan was in Kerry. The despatch rider had been unable to contact Moylan, such was the secrecy of his movements and that of his men. When the rider did eventually make contact, the first men he met were the Musketeers. They told him Moylan would be arriving at their position directly. During the course of his conversation with the Musketeers, the despatch rider mentioned that Lynch was 'in a towering rage' over Moylan. Lynch, he said, was highly put out that he had not received a written report from Moylan in over a week. He and his fellow Council members were also outraged at having been kept waiting at brigade headquarters for Moylan and Commandant O'Brien for the past two days. The Musketeers, it seemed, were less than impressed with a man who seemingly put a greater emphasis on receiving written reports from men who were being constantly hunted and harassed by the enemy. They suggested to the rider that if the brigade commanding officer was so interested in reading reports, he should buy a newspaper on the following Monday morning and he would be able to read a report that might well be better than any others he had read in the past. With that, Moylan arrived and dismissed the despatch rider with a brief explanatory note before returning to the more pressing matters at hand.

* * *

By seven o'clock there was nothing else to do but wait. Moylan walked along the line on the northern side of the ambush site until he came to where the Charleville men were positioned. They showed Moylan a newspaper report of the death of Sean O'Brien, the chairman of the Charleville District Council, who had been murdered by the Black and Tans in his own home. As well as being a good friend of Moylan, the slain O'Brien had also been friendly with the Charleville men and Moylan knew by their grim expressions that they were determined to exact an appropriate revenge.

At about ten o'clock Moylan got word that the British were approaching on a road leading from the west. Turning his field glasses on them, Moylan could see three wire-covered lorries and, on one of them, a man was playing an accordion while his comrades sang. Moylan thought to himself:

> Poor devils, they little knew how close to disaster they were. What a horrible thing is war. Here were men against whom we had no personal hatred. Yet, because of the unwisdom of a statesmenship that refuses to recognise right except when it is backed by force, a single shot fired by accident, or by a nervous or excited youngster, meant swift dissolution for all of them.[52]

As it transpired that fateful shot was not fired on this occasion and Moylan saw it a fine test of his men's discipline, despite the fact that they had been lying in wet ditches, on and off, for the best part of week. The lorries continued on their journey going over the crest of the hill before disappearing. All was silent for a short time before the murmurings of Moylan's men could be heard as they questioned the wisdom of allowing the enemy to pass by unhindered. They all wondered if they would get a second chance and even Moylan had some doubts about his decision not to engage with the enemy given the opportunity that he had been presented with. The men went back to their positions to continue their wait. Nothing happened until just after two o'clock that afternoon when a signaller came with the news they had all being waiting for. This time the enemy was again coming from the west. Moylan recalled the moment vividly:

> The signallers on the hill behind us had seen them. They were not yet in view from the position in which I stood. I focussed the glasses on the hill crest. In a few moments the first lorry appeared, then two other vehicles, next came an armoured car,

> behind that again three more lorries. They were spaced at such intervals as to cover a half mile of the road. We had expected this and had spaced our section and the road mines accordingly. I watched the coming of the armoured car. The mine in the centre of the ambush position was destined for it. As it passed over the mine, I pressed the switch on the battery. I got a shock that almost knocked me over. It had short circuited. But all the others were watching too and at once a burst of rifle fire rang out. The leading lorry was ditched. And now we had a slice of luck; Liam Moylan with his Hotchkiss gun had concentrated on the armoured car and one lucky shot had got through the slit in front, wounding the driver. The armoured car, too, was ditched. The British dived for cover.[53]

With the advantage of surprise now lost to Moylan and his men, the British found themselves in a position of equality and what turned out to be a long fight began in earnest and only came to a conclusion as dusk began to fall. Moylan recalled how he and his men suffered from one major disadvantage, the lack of ammunition. Moylan was later of the opinion that had he twenty good marksmen that day the fight would have been much shorter and that he and his men would have had an even greater success. While both sides were equal in numbers, the British had the advantage of a Lewis gun and a heavy Maxim, which roared continuously from the armoured car. The Charleville men made several attempts to drive in the British right flank. Moylan and some of his men attempted the same manoeuvre on the left, but also failed. The armoured car commanded the whole area and Moylan and his men had to constantly take cover. In fact, stalemate seemed to set in very quickly.

According to Jimmy Cashman in his witness statement, Moylan took three men and crossed to the south side of the ambush site where the Kerry men and the Millstreet Active Service Unit were positioned about 200 yards from the road on a sharp rise of ground. A deep ditch and several houses gave the British excellent cover against an attack from that side and they had a fine field of fire against the IRA position. Yet Moylan and his comrades were able to keep the British pinned in their position, and he recalled how:

> The fight started about 2.30 p.m. It seemed to me that it had been in progress less than an hour when I looked at my watch. It was 5.30 p.m. My worry then was British reinforcements,

> Kanturk and Newmarket, where there were strong garrisons, were but a few miles distant. Buttevant, the main British garrison, only twenty-five miles away. The sound of firing could be heard (it actually was heard) in Newmarket and Kanturk. The reinforcements were overdue. Con Meany and Tom McEllistrim took a section to cover the road from the East. The fight went on and still no reinforcements arrived. I heard afterwards that a lorry with troops left Newmarket and, hitting a fence, overturned a mile from the town. The soldiers in Kanturk, in no way anxious to participate in the brawl, dug themselves into the various publichouses in the town and were with difficulty collected. It was not until darkness was falling that the reinforcements arrived and when they came, they came in strength. Talk about the taxicabs of the Marne, the line of lorries was like the parked cars in O'Connell Street.
>
> As darkness fell, we moved away. Millstreet and Kerry troops to the West. Those from Charleville and Newmarket retired North to Kiskeam.[54]

Moylan and his men in the 5th Battalion section crossed the fields at Dernagree and as they did so saw a large group of men following behind them. They took them to be comrades and slowed down to wait for them, only to realise in due course that they were British soldiers. The soldiers opened fire but luck was on Moylan and his men's side as dusk had already fallen and the British decided not to pursue them. Moylan and his men eventually fell in with other Volunteers from one of the local companies. They had the news that a British general had been killed and everyone assumed it was Strickland.

As it transpired, the 6th Division Record eventually confirmed that the senior officer who lost his life was Colonel Commandant Cumming along with another officer, Lieutenant Maligny. The record also stated that another officer and seven other men, mostly members of the East Lancashire Regiment, were wounded and it described the ambush as:

> One of the worst reverses suffered by the army and, making all allowances for the elaborate and undoubtedly skilful preparations made by the rebels, there is no doubt that the two facts which were more or less responsible for the disaster were (1) finding the original ambush position, of which information

> had been received, evacuated, precautions were somewhat relaxed; (2) owing to the armoured car, in its efforts to avoid a collision, getting ditched, it never properly came into action.[55]

The bodies of Cumming and Maligny were taken to Buttevant Barracks and brought to Dublin the following day. The next morning the bodies were placed on gun carriages and taken from the King George V Military Hospital at Arbour Hill along the Dublin quays to a ship waiting at the North Wall. The funeral cortège consisted of senior officers acting as pallbearers. Behind them walked General Macready and hundreds of officers and soldiers. Traffic was stopped by Auxiliaries and it was reported that any bystanders who failed to uncover their heads had their hats knocked to the ground.

Some hours after the ambush, which Republicans claim cost the lives of 13 British soldiers and wounded 15 others, Moylan and Commandant O'Brien made their way to Nadd, where the postponed Brigade Council meeting was to be held on the following day. On the way they went back to Clonbanin and made contact with members of the local company and, with their help, recovered the mines that had failed to detonate during the ambush. It seems the British had either overlooked them or decided not to attempt to deactivate them. When Moylan and O'Brien arrived at Nadd, they found Liam Lynch engrossed in the newspaper reports of the ambush and clearly in a better mood than he had been prior to it. Immediately after the meeting, Moylan left for Lisgriffin, where men of the Kanturk Battalion were lying in ambush for a police patrol at Father Murphy's Bridge near Banteer. With that in mind, Moylan crossed the Blackwater river at Roskeen Bridge and had it in his mind that it was the right time to destroy the bridge.

* * *

The destruction of bridges and the trenching of roads had become a major tactic in the disruption of enemy movements and Moylan was always on the lookout to engage in such actions. He called at the home of Tom Frawley, the local company captain, where he had a meal and waited until dark to begin the demolition job. Together with local company members, they carried out the task with picks, wedges and bars as they had no explosives. It took longer than expected to complete the job and make a satisfactory breech. As they worked, they received news that the ambush at Father Murphy's

Bridge had been a successful one with the RIC and Tans patrol attacked and disarmed.

Once the work on the bridge was completed, Moylan cycled the fifteen miles to Dromagh. When he reached Dromcummer, he stopped beside the main road while a convoy of British Army lorries passed by. It was about 4 a.m. and Moylan instinctively knew something rather big was in the offing. He cycled for a while behind the convoy before leaving the road to cross some fields, only to rejoin the road sometime later. At Dromagh he met Maurice Clancy, captain of the Derrygallen Company, who confirmed he had heard but not seen the lorries. Moylan, after leaving Dromagh, cycled south towards Rathcoole, where he called to the house of a friend and found three members of the Kanturk Battalion, who had been at the Brigade Council meeting with him at Nadd. They had heard rumours of an imminent British round-up at Nadd but could not offer any details.

It had been an arduous period for Moylan, who was feeling the physical effects of his efforts. In later years he looked back with a kind of amazement at the response that the human body is capable of making when difficult demands are made on it. During the weeks and months prior to Clonbanin, it has to be acknowledged that Moylan was not always in the best of health and for months he existed on a few hours' sleep each night. However, like many good leaders before him down through history, he did adapt to the conditions he worked under, as did the men he commanded, all of whom displayed a marvellous capacity for untiring, vigorous effort whenever they were called into action.

In his witness statement, Moylan later reflected on the British military leadership in Ireland during the revolutionary era and maintained it did not possess the same untiring, vigorous quality evident in the IRA men. He was convinced that, for whatever reason, the British never developed a soldierly aggressiveness. They replaced that attribute by introducing the undisciplined Black and Tans and Auxiliaries into Ireland to carry out attacks on property and on the civilian population. In Moylan's view there was only one real answer for the British and that was to employ like for like in the field. Rather than concentrating large bodies of soldiers in barracks around the country and staging intermittent forays and raids into the countryside, they should have employed smaller units, like the IRA Active Service Units, and lived off the land while constantly seeking battles against the enemy. They would have had to suffer the same discomforts as the IRA men but would have become battle hardened like their opponents. He went on to make a final comment on the quality of the British military in Ireland when he wrote:

> Of course, such commandos are not easily created, fighting men of the type necessary, sufficiently self-reliant to be capable of individual action, are few and far between; the average Englishman was war weary and disillusioned; Britain had many pre-occupations other than Ireland but, even when all this is considered, French, Macready and Strickland were no more to be commended for their work in Ireland than were Burgoyne, Howe and Cornwallis for their achievements in America. But even had the British adopted the commando system and had successfully dealt with the IRA, that was not necessarily the end. Determined, earnest men, familiar with the face of the Grim Reaper, would have devised alternative methods of embarrassment for Britain. And while the dice would be always heavily loaded against them, Imperial strategy never succeeded in manipulating these with skilful unerring hand.[56]

One has the sense from the above observation that Moylan felt his tactics at Clonbanin were justified and the success he and his men achieved could also be put down to their greater determination to win. They had become, over many months, battle-hardened individuals and the difficult and demanding regime they lived their lives under stood them in great stead that day. In essence they were tougher than the enemy and more committed to the cause they were fighting for. More than a century after the event, the ambush at Clonbanin has gone down in modern Ireland's folklore as a great victory for gallant Irishmen against the British and remains, to this day, a fine testament to Moylan's organisational and leadership skills.

Chapter 10

The War Moves Towards Stalemate

In the early days of March 1921, the Cork No. 2 Brigade established its headquarters at Nadd, a small place 1,000ft up on the slopes of the Boggeragh mountain almost equidistant from the towns of Macroom and Millstreet. According to Moylan, the location was perfect for the headquarters because it afforded a fine view of the surrounding countryside made up of rugged hills and glens. It also had the advantage of many loyal locals, all of whom were prepared to house and feed the men from any of the five battalions based in the region. The nature of the locality and its terrain facilitated the placing of outposts and made it very difficult for the enemy to approach unseen. The brigade headquarters was staffed at times by men from the Kanturk and Mallow battalions supplemented by members of the local and nearby companies who took their turns on outpost duty. All in all, there was a very good and cohesive set-up in Nadd and all the men were committed to the cause of independence and prepared to take on the British at any time.

On the morning of 9 March their commitment was tested to the limit when before the light even came upon the sky, a Volunteer rushed to the houses where members of the brigade staff were billeted to wake them with the news that the British were approaching and surrounding the area. It wasn't long before machine and rifle fire was heard. As the British appeared, they were fired on by men on outpost duty, forcing them to take cover. While the British advanced carefully under cover, the IRA men began to retreat all the time, keeping up their rifle fire. As a result, the British were delayed in their progress. The delaying tactic allowed the brigade staff to make their getaway with all their material and documents accompanied by many of the Volunteers. Three men, David Herlihy, Edward Waters and Timothy Kiely, were killed in the firefight, while a number of others who were wounded were helped in their escape across the hills by loyal comrades.

Moylan was later of the view that the British attempt to capture the Nadd headquarters was, in essence, a failure because they met a sturdy defence and were deprived of the end result they had set out to achieve. He maintained their lack of success:

> was due to the failure of one party of troops to arrive in time. While I was engaged on the Buttevant-Kanturk road a party of Volunteers of the Mallow Battalion were digging a trench wide and deep, on the Mallow-Banteer road.
>
> The armoured car leading the lorries loaded with troops and advancing on Nadd skidded into the trench and was overturned. By the time the British had decided that their efforts to haul it onto the road were useless and had filled in the trench to enable the lorries to cross, several hours had been lost. The party that had arrived on time advanced at the appointed hour and before all exits from the hills were blocked; the IRA, familiar with all the mountain paths, got clear away.[57]

The British, it seemed, had planned their operation well but had not anticipated the trench disruption on the Mallow–Banteer road. The question was soon raised among Moylan and his comrades as to how the British got to know of the whereabouts of the brigade headquarters. As it transpired, the answer was very quickly found. There was an individual living in the locality by the name of Shields, of whom Moylan had some knowledge but did not know him personally. He had served in the British Army for a short period of time. According to Moylan, the man was big and clumsy and very uncouth, and was in every sense a blackguard who was given to drink. He had a cast in one eye that gave him a sinister appearance and Moylan professed he had a real disliking and distrust of the man. He recalled how he was very shocked when he heard Shields had been recruited into the Kanturk Battalion. It seems he had convinced that battalion's leadership of his bona fides and was readily accepted into the ranks.

It soon became clear to Moylan that Shields played an instrumental role in the British operation on that fateful day. On 8 March, a young Volunteer and a native Wexford man called Martin McGrath was in Kanturk on Volunteers business. McGrath had been attached to the Volunteers in his native county and had come to Cork on transfer when he secured a job teaching Irish in Kanturk. His father had been an RIC sergeant in the town and still stationed there was a policeman who had served with him. The policeman was also a native Irish speaker and he and the young McGrath often spoke to each other in their native tongue. Late, on the evening of

8 March, the policeman, seeing McGrath, called him down a side street and informed him that Shields was in the RIC barracks. It seems he had arrived at dusk and was still, up to that time, in conversation with the officer in charge of the British troops in the district. McGrath immediately left for Nadd and passed the information on to his superior officer and asked to be permitted to talk to the brigade Officer Commanding. His request was turned down as his information was considered to be of little consequence. Moylan, looking back on the incident in his witness statement, was clearly still angry about that decision when he said:

> Neglect to enquire into the character of a man who turned out to be a traitor, lack of intelligence to understand the vital nature of the information, or careless neglect in making it known, were responsible for the deaths of three men and might have resulted in the complete disruption of the Brigade. Luckily we escaped this major disaster.[58]

Moylan recalled some more ambushes during the month of March. A week or so after Clonbanin the IRA launched an ambush at Castletownroche that resulted in the death of an RIC constable called Elton. Over in West Cork, Tom Barry led an engagement at Crossbarry, inflicting and sustaining significant casualties. It was one of the largest engagements of the War of Independence and there were many conflicting reports of the casualty toll. Barry claimed he lost three men, while the British claimed he lost up to six men. Barry and his comrades also claimed some thirty of the enemy died in the firefight, though the British officially accepted they lost ten men. On 22 March there was an engagement at Clogheen that resulted in six IRA men from the Cork No. 1 Brigade losing their lives. It was rumoured the British were able to locate the IRA men with the help of an informer who was allegedly paid £150 and sent on his way to England.

* * *

On the last day of the month, Tom Barry was once again in action when he and his men attacked the Rosscarbery RIC Barracks. They blew a hole in a wall of the barracks and a gun battle ensued that cost the lives of Sergeant Shea and Constable Bowles. The other eight RIC men in the barracks eventually surrendered as the building was engulfed in flames. By the beginning of April 1921 there was something of a stalemate in North

Cork. The RIC increasingly confined themselves to barracks for fear of being ambushed and the British Army only ventured out in large convoys and always varied their routes. The British were further inconvenienced by the fact that a telephonist at the Mallow exchange, Annie Barrett, was intercepting their messages and passing the information on to the IRA, which resulted in a number of their planned sweeps or round-ups being foiled. On the other hand, Moylan and his men were often frustrated in their own attempts to ambush the enemy and, on many occasions, were forced to endure long hours waiting to strike in all weathers without success.

Around that time Moylan cycled to Knockacluggin to call on Mick Sullivan and on the way visited Jack Mahony at Umeraboy and Jim Riordan at Knockavoreen. Sometime previously, Moylan had arranged with Mahony that they would build a dugout in a bog adjoining his farm and he wanted to discuss the project further and make a start on it. They had come to the conclusion that as the pressure on them from the enemy intensified they might have occasions to disappear for a while. With that in mind, they had discovered a large bog-hole with a gravel subsoil that did not retain water. It was ideal for an underground chamber and so they decided to build one with a subterranean exit into a smaller hole some distance away. Charlie O'Reilly was put in charge of the project and he selected trustworthy and qualified men capable of helping him. Moylan and O'Reilly also decided to build another dugout, which they would allow the public to know about, in a less remote place by way of a cover to their real intention. The work got under way and Moylan joined the men during the week to help them out.

On the Saturday night, Moylan took some of his men to Newmarket in an attempt to demolish the Clonfert Bridge, which was about half a mile from the town. They had no explosives and had to rely on sledges, pickaxes and bars. Moylan really had little hope of completely demolishing the bridge but he hoped the ringing sound of the sledge on steel in the stillness of the night would induce the police and military to investigate. In the hope that his plan might work, he placed six riflemen close to and covering the military and police barracks. The work on the bridge went on until early in the morning and while lights were switched on in the barracks and people moved about inside, no one ventured outside. With there being little likelihood of a patrol coming out of the barracks, Moylan and his men returned to Knockacluggin at daybreak.

* * *

While the work on the dugout continued there was a need to go into Newmarket for tools and materials. Moylan arranged for his uncle, Con Moylan, to collect the supplies and then, together with Mick Sullivan, decided to take the horse and car to collect everything. As they were leaving, Charlie O'Reilly decided to travel with them as he needed something from the chemist for a heavy cold. They left the horse and car at Horgan's of Coolagh and walked the final mile into Newmarket while all the time keeping an eye out for any military or police. They arrived into the town without meeting anyone and collected the tools as well as the medicine for O'Reilly. When they arrived back at Horgan's they checked the tools and found one was missing and it was assumed it had been dropped on the journey home. Sullivan decided to go back along the road in an attempt to locate the tool and O'Reilly stepped on to the car with him. Moylan decided to walk slowly back along the road in the hope he might see the tool. It wasn't long before he heard the sound of rifle fire and bullets began to whistle past him and ricochet off the road. Moylan recalled the incident in his witness statement when he said:

> I dived for the fence and pulled my gun. My anticipation was too correct.
>
> The British had laid an ambush and had arrived almost simultaneously with Sullivan and O'Reilly. There was another volley, then a scattered fire and I heard the horse galloping on the road below making for home by his usual route. I crept across the road and over the fence, across a field and on to the Rockchapel road, across this and into the fields again. I had little hope that my comrades had escaped but there might be some chance that they might have been wounded and had got away somewhere and needed my help. It was bitter cold as I crawled through the sodden field, revolver in hand and seeing a British soldier in every swaying bush. I got to the bridge and could hear the tramp of the troops as they marched back to the town. I waited, examining the roadway and fences outside. Finally, I came out on the road and searched for any traces of my friends. Not a sign anywhere.[59]

Moylan walked along the Rockchapel road for about three quarters of a mile, eventually coming to Jerry Doody's cottage. Doody was a loyal friend but his house was in darkness as it was two o'clock in the morning. Under the circumstances, Moylan was reluctant to knock on the door, believing all inside to be asleep. What he did not realise until later was that Charlie O'Reilly happened to be inside the house suffering from great pain, having taken two bullets in the earlier shootout, one being to his liver. By that stage, Jerry Doody was making his way across fields to fetch doctor Algie Verling, a former British Army officer who had served all through the Great War in France. Verling, though not a notable supporter of the republican movement, was a good friend and was not to be deterred from going to O'Reilly's aid.

* * *

Unaware of O'Reilly's plight, Moylan searched the Kingwilliamstown road and eventually found his first clue as to the whereabouts of his comrades. He located a saw in the middle of the road that had fallen from the horse and car. Along the road he found a hammer and at various intervals he picked up other tools. Around five o'clock, he arrived back at Mick Sullivan's house. He later recalled:

> I went to the bedrooms where O'Reilly, Mick and I had slept on the previous day. The rooms were empty and the rifles which had stood by the bedsides had gone. I sat on the bedside to think. I concluded that the boys had escaped, had at some time arrived home and not finding me had taken their rifles and gone to look for me.
>
> I found somebody shaking me and looked up to find Mick Sullivan. In sheer weariness I had dropped off to sleep. Mick had spent the night after his escape from the ambush in search of O'Reilly and of me. He had been over the same ground as I had covered but at different times and had finally decided that he could only get news of us by coming home.[60]

Sullivan was relieved to see Moylan but he could not explain the absence of the rifles. However, that mystery was soon cleared up with the arrival of two of Moylan's men, Johnnie Jones and Liam Moylan. They had been sleeping in the house of the man who owned the horse that Moylan and Sullivan had driven to Newmarket and were woken up when it trotted back into the farmer's yard. Jones and Liam Moylan immediately realised something untoward had happened and made their way to Sullivan's house to look for their comrades. Not finding anyone in the house, they feared the worst and departed for Newmarket, taking the rifles with them. They eventually heard that O'Reilly had been shot and he was being guarded by the British in his own home. Unfortunately, the gallant freedom fighter lost his final battle the following day and passed away. A distraught Moylan later recalled his friend's funeral as the occasion:

> of a great demonstration of force and intimidation on the part of the British. But in spite of this its dimensions proved where the sympathies of the people lay and their respect for the dead soldier.[61]

O'Reilly's death had a profound impact on Moylan and caused him to reflect on the situation he and his comrades found themselves in. He mused that a soldier's sorrow for the death of a comrade is neither insincere or evanescent, but in war, death is a clear possibility if not an inevitability. O'Reilly's death and, indeed, the deaths of the men at Nadd earlier that week, did not, however, affect Moylan's routine and that of his men's existence. They were all aware there was still a job of work to be done and any personal feelings, no matter how sad and upsetting, had to be set aside. In fact, Moylan was of the opinion that they had all developed a kind of philosophy around the notion of wartime death. They were all caught in a trap of their own making, from which there was no escape and from which they had no desire to escape.

* * *

It wasn't long before Moylan came up with another plan of action when he decided it was an opportune time to destroy Barleyhill Bridge, two miles north of Newmarket, and to lay an ambush there. He was aware the number of attacks they had actually carried out up to that time bore no relation to the number of attempts they actually planned and organised only to be thwarted at the last minute by some unforeseen obstacle or event. During all the aborted operations the men had to endure endless weary hours in all weathers without experiencing the thrill of success. Moylan hoped the planned ambush at Barleyhill Bridge might deliver another success to savour.

He set about assembling thirty riflemen at Kiskeam and ordered the Newmarket company captain, Jeremiah Sheehan, to mobilise his men for drills every night during the week. On the evening before moving into the ambush position, Moylan sent for Sheehan and ordered him and his men to demolish the bridge at Barleyhill. After dark, Moylan and his riflemen left Kiskeam and marched westwards across country until they reached the Newmarket–Meelin road half a mile south of Meelin. They continued in single file along the road from Meelin to Barleyhill, moving cautiously for fear a sudden appearance on their part might be taken to mean the arrival of a British party by the men demolishing the bridge. Moylan recalled:

> When we got within half a mile of the bridge we halted, lay against the fence and listened for the sound of pick or sledge. All was silence. We sent forward two scouts. These disappeared into the fields and we waited their report. They were back in twenty minutes. Half the bridge was down, picks, sledges and shovels were thrown on the road and the fence was lined with discarded overcoats. They had either been surprised or had taken alarm. We moved carefully forward, examined roads and fences on both sides of the bridge, finally came out on the road beside the bridge. Sure enough, half the bridge was down and the road was strewn with instruments of demolition. These boys had left hurriedly. We gathered up the tools and waited. While waiting, I noticed two men sling their rifles and stooping in the centre of the fence, make a careful examination of the discarded overcoats. Satisfied apparently with the examination, they divested themselves of the coats they were wearing and from the fence appropriated two which, I assume, they felt better suited to their condition. I made no protest. I felt now that there had been a panic dispersal as a result of a false alarm and hoped that the loss of the coats might be a lesson to their owners on the evil consequences of panic action.[62]

It transpired that Sheehan had been unable to control his men and had moved away with them before returning alone to discover those who had arrived were Moylan and his men. There was no hope of rounding up the men who had fled, leaving Moylan and his riflemen to tackle the job themselves. When the work was completed, they gathered up all the tools and left the scene.

The houses that were to be used to billet Moylan and his riflemen had already been selected and when they arrived at the first house they knocked the door but there was no answer. There was nothing for it but to open a window and send one man through it, and he opened the front door. It was obvious the occupants of the house knew the men were there but no one emerged from the inner rooms. A workman was found in an outhouse and he made a fire and put a kettle on to boil and soon a breakfast of ham and eggs was prepared. After having their fill, they all adjourned to a house they knew they would be sure of a welcome where they gathered around a blazing fire and waited for the dawn. It wasn't long before Moylan became very ill, suffering a reaction to the ham he had eaten. Since his recovery from his debilitating illness of the previous year, he had been very circumspect about his food. He found he could not tolerate meat and the little amount of ham he had eaten caused an adverse reaction. He recalled:

> My stomach felt as if I had some demon surgeon operating on it with a red hot blunt scalpel. My head ached violently and cold sweat oozed from every pore. I was put to bed, where I lay helplessly. I had scarcely strength to speak yet I forced myself to discuss the proposed ambush with Mick Sullivan. He was quite as familiar with the ambush position as I was. He listened to and approved of my plans. As he left with the others to take up their positions my last instruction to him was to send for me at once when he had word of the arrival of the British and under no circumstances to leave his position until after dark.[63]

Moylan spent the day in bed in great pain waiting to hear the sound of rifle fire but it never came. As darkness fell, a downcast Mick Sullivan appeared to say he and the men had waited until dusk but there was no sign of the British. Just then, a Volunteer arrived on a bicycle bringing news that very soon after the men had vacated their positions the British arrived and they examined the damaged bridge before returning to Newmarket. It was, of course, too late to pursue them and everyone was extremely disappointed. Moylan refrained from pointing out that his orders had not been carried out to the full and had they been, the men would have been in position when the British eventually appeared. The following week was spent making nightly forays in and around Newmarket in the hope that they might encounter a British patrol but to no avail. It was clear they had no intention of being caught away from their barracks as darkness fell. Eventually, Moylan moved back to Kiskeam, disappointed that another opportunity had been lost to strike at the heart of the enemy.

* * *

Once back in Kiskeam, Moylan set about carrying out the final trial of a gun that he hoped would blow a hole in the steel shutters of the RIC barracks. The cannon, which had been seized from Ross Castle in late January, had been put to one side because of more pressing projects. Since January, it was housed in a barn and so it was trundled out and moved into position. The powder was tamped in place and a newspaper wad rammed home. The bore was, however, very rough and jagged, eaten by the rust of years, and in hindsight, the gun was an accident waiting to happen, a fact later confirmed by Moylan when he said:

> As I placed the iron projectile in the mouth of the gun there was an explosion. The piece of iron was torn from my hand. I was blinded with smoke. My hands were numb and as I looked down, I found my left hand covered with blood and gobbets of flesh hanging from it. That, for me, completed the day's experiment.[64]

The mangled hand was later treated by Dr O'Riordan in Boherbue, who stripped off the bandages and took one look at the mess before producing a bottle of whiskey. He gave Moylan a stiff drink of it, by way of an anaesthetic, and then proceeded to operate. According to Moylan, the doctor performed a fine job that turned out to be as good as any that might be carried out by an eminent surgeon. Despite all of O'Riordan's good work, the pain was immense and left Moylan weak and exhausted. However, the discomfort had to be ignored to a certain extent because Moylan had an important meeting scheduled for the following day with the brigade commanding officer near Millstreet. It seemed the 1st Southern Division was about to be formed.

Chapter 11

Promotion and Added Responsibilities

In his witness statement, Moylan discussed the IRA and the units that made up the organisation. He made the point that though the terms company, battalion, brigade and division were used to describe the different elements of the army, the terms did not denote numerical strength or units designed to a specialised service. The basis of the organisation was the parish and in every parish a company was formed and the battalion area was a grouping of parishes. Cork county was originally a brigade area but later still it was divided into five brigade areas. Each brigade was self-sufficient, depending on its own resources, and was only recipient of a general direction from headquarters. According to Moylan, the brigade was sacrosanct and any intrusion within its limits was often resented by both the brigade staffs and the fighting units. Moylan recalled one such intrusion in November 1920 when the Cork No. 1 Brigade saw a real opportunity to inflict some hardship on the British. They had carefully planned the operation and Moylan was asked to send certain reinforcements to help them out. On the selected day some of his men with two machine guns travelled by arrangement into the Cork No. 1 area. They arrived back the following day after the planned action had been cancelled because of the Kilmichael ambush. It seems the Cork No. 1 Brigade had no idea the Kilmichael operation was taking pace almost on the same ground as their proposed action was to be attempted.

Moylan also provided two other incidents that highlighted the lack of co-operation between different elements within the organisation. At Clonmult in February 1921, a small party of IRA men were surrounded by a British column. They fought a magnificent rearguard action until their ammunition was exhausted and a number of them were killed or wounded. Most of those who were wounded were later executed and the whole operation was deemed in the end to be a disaster. Moylan claimed that at the time, though he had no real proof, that another IRA column found itself within sound of the guns and made no attempt to discover what the cause of the shooting was. He also gave the example of the ambush in March 1921 at Headford in

Kerry where the IRA leader, D.J. Allman, was killed. Moylan claimed the operation might have been entirely successful had there been co-operation forthcoming from the North Cork men, who were based at that time only a few miles across the border and who would have only been too glad to lend a hand and participate in the fight. It was for these reasons that Moylan welcomed the formation of 1st Southern Division, believing the goodwill between brigades and their understanding of and respect for each other could be hammered into a closer co-operation effort.

* * *

The meeting that set the ball rolling was held at Kippagh near Millstreet on 26 April 1921 and it involved some of the most senior IRA men in the south-west of the country. Moylan vividly recalled the day of the meeting:

> The cold of Winter was gone, the sun shone with a comforting warmth, the scent of the furse blossom was heavy in the air, there was a lazy drift of smoke over Claragh as I travelled south from Cullen to Kippagh where the meeting was to be held. Here Paddy McCarthy's body had lain the previous November, and here now were gathered IRA leaders from all the Cork, Kerry, Waterford and West Limerick Brigades. Some were old friends and associates of long standing, others were strangers known to me only by reputation. Sean Hegarty, O.C. Cork No. 1 Brigade, I hadn't seen for several years. He was now bearded, with a homespun trousers and blue coat, the whole ensemble roofed in a bowler hat. He looked like an old time music hall artist; a stranger seeing him would not be surprised if he broke into song. He was, however, no comedian but a serious man of keen intellect. If he had a sense of humour, it was of that sardonic and devastating type peculiar to Cork. I had heard so much of Tom Barry and of his high reputation as a leader of troops in action that I was anxious to see him.
>
> Here he was; like Ernie O'Malley, he looked a soldier and didn't care a damn who knew it. He was slight and erect, his smart coat, riding breeches and gaiters giving an impression of uniform. Later as he sat across the table from me, I watched him.

> His face was that of an intelligent, earnest, determined and intolerant man, one whose mind was closed to all issues other than that with which he was concerned.
>
> I don't think his appearance belied his character. A few weeks before he had had at Crossbarry a great success against the British.[65]

Others who attended the meeting included Florrie O'Donoghue, adjutant of Cork No. 1 Brigade, who Moylan described as shrewd and brainy. Liam Deasy of the West Cork No. 2 Brigade was there, as was Pax Whelan from West Waterford. Garrett McAuliffe, the newly appointed West Limerick Officer Commanding, attended, as did Humphrey Murphy from Kerry. Liam Lynch was accompanied by George Power and Ernie O'Malley represented General Headquarters and was designated to preside over the meeting. It had been agreed before the meeting to appoint Liam Lynch as the new divisional Officer Commanding and the meeting was ostensibly called to obtain a formal agreement from the brigades to the proposal to arrange the appointment of a divisional staff and to discuss a new way forward in the south of the country.

* * *

Moylan recalled how the meeting opened with the reading of a communication from General Headquarters. For most of those in attendance the missive contained impractical military proposals that only served to arouse their anger and to their minds had been put forward by people who had little experience of battle. It seems that Sean Hegarty who, according to Moylan, 'was a master of invective', tore the communication and its authors to ribbons. Tom Barry also registered his disdain, as did others among the gathering. Moylan and others sat back, said nothing but enjoyed the fun and Lynch attempted to pour oil on the obviously troubled waters.

Once all that was out of the way, the meeting discussed the appointment of divisional staff and the necessary readjustments in the various brigades. This resulted in Moylan losing one of his most trusted men, Con Moylan, to Division. There was also a discussion on tactics and when it became clear that GHQ was attempting to place them all in a tactical straightjacket, there was a furious reaction from the body of the meeting. Many took the view that those at GHQ had too much time on their hands and too little military experience.

Moylan was especially impressed by the contributions made by those from the Cork No. 3 Brigade to the debate on tactics. It was clear the local commanders had their own views and how to prosecute the war against the British. Even Moylan, it seems, showed his displeasure at the directive coming out of GHQ, when, according to Tom Barry, he jumped to his feet and exclaimed:

> We started this war with hurleys, but, by heavens, it seems to me, we will all finish it off with fountain pens.[66]

The meeting also discussed the question of the torture and shooting of IRA prisoners by the British, most especially in Cork. At that time there were five prisoners awaiting their execution at Victoria Barracks and Tom Barry suggested that a letter be sent to Major General Strickland threatening reprisals. He also suggested that 14 May be designated as a 'shoot-up' day if the executions were carried out. While the meeting broke up in a reasonably amiable atmosphere, there continued to be some lingering personal dissatisfactions for some years after it. Moylan and Barry continued to be very critical of GHQ and its role during the meeting. Barry, in particular, regarded the new divisional structure to be a waste of time and declared:

> not a gun, a round of ammunition, a shilling or a plan of action came out of it.[67]

When the meeting concluded, Moylan prepared to return home somewhat disgruntled that he had lost Con Moylan, a man he depended on so much, to Division. As he was about to leave, Lynch called Moylan back for a chat and he recalled how the new division Officer Commanding was:

> delighted with his new post and expressed that delight to me. He had an amiable boyish touch of vanity which did not detract from his earnestness and determination.
>
> 'You'll take over the Brigade,' he said. I was not prepared for this. A Brigade O.C. has to concentrate on staff work and cannot personally concern himself with the clash of arms. It seemed to me that life as a Staff Officer would be intolerably dull for one of my experiences. It seemed to me that George Power of Fermoy should be appointed.
>
> He was Deputy Brigade Commandant. He had done his work well and was the obvious choice for the vacant post. I had no desire for a change for the vacant post. I had no desire

> for a change that would take me out of the fighting line and relegate me almost entirely to staff work and organisation.[68]

Moylan objected vehemently to his promotion but his views were rejected out of hand. Lynch said he had discussed the matter with George Power, who was anxious that Moylan take the post on the basis that he was older and had much more experience. Power's attitude was similar to that of so many IRA men, all of whom felt it was not their place to seek rank or position but to do the job they were asked to do. Power, it seems, felt Moylan was the better man for the job and he was adamant that he should step aside and allow him to occupy it. He was also more than willing to give Moylan his fullest co-operation in carrying out that onerous task.

In later years Power recalled he had been offered the post as brigade commander but had declined it in favour of Moylan because he seemed to be the natural choice. Moylan, of course, was eminently qualified for the job because of his reputation for sound judgement and his undoubted leadership qualities. He had also trained and kept together a battalion of Volunteers and turned them into a fine and very effective fighting force. He had established a major reputation for himself by his involvement in ambushes at places like Tureengarriffe, Ballydrochane and Clonbanin among others. In every engagement with the enemy he maintained a cool and shrewd countenance, never flinching in his duties as a leader. He had proven himself to be a keen strategist with an ability to adjust and adapt to unexpected developments or obstacles.

There was one other very important factor when it came to promoting Moylan. It had not gone unnoticed that his casualty rates during engagements with the enemy were low. In ambushes led by Moylan there were no fatalities among his men and he had a reputation for being cautious with their lives. Invariably, the ambushes he oversaw were carried out at sites of his choosing and, very importantly, only when he was satisfied that he and his men had sufficient arms and training to carry out the ambush. Moylan also had that rare ability as a leader to make sure that he and his men survived any engagement and in the eyes of his superiors that very significant factor was taken into account when he came under consideration for the position of brigade Officer Commanding. Moylan also had one other very important attribute; he was able to avoid capture, whether it was by sheer good fortune or by having an uncanny ability to do so. He survived the Spanish flu despite being very ill when he was struck down by it. He survived many days and nights out in the most inclement weather imaginable and he survived being struck down by a bullet while engaging with the enemy. In essence, Moylan had staying power and he seemed destined to survive all the dangers he was confronted with.

Moylan's objections to his promotion were dismissed and he was left with little choice but to accept and get on with the job. Once in situ he determined his first task was to reorganise the brigade. The Cork No. 2 Brigade covered a wide area from north of Midleton from Ballynoe to the Kerry border west of Millstreet and Newmarket. The northern border was the Limerick county boundary and, in the south, it was the Boggeragh Mountains. There were eight battalions in the brigade: Fermoy, Castletownroche, Mitchelstown, Charleville, Mallow, Kanturk, Newmarket and Millstreet, all of which comprised around 5,000 Volunteers. While only a fraction of the men would be active at any one time, it was clear that Moylan had the responsibility of looking after all of them.

Moylan, despite his initial protestations, was pleased with his appointment because for some time he had been pressing for a reorganisation of certain battalions. He was also anxious to determine the reasons for a number of failures and disasters, including the one at Nadd, and apportion blame if he deemed it necessary. Essentially, what he wanted to do from the outset was to turn the brigade into an efficient fighting unit. Moylan did not intend to proceed with his plans without proper consultation and deliberation but he did feel he had sufficient facts to justify any actions he proposed to take. Before doing so, however, he had to attend to his own battalion. He replaced his vice-commandant, Paddy Murphy, with Sean Nunan. Murphy had been a very loyal, effective and hardworking comrade and a pioneer in the movement. Though physically big and powerful, an accident while in Belfast jail, when he almost bled to death, had lessened his vigour and vitality so the time was right for him to step down.

Murphy's replacement, Nunan, was an energetic individual whose countenance exuded authority and character. He had a presence that seemed to set him above anyone else and Moylan was often known to say he knew of no better man. Jim Riordan from Kiskeam replaced Nunan as quartermaster. Riordan's home had been Moylan's headquarters for some months and the man was always at his beck and call. He was very familiar with the work of the battalion and so was eminently qualified to do the job. Both Nunan and Riordan applied themselves wholeheartedly to their posts and lessened the burden of responsibility on Moylan's shoulders. Both Moylan and Nunan spent a couple of days at Geoffrey Sullivan's of Knockilla, where they discussed battalion reorganisation. The debacle at Nadd still rankled with Moylan and he decided to take retrospective action. He was convinced what happened at Nadd was due to a failure of intelligence and it could not be overlooked. He decided to replace the battalion Officer Commanding at Kanturk who had permitted the informant Shields to be recruited into the ranks and who had failed to act decisively when suspicions were raised.

While at Sullivan's a very funny incident took place that Moylan felt he could share with the wider public in his witness statement. Sullivan had a few good horses in his stable and they very often provided transport for Moylan and his men. One morning, Moylan and Nunan came out into the farmyard while Sullivan was training a colt. They stopped to watch the proceedings and Moylan happened to mention that he never had the opportunity to learn how to ride a horse. Sullivan stopped what he was doing and went into a stable before re-emerging with a fine big chestnut horse. What happened next turned out to be an escapade of pure comedy for those lucky enough to witness it. Sullivan, according to Moylan, put a saddle on the horse and said:

> 'Up you go.' My idea of learning horsemanship was to secure for the purpose a smaller animal which the years had deprived of any ambition for undue effort and I was rather taken aback at the power, size and rolling eye of my proposed mount.
>
> Well, I had brought it on myself. I was hoisted into the saddle. The chestnut proved to be a not ungraceful ballet dancer. I was perched insecurely at a height which seemed to me to be about ten feet off the ground. Paddy led the animal out of the yard across the road and into a field. He then flicked the horse with his whip and away we went across the field. As I lifted into the air and came back with a thud on the saddle the exclamation that left my lips was a compound of fervent prayer and lurid profanity. When the hooves hit the ground each time I floated in a beautiful parabolic curve on the horse's neck; as they left it again, I clashed with the saddle so hard that I thought I'd finish with my backbone protruding through my scalp. A low bank divided the field in which I was from the next field. My mount faced it, hit it beautifully with his hind feet, sailed over and continued

> his lunatic career. The next fence was high and topped by a thick growth of thorn. We pounded towards it. In midfield it dawned on me that if I pulled hard on the rein the beast might forego his intention to murder me. I did so; he swung round in a wide curve and faced back for the fence we had crossed. He and I repeated our previous performances and as he landed he broke into a trot which was for me a more excruciating experience than his gallop. At the end of the field where my audience waited in a gale of laughter he halted and my heart dropped back into place. Paddy, choking with merriment congratulated me on my success and turned the horse around again for another trial. While the jarring of my backbone had not decreased, I had now much more confidence in my mount. I assume he realised, as I did, that I was a damn fool and decided to take care of me. Each further trip made me more confident but after an hour I felt it was time to call it a day.
>
> I dismounted, tried to walk and failed. Every muscle in body ached.[69]

A little while after his initiation into the world of horse riding, Moylan was visited by Liam Lynch while he was on his way to Kerry. He informed Moylan that some politicians were becoming more and more uneasy about the outcome of the war, and one in particular, Eamon de Valera, was particularly anxious to see for himself what conditions were like outside the confines of Dublin. He proposed to spend a month in the field with an Active Service Unit in Moylan's Cork No. 2 Brigade. While Moylan was pleased his unit had been selected, he was, nevertheless, worried about the safety of the man who was the unquestioned political leader of the majority of the Irish people. Guerrilla warfare was uncertain at the best of times so, having a man who was much revered, in the thick of it or, at least near the action, brought its own problems.

* * *

Moylan informed senior officers of the impending visit and a number of capable and trustworthy fighting men were assembled to prepare for the task of maintaining security around the esteemed visitor. Moylan sent Michael O'Connell, another trusted comrade, to Dublin to meet with Sean

O'Connell, who was a member of Collins's staff. When he returned, he informed Moylan that de Valera was scheduled to arrive on a particular train two days later disguised as a railway guard. On thc appointed day, Moylan and his men moved into position very early in the morning. Trains passed through the station but there was no sign of de Valcra. Thinking that he might arrive on the following day, Moylan again moved his men into position and as he did so he received a message from Liam Lynch to stand his men down and to meet him in Lombardstown. Moylan learned from Lynch that de Valera's visit had been cancelled because the first tentative approaches for a truce had come from the British.

Chapter 12

The British Step Up Their Presence

When the 1st Battalion of the Gloucestershire Regiment arrived into Kanturk near the end of April 1921 it was clear to everyone that the British were about to step up their presence in the region. Under the command of Lieutenant Colonel F.C. Nisbet, the battalion comprised of eighteen officers and 572 other ranks. They were based, in the main, in Kanturk, while smaller units were sent to Newmarket and Banteer. When the advance party arrived it was led by Lieutenant R.M. Grazebrook, who was given temporary transport in the guise of a purple tourer that had been used by the late Brigadier General Hanway Cumming, who lost his life at Clonbanin. It seems Grazebrook was somewhat disconcerted by the fact that the car had a number of bullet holes in it.

The main body of men were billeted in the Old Union Workhouse on Coolacusane Hill, which conveniently overlooked the town of Kanturk. Grazebrook later recorded his initial impressions of taking over the building when he said he was:

> armed with the authority to take over the building and to eject within a certain number of days all the inmates and attendants. To one who doesn't know Ireland, and the squalor and filth of the cottages and of that country, it would be impossible to describe the condition of the building and the inhabitants. There were about a hundred or so male and female inmates of all descriptions, some absolutely bedridden, others stone deaf, many real imbeciles and continually creating ghastly noises.
>
> Besides this there was one block full of orphans and one set apart for fever cases.[70]

The workhouse was run by a man called Pat O'Keefe and it was under the auspices of the Board of Guardians and, by all accounts, O'Keefe was not that keen to co-operate with the British. The fact that the inmates had to

Above: Liam Lynch's handkerchief with bloodstains. (© Sheila1988/ wikicommons)

Right: Moylan and General Sean MacEoin.

Below: Clonbanin ambush commemoration stone.

Anti-Treaty IRA Convention, Mansion House, Dublin, April 9th 1922. Moylan is three from the right in the front row.

Kiskeam Church, built by Moylan.

Moylan's former home in Kiskeam which he built himself.

Moylan's grave and headstone in Kiskeam cemetery.

Welcome to Kiskeam mural in Kiskeam village

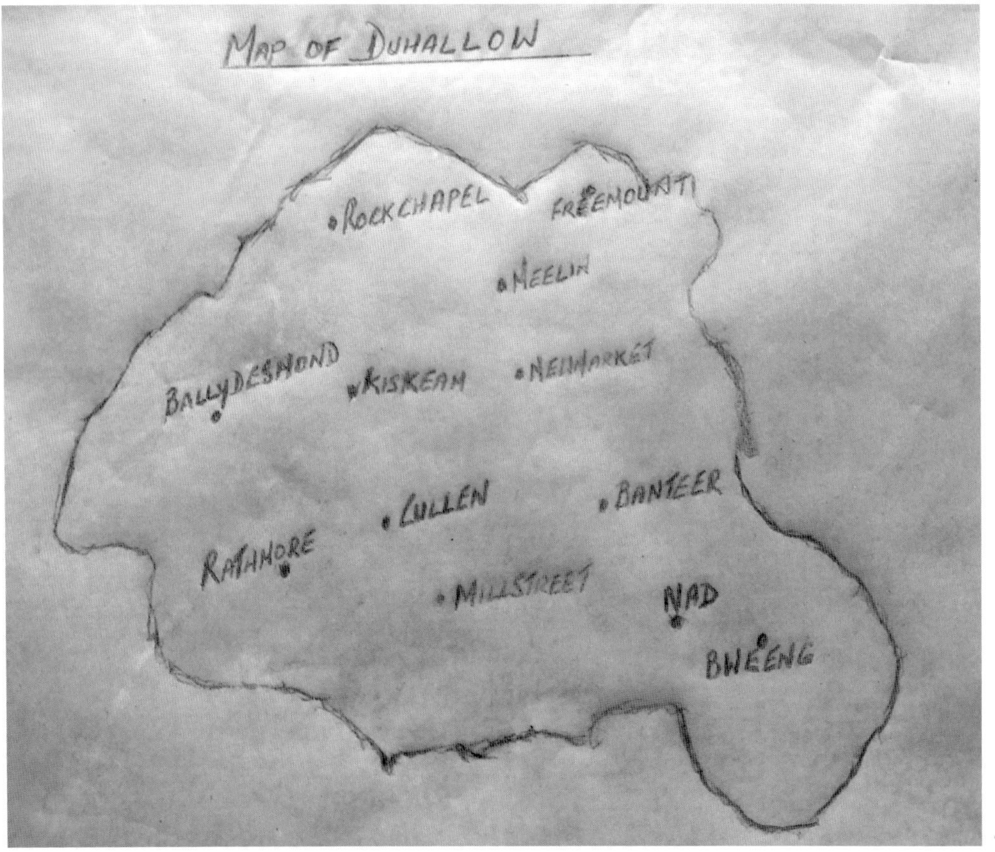

Map of Duhallow. This is a hand drawn map by myself. This is the region Moylan operated in during the War of Independence.

Dáil Éireann meeting in the Mansion House, August 1921.

Seán Keating, *Men of the South*, 1921-22. Collection Crawford Art Gallery, Cork. (© Estate of Sean Keating, IVARO Dublin, 2024)

be moved proved to be too much of a trauma for some of them and they unfortunately passed away.

The workhouse appears to have been chosen because the building was big enough to accommodate many soldiers and because it was in a strategically important place just outside Kanturk, which, of course, was a hub of IRA activity. The two-storey workhouse was easily defended and had a yard surrounded by a 14ft wall. There was a single gate entrance big enough to allow a lorry through and a narrow gate to a recreation field. The soldiers were billeted in the old hospital block while the boardroom was used by the sergeants and the officers used the fever hospital annex. There were many complaints from the men and officers about the poor condition of the building but it was all that was on offer to them.

* * *

While the soldiers may have been unhappy with their billet, they did, it seems, attempt to integrate into the local community. One officer, Captain A.H. Richards, later recalled how:

> The locals were quite affable and we did drink with them knowing full well that they were at least IRA sympathisers. They were nearly always able to tell us where we had been on our latest operation and what we had been doing whether it was by day or by night.[71]

The remit of the regiment was essentially to restore order, arrest known IRA men, especially Moylan, and seize their arms. They were also to provide escorts for lorry convoys. The arrival of the Gloucestershire Regiment was not helpful for Moylan and his men and only served to make their lives even more difficult. He recalled:

> Our difficulties had been augmented by the fact that a Battalion of the Gloucester Regiment had come to Kanturk … I lay one sunny afternoon on a hillside watching a column of troops pass by on their way to Kerry. The column consisted of twenty-five lorries and two armoured cars. They proceeded slowly, stopping to search roadside farmhouses and to make excursions into the fields to search the farmhouses at some distance from the road. They held up and questioned everybody they met and after

> several hours passed out of my sight. They were proceeding at a rate of not greater than one mile an hour.[72]

It soon came to Moylan's notice that the Glosters (the name given to the regiment by the local people) always carried metal girders to get their lorries and armoured cars over the many trenches that had been dug into the roads in the Kanturk and Newmarket areas. They also began a new trend of taking farm carts or even their wheels as a way of persuading local farmers to fill in the trenches. They were also not averse to rounding up locals and forcing them to repair the roads. Despite all that, the local Volunteers were more than willing to go out and re-dig the trenches, so it essentially became a game of cat and mouse. The Glosters also resorted to using bicycles to get themselves around the area, which of course made them more vulnerable than when they travelled in motor vehicles. To counteract the bicycles, the Volunteers busied themselves by covering many roads with glass and tacks. Fires were lit across the countryside to signal troop movements and a curfew was strictly enforced by the Glosters. On occasions they forced people who were caught outside after curfew to walk all night with them on their patrols. On other occasions curfew breakers were forced to spend the night locked up in the barracks.

The Glosters took a different view to other regiments when it came to patrolling the region; in fact, they spent most of the time in barracks or very close to it. This meant Moylan and his men had really only one option and that was to snipe at them when the opportunity arose, and he was not keen to involve his men in that type of activity. The lack of contact with the enemy was evident on 14 May, the day designated as 'shoot-up' day by the IRA Executive Council, when Moylan took twenty men into Newmarket and found there was no movement forthcoming from the Glosters. The war was taking on a new and very frustrating dimension and, to Moylan, it seemed the days of open conflict with the enemy were coming to an end.

However, the Glosters were not finished. They had one more large-scale operation still left in them and were determined to make their presence felt in the region and round up as may IRA men as possible. It did not take the officers of the Glosters long to notice they were being observed anytime they ventured out of the barracks, not helped by the fact there was only one exit from the building. To counteract that problem, Grazebrook began to billet some of his men in tents in the adjoining field, which made it easier for them to leave at night unobserved. At first, the Glosters had little knowledge of the region and of the people and were forced to rely on information from the RIC. However, they soon managed to find informers and began to put together a very precise knowledge of the IRA structure in the region. It wasn't long before they knew who were the most active IRA men around and were using the informant Shields to provide them with up-to-date information. By then Shields was wearing a British uniform, was operating under a new name and was very conspicuous in the area. He even assisted in interrogating IRA men and often gave evidence at courts martial.

Moylan and his fellow officers and men soon became aware of the intelligence work being put in by the Glosters to build up a clear picture of the overall situation in the area. Members of the regiment had been observed, often in plain clothes, drawing up maps, helped by spotter planes and sophisticated binoculars. The Glosters began to round up individuals almost on a daily basis and one of the best ways they found to do so was to surround a church on Sunday morning and take out a suspect from the congregation. Arrests were made and documents were seized and often the end result was a court martial, with the suspect more than likely sent to the Spike Island prison.

It wasn't all one-way traffic of course, as the IRA actively engaged in their own intelligence work. They soon began to identify the informants in each community, and telephonists like Annie Barrett continued to pass on very important information, and, whenever they could, make it difficult for the military to access the telephone system. Moylan and his men also continued to cut telephone wires and raid the mails. Moylan continued to be a prime target of the military because of his association with the Tureengarriffe and Clonbanin ambushes. As a result, his mother's home and shop in Newmarket was continuously under observation and even raided, though there was never any chance of finding Moylan there. It seems the British believed, probably because of local gossip, that Moylan was dying of consumption, which was not correct. We know from his own admission that he was in poor health but he certainly wasn't dying. He did admit in later years that at the time he really was unwell and that people in GHQ constantly pleaded with him to go into hospital in Dublin for treatment and an assessment of his health but he rebuffed their pleas.

The British were also consumed by a rumour that Moylan was often seen travelling the Tullylease to Kiskeam road every Saturday night in a black trap and that he was about to get married. In fact, Moylan, as far as the British were concerned, was taking on the aura of a Scarlet Pimpernel-like character and they were becoming obsessed with tracking him down. We do know, of course, from his witness statement that Moylan had set up his brigade headquarters at Knockavoreen, not far from Kiskeam, and that he did spend most weekends there. According to Aideen Carroll, there may well have been a very normal social reason for his presence in Kiskeam at the weekend because it was known that he was friendly with Katie Murphy, the principal of the girls' school in Newmarket, as well as her sister Mollie.

After meeting Liam Lynch, as arranged, at Lombardstown and seeing him and his entourage leave for Kerry to continue their inspection tour, Moylan made for the Millstreet Battalion area. Rumours were beginning to abound that the British were about to embark on a huge operation designed to find Moylan and as many other prominent IRA men in the region as they could lay their hands on. Moylan's arrival in the Millstreet area was not expected and no billet had been prepared for him so, that night, he found himself sharing a bed with 'Big Con Meany' and Paddy Healy. Not a sound sleeper, Moylan spent an uncomfortable few hours between the two men before hearing footsteps outside in the yard. He then heard a soft tapping on the door and someone entering the kitchen. The rule was that doors were never locked in the safe houses where IRA men were billeted because scouts required swift access if they needed to warn their comrades of impending danger. Moylan slipped out of bed and into his clothes, and he was half dressed when the intruder reached the bedroom door and called to him. He informed Moylan that three large fires were burning at various points across the surrounding hills. One was to the east while the second was a few miles to the west. A third blaze seemed to be even nearer to the house. Moylan's first instinct was to assume the big expected raid was in progress.

He and other men who were billeted in the vicinity gathered in the farmyard and the suggestion among everyone was that the British operation was a very significant one and probably much bigger than Moylan had bargained for. It did not come as a real surprise to him as intelligence had suggested for some weeks that such an operation was in the offing. Preparations to counteract it had been carried out meticulously as combustible material of many different kinds had been made ready on the hilltops. Company captains and intelligence officers had been given detailed instructions as to what should be done in the event of a raid beginning. Moylan kept a calm head, believing there was no need to panic because many roads in the area had already been trenched or blocked in some fashion, making it very difficult for the enemy to effect a speedy advance. He was, however, concerned the British might attempt to travel over fields instead of the roads because the weather for the time of the year had been very dry for weeks. Good drivers, he felt, could drive their lorries over terrain that would have been very wet in normal years and, as it transpired, that is exactly what happened. However, because the plans put in place by Moylan and his staff were more than adequate to counter all eventualities, a disaster was averted.

The men of the local Active Service Unit began to gather, a few with rifles while others had shotguns. Two Active Service Unit men were sent to each surrounding townland to warn every one of the impending danger and Moylan went back inside the house. He produced a map of the area and, under a lit candle, he spread it out on the kitchen table. He was of the opinion that one may have the perfect knowledge of any terrain but the lines of a map can jog the memory of important little details often overlooked during a period of pressure and stress. His examination of the map enabled him to make an important decision. There was an opening to the north, towards a mountain district where, he believed, the enemy would find it hard to pursue him and his men. He was also of the opinion that the only force that could intercept them was a brigade of British military garrisoned about thirty miles to the west and they were unlikely to have made an uninterrupted journey across country. Nevertheless, in order to get to safety, Moylan and his men had no option but to cross open country intersected by many roads; there was no other course of action open to them.

Once Moylan made his decision, he and the men who were known to or wanted by the British fell in and prepared to move out. The other Volunteers who had so far evaded the interest of the enemy began to scatter across the area and soon disappeared from view. Moylan decided he needed one man to be on the spot in order that he could be appraised of any enemy activity. The man had to be reliable and in possession of a good knowledge of the area. At once a despatch rider called Taaffe stepped forward and he had the distinct advantage of looking much younger than he was. He went into the house and some moments later reappeared barefooted and dressed in an old jersey and short trousers belonging to a school-going son of the farmer in whose house Moylan had slept. To Moylan, he did not look more than fourteen years of age. With that, Moylan, together with members of the Active Service Unit and a contingent of Volunteers, moved off in single file, well extended, and, as the dawn broke, they reached their destination without encountering any trouble. Moylan later vividly recalled that early morning, saying:

> We lay until the forenoon in a deep glen with the heather high above us and with hidden outposts placed at the strategic points. Children passed to school on the road above us. Farm

> carts rattled on their way to the Creamery. It was as yet too early for news. Then the creamery carts began to return. It was noticeable that the drivers were the older men. The younger men had gone to ground. We waited and at last came a man we knew. The Company Captain of the district from which we had started stepped out on the road to talk to him. Had he seen the British or had he any news?
>
> He had. The roads were black with soldiers and police. They were searching everywhere, firing on anyone who failed to halt when called upon.[73]

The man confirmed that three men had already been shot, one an old man working in a field. He also confirmed the British did not seem to be coming the way of Moylan and his men; in fact, they seemed to be heading back towards the east. To Moylan, the news seemed reliable but he was inclined to wait a bit longer before moving on. He asked the man if he could organise any food for him and his men and within an hour it arrived. A group of women and young girls appeared on donkey carts with mountains of bread buttered in huge slices and lashings of tea with mugs, cups and bowls. They left everything in jars and baskets at a gap in the roadside fence and departed. After the food was consumed, Moylan recalled how he and his men:

> lay all day in the sun-drenched heather, the hum of innumerable bees a lullaby in our ears. Smokers were restless without their tobacco. But most of us had long arrears of sleep to make up and took advantage of the opportunity. An aeroplane zoomed over us, turned in a great circle and came back, emphasising the need there was for refraining from any action that might betray our position. For this reason too, I had issued a warning against a second visit by the food suppliers ... At last darkness fell, the local Volunteers slipped in among us; we divided into parties and went off to eat a prodigious meal in the surrounding houses.[74]

As Moylan finished his dinner, news of what the British were up to in the area reached him courtesy of the farmer in whose house he had spent the previous night. It seems Taaffe, the despatch rider, helped the farmer and his family with the usual daily chores around the farm and at noon the

British appeared, coming from the north. Armoured cars toured the area as local men were conscripted to fill in the trenches on the roads and clear barricades. Road blocks were put in place and all civilian movements were brought to a standstill. Soldiers, in extended order, moved across the fields, beat the fences and searched farm buildings closely. In the afternoon they arrived at the farmer's house and they searched it thoroughly as if they were aware Moylan had been there the previous night.

Taaffe then jumped into action and blurted out confirmation of everything they already knew. He guided them to all the houses and was entirely helpful. Rumours abounded that the British numbered somewhere around 6,000 men all across the region and they were camping out in the open. The 'informer' departed the farmer's house with the British and Moylan moved back to it that night. By dawn he was in position on a hilltop with a wide view of the valley as the morning mist arose. He saw for himself tent after tent for miles around and he thought it a truly vast demonstration of force. Somewhere in that British force was his despatch rider, the practical joker, who was feeding the enemy a tissue of lies and false information.

* * *

News came confirming the deaths of the three men they had heard about the previous day and also confirmation that a number of other men were being held for questioning. As it transpired, the British packed up later that evening and departed in their lorries and armoured cars. They took with them some five lorry loads of prisoners courtesy of the despatch rider. The next morning he arrived back at the house full of self-satisfaction and still clad in the schoolboy's clothes. He had been everywhere with the British and had been treated royally by them as he fed them with what turned out to be useless information. Moylan asked him about the prisoners:

> 'Oh, them', he said, 'they'll be alright. My father is arrested too.' 'How did he come to get arrested?', I asked. 'I told the Tommies that he was the Chief Intelligence Officer of the district.' 'Why the devil did you do that to the poor old man?' I said.
>
> 'Well,' he replied, 'my father was always boasting about how good an Irishman he was and I wanted to give him an opportunity to prove it. All the other fellows in the district are gone off with him to Cork.'[75]

It wasn't long before Moylan realised everything Taaffe had told him was correct, although he was somewhat annoyed the young man had exceeded his brief. He believed Taaffe had endangered innocent people, including his father, and had come to treat what he had done as a great joke. As a result of the information supplied by Taaffe, the British rounded up men who had no association with the IRA and they were all taken away for questioning in Cork. A few days later the British realised they had been tricked by the cunning despatch rider and all the 'dangerous' prisoners were returned to their homes. However, the general information he brought back to Moylan in relation to troop numbers and their equipment as well as the different bases they had started out from proved to be invaluable in the remaining months of the conflict.

The records kept by the Gloucestershire Regiment about the raid, even to this day, still make interesting reading and concluded that:

> As far as we were concerned the operation was almost a blank. We rounded up ninety-one men but there was a surprising lack of young men – all we got were practically over forty. The spotter plane was also ineffective and the only message dropped in the course of the round-up said, 'No enemy visible, is it time to go home?
>
> In none of these cases were any very good results achieved … most of the worst characters slipped away.[76]

The end result of the 'big raid' was the interning of one man and no mention was made in the report of any discovery of arms or ammunition. The three civilians who died may well have been fleeing the soldiers in panic, causing them to be shot on sight. As for Moylan and his men, they had managed to evade what was a very significant attempt by the British to capture them. However, it wasn't long before Moylan's luck ran out and the British eventually caught up with him.

Chapter 13

The Net Closes In and Capture

With the 'big raid' over and all dangers from it having receded, Moylan decided to visit Liscarroll, where he spent a couple of days in the home of the O'Donnell family at Aughrim. There he met with Paddy O'Brien and Seamus Brislane to discuss what was happening in their battalion area. Moylan quickly concluded there was little need for him to interfere with any of their plans because both men were experienced and very capable leaders. He found the morale of all the men in the area to be very high and when he left the area he was very satisfied that everything there was in good order. Even though, in this case, there was little to be unhappy with, Moylan believed there was merit to be found in his visit. Discussion with fellow officers was always good and the kicking around of ideas never did harm to anyone. Moylan was aware that strong leaders like O'Brien and Brislane held trenchant views of their own and he was always inclined to listen to what they had to say and even take on board some, if not all, of their suggestions or requests.

On the other hand, Moylan had different plans for the Kanturk Battalion. While the fighting men of the battalion were, of course, very earnest and in no way lacking in soldierly qualities, Moylan was concerned those directing them lacked drive and initiative. Therefore, it was his intention to make some long overdue changes in the leadership of the battalion. While on his way to Kanturk he was the recipient of news about an ambush carried out at Rathmore by the men of the 5th Battalion out of Newmarket, in co-operation with the men from the Kerry No. 2 Brigade. The ambush took place on a remote section of the Bog Road near Rathmore village. It seems Moylan's comrades left the body of an informer on the side of the road and stayed around the area to see what might develop. They discussed among themselves the possibility of staging an ambush and checked if they had enough ammunition to carry it out before deciding the opportunity was too good to pass up. An RIC patrol came out to investigate the body and no sooner had it arrived than the ambush began, which resulted in heavy losses for the police. Constables Thomas McCormack, Walter Brown, William

Clapp, Robert Dyne, Alfred Hillier, James Phelan, Samuel Watkins and Headley Woodcock all lost their lives in the engagement. One constable managed to cycle to safety and raised the alarm. Of course, reprisals ensued that saw a number of farmhouses as well as the creamery in Rathmore burned down.

Once he heard that news, Moylan changed his plans and concluded that his presence in the 5th Battalion area was required, so his visit to Kanturk was put on hold. He found the men of the 5th Battalion in a very happy and satisfied mood. Some half a dozen men on the Active Service Unit waiting list found themselves newly armed with rifles secured after the ambush and they displayed a real desire to involve themselves in further engagements with the enemy. Moylan mused at the time that the morale and aggressiveness displayed by the men of the 5th Battalion was comparable to that of every single fighting unit in Cork, Kerry and Limerick. While the men of the 5th Battalion basked in the glory of their Rathmore success, the other side of war was played out a few days later in the house where Moylan had met Paddy O'Brien and Seamus Brislane. It seems that O'Brien, his brother Dan, and Jack Regan were all sitting down to breakfast when the house was surrounded by British troops. Jack Regan, according to Moylan, was riddled with bullets while Dan O'Brien was captured and executed a week later. Paddy O'Brien somehow and miraculously managed to shoot his way out and escaped under a hail of bullets.

* * *

Moylan, by that time, was continuously struggling with poor health and he later recalled how it reduced him to a pale shadow of his true self. As mentioned before in this volume, Moylan refused to enter hospital in Dublin at the request of those at GHQ, who were increasingly concerned about his well-being. He was of the opinion that retirement from active service for any reason might well have been misunderstood by his comrades and would have adversely impacted them. He did accept he had not fully recovered from the illness that he had contracted in 1918, the return of which had also kept him out of action in the early months of 1920. That same illness returned in March and April of 1921 and it resulted in major stomach problems and a constant bleeding of ulcers. In his own words, Moylan saw himself at that time as a sad case.

In his witness statement, Moylan spent some time discussing the quality of the food he had to eat during his time moving from house to house. He was of the opinion that good food was essential for the maintenance of good health and he did not always have access to it. He somewhat sarcastically recalled:

> In my 'Rambles in Eireann' it had been my good luck at times to have my needs supplied by those who understood the art, but it has also been my misfortune to suffer at the hands of those whose real vocation was research chemistry. The consistency with which these latter could transmute good class beef into better-class sole leather; their capacity for changing fresh vegetables into synthetic rubber showed that their vocation lay in the laboratory rather than in the kitchen.[77]

Moylan was not just a military man consumed by a passion to relieve Ireland of British rule. He was keenly aware, during those heady days of soldiering, that the new Ireland that might emerge once independence was secured would have to be a place of equality, fairness and compassion. His love of reading and books and his willingness to engage in conversation with his elders in Kilmallock and Newmarket as he matured into a young man undoubtedly contributed to his cultivation of the social conscience that became the hallmark of his later political career. As he traversed the country during the revolutionary era, he took time out to note and, to pass judgement, on the prevailing living conditions of his fellow citizens, most especially those who resided in rural areas.

He constantly called out the poor living conditions that he witnessed almost every day but he was also keen to reiterate his admiration for the good people who welcomed him and his comrades into their modest and, often, shamefully inadequate homes. They always made Moylan and his men entirely welcome and never wavered in their belief that each and every fighting man was entitled to the best that was in their power and ability to give him. For his part, Moylan made sure to let those who gave him and his men refuge and sustenance know just how grateful they were for all that was done for them and, in later years, he and those who soldiered with him never forgot the kindness and generosity of the civilian population. However, having made those salient points, he still had the underlying concern that his people, as he believed them to be, were living in conditions that were long deemed unacceptable elsewhere in the modern world. For Moylan, it was essential the independent Ireland he was fighting for should join that very same modern world and afford its citizens a decent and acceptable standard of living. Without it, he believed, an independent Ireland would be little different to the Ireland that had endured centuries of British subjugation and oppression.

Moylan, the politician, continued to exercise his social conscience long after his revolutionary days. In his witness statement, made in 1953, he continued to lament the unacceptable living conditions endured by the people of Ireland in the first half of the twentieth century. His obvious angst was there for all to see and he maintained an abhorrence of the difficulties his fellow countrymen and women were forced to contend with for some thirty years after the attainment of independence. He recalled how:

> Food was coarse and in general not well cooked. The facilities for cooking were primitive. A fire on the hearth, a large pot hanging on the crane and a bastable were the basis of equipment. Any graduate of Cathal Brugha Street forced to work under these conditions would have retired from culinary effort. Furnishings in general were inadequate, of poor design and craftmanship. Houses were damp, airless, inconvenient; outhouses entirely unsuitable to their purpose. The evil system of land tenure under which the country had so long suffered had left its foul mark on the economics of the nation. Money that in a normal country would be put back in the land, into the purchase of badly needed amenities, was, where it existed, hoarded away in banks to be utilised outside the country as the capital of Industry and Commerce for the enrichment of other nations. The effects of any great national evil reach far into the future and, because of tradition and experience, the Irish farmer could envisage no real security for his family, only in his bank deposit, wrung with hardship from his land and gathered in an unjustifiable self-denial; discomfort and wearisome effort.[78]

Moylan went on to make the point that work in the home and, especially in the kitchen, under reasonable conditions and with adequate equipment can often be a pleasure. However, it seemed to him that the never-ending labour with very modest equipment in Irish farm kitchens only served to ensure Irish women remained in a state of serfdom. Farmers and their workmen, he claimed, engaged in a laborious occupation that ended at some point during the day. However, for the farmer's wife and, most particularly for the female farm servant, there was very little respite. He was particularly concerned for the welfare of the very many female kitchen servants across the country, most of whom, he believed, were worked to the bone, with little thanks or appreciation ever afforded to them. In his statement, he alluded to the life of the traditional female servant and how:

> From the dawn's early light to the sunlight's last gleaming she was still unflaggingly engaged. And fatheaded economists talk about the cause of emigration! It amazed me to see a slight young girl lift a huge pot of boiling potatoes from the fire and lug it into the farmyard to feed pigs and poultry. The carrying of these awkwardly shaped pots, weighing over fifty pounds, necessitated a posture that surely wrenched every organ in the body out of its proper alignment, with evil effects in after years. There should have been no need for such strenuous effort, for such continuous labour.
>
> Nowadays, when State recognition of the need for farm improvement is an accepted thing, it is high time to lighten this burden of effort that had borne so heavily and so long on the mothers of the race, whose lot on Irish farms is cast in any but pleasant places.[79]

Moylan continued his nomadic life in April and May of 1921 moving from farmhouse to farmhouse as he attempted to evade the clutches of the Gloucestershire Regiment. The battalion intelligence officer, Lieutenant Grazebrook, viewed Moylan as an ephemeral and elusive character who was almost impossible to capture, and he wrote in his diary that:

> one always found him leading the most violent outrages … without doubt he was a most clever and able man.[80]

Grazebrook also garnered information from informers that allowed him to follow Moylan's movements with a degree of accuracy. The 6th Division Record of that time recorded how:

> In the middle of May, the Gloucester [sic] Regiment carried out a round-up in N.W. Cork with a view to catching John Moylan, a well-known rebel commandant … it was believed that rebel forces were billeted about the townland of Knockavoreen,

> one mile south-east of Kiskeam. The locality of a dugout where four men lived had been roughly given, and lastly John Moylan had passed through Meelin supposedly for Kiskeam and Rockchapel. The object of the operation was to carry out a round-up of the Knockavoreen area, and during a weekend when there would be more chance of finding Moylan.[81]

The Glosters put a plan in place but they were faced with a number of difficulties. They were unable to use motor transport because most of the roads were being continuously trenched by the IRA and, if they were to use bicycles, they would most likely be spotted as soon as they were on the roads. With just the one entrance to the barracks, a departing patrol was certain to be watched closely by IRA scouts and intelligence officers, thereby removing any possible surprise element. The plan involved the deployment of four officers and fifty-eight troops backed up by four RIC sergeants. They settled on moving out at 1 a.m. on Sunday, 15 May from the adjoining field where they had been billeted in tents for a number of nights. Once out of the field, the Glosters made their way slowly on foot across fields and ditches, taking three hours to cover seven miles. They eventually arrived at a copse they had previously chosen, however, they found some of the trees had been cut down so they took cover in a nearby barn overlooking the village of Boherbue. In the meantime, the telephone wires at Newmarket were cut to prevent Moylan from hearing about troop movements. Having settled into their hideout, the Glosters watched the villagers come and go about their business, including attending Mass, as it was a Sunday. At one stage they were discovered by a man who arrived to milk cows. They could not take him prisoner because he would have been missed by his family so he was threatened by the RIC sergeants, who promised there would be dire consequences for him and his family if he raised any alarm in the village or locality.

* * *

The GHQ of the IRA had, some weeks earlier, issued a general order to all brigades for an attack to be carried out everywhere on the British Army on 14 May. Moylan was of the opinion the order was sent out to appease certain political figures in the republican movement and from a military point of view he felt it had not been very well thought out. As it happened, the results of the order did not produce any more effective activity on that day that would distinguish it from any other day. In compliance of the order,

Moylan took twenty men to Newmarket on the night of 14 May but there was no movement of British troops, Black and Tans or RIC in the town. Consequently, no opportunity presented itself for Moylan and his men to strike at the enemy. They could have sniped at the barracks but Moylan was not willing to do so because it probably would have endangered civilians. There was nothing else for them to do but return to Kiskeam as dawn broke on the morning of 15 May.

Moylan had other plans for that day and he decided to put them into motion. Sean Finn, the Officer Commanding of the West Limerick Brigade, had been killed some months earlier and Moylan had arranged to travel into that brigade area to meet with the new Officer Commanding and discuss some proposed activities that they had tentatively planned some weeks earlier. Arrangements were made for Moylan to travel into West Limerick later that evening. It was decided that he and his men would travel in small parties and meet at a place called Taur, where transport would be available to take everyone to Mount Collins. Moylan, together with a number of his men, started out from Knockavoreen and they had travelled only few miles when they were overtaken by a messenger on a bicycle. He informed Moylan that some officers from Kerry had arrived at his headquarters and were anxious to speak with him. Because no one had exact knowledge of his whereabouts, messengers were, at that time, cycling in different directions looking for him. Moylan then made what turned out to be a fateful decision and returned to Knockavoreen, arriving about midnight. He had a discussion with the men from Kerry and when it was finished he decided it was too late to set out for Limerick and retired to bed.

While Moylan and his men were going about their business during that day, the Glosters, from their hiding place, had identified two suspicious farms in the area owned by the Mahoney and Riordan families. The British were of the opinion that Moylan was probably hiding out on one or the other of the farms. The troops planned to surround three sides of each farm while another patrol on bicycles moved up to close off any escape routes. When darkness descended, they moved off in the direction of both farms. As they approached and circled round to the north, a party of eight men was dropped every 400 yards. A search of Mahoney's farm was inconclusive as far as arms and information was concerned. However, two men in the house were seized and taken on with the raiding party towards Riordan's farm. At that point, it seems, an alarm was raised and the British cover was effectively blown. As the raiding party closed in on Riordan's farm they ran into heavy rifle fire, most probably, in the confusion, coming from some of their fellow Glosters approaching the farm on bicycles. It was, by then, around 3 a.m. and Moylan was awoken from his sleep and informed that the British had passed through Boherbue, four miles away, and that there was every likelihood his billet was about to be raided. In his witness statement he vividly recalled the events that then unfolded:

> I got out of bed, went into the yard where half a dozen others were collected.
>
> They expressed the opinion that the British were much closer and suggested that we should move off to the West at once. I decided that it was a good idea.
>
> In view of the fact that the Active Service Unit had left the district, the usual care in regard to sentries and signals had not been taken and it was quite possible we might have been taken unawares. We went out on the roadway and at the yard gate we met a Volunteer who informed us he believed we were surrounded. Fifty yards away, in the passage leading to the next house, he had heard the rattle of rifle butts which led him to believe that the British had arrived. I ordered those who were with me to get inside the fence on the North side of the road and decided to investigate. If the British were here the sooner we knew it the better and the only way of finding out was for one man to walk into the trap, if a trap it was. This at least would give the others a chance to get away. I walked down the dark passage about 20 yards and then heard a shout, 'Halt, hands up'. I halted and put up my hands and was then instructed to come forward. I advanced one step forward, turned swiftly, ran a few steps and dropped on the ground. I jumped to my feet and got round a corner of a fence before the second volley came. The volley was sufficient signal to my comrades to get away swiftly, which they did and luckily they got out of the ring before it was finally closed. I ran towards the East.
>
> I was again fired at and doubled back and went to the North. Here again I drew fire.
>
> Finally I went towards the West. The ring had closed and the air seemed to be alive with bullets as I appeared. Escape was hopeless. I crawled back again into cover and got on top of a fence between furze bushes. As the day broke brightly, I could

> see everywhere around me khaki clad figures of the British soldiers. It was Nunc Dimittus for me. I lay down and fell asleep. Possibly an hour later I was dragged from the fence by the British soldiers and brought into the yard which I had left a few hours before. Here a number of troops were drawn up. Among them was a group of civilians whom they had picked up in the various houses. Most of these were local farmers and workers. A few were Volunteers but none of these were prominent and none was likely to be known for his activities to the RIC.[82]

The owner of the farm, Johnny Riordan, was questioned as he sat up in bed and Moylan was brought in and the old man was asked to identify him. It seems Riordan feigned deafness and eventually the soldiers relented. Moylan was interrogated just after dawn out in the farmyard under a heavy guard. Moylan and other captured men were brought in turn to a table and questioned. Moylan gave the name O'Connell when first questioned but he was immediately identified by the RIC men in attendance. Moylan said little in his defence and did not deny possessing a revolver and a Mills bomb. He did not say where he had stayed the previous night and implicated no one in any activities that had taken place over the previous hours and days. Moylan later recalled his interview with the officer sitting at the table:

> An officer sat a table in the yard. Beside him stood an RIC man. This man recognised me and gave to the British Officer a history of my activities. The British Officer questioned me and while he was questioning me, I was busy reading the list of names which lay before him on the table. He seemed to have the names of every member of the Active Service Unit and also the names of some of the prominent under-cover men, at which I was surprised. When the questioning was over I was taken away by a party of British soldiers to be held under guard until the completion of the raid.[83]

The officer who questioned Moylan was most likely Lieutenant Grazebrook and he later made the observation that:

> very little could be got out of Moylan, he looked decidedly ill and frightened ... he obviously expected to be court-martialled and shot right away.[84]

Moylan was certainly very ill at that time and one could understand that he feared he was about to be shot just as many other IRA prisoners before him had been. The search of the Riordan farm led to the arrest of fourteen other men, all of whom the Glosters believed were members of an Active Service Unit. Moylan later disagreed with that assessment because, as he remembered it, the Active Service Unit had, to a man, left the area prior to the raid. He claimed that only a few of those arrested were Volunteers and were only low-ranking personnel at that, with the rest being farmers and labourers. In the end the only individuals charged were Moylan and Johnny Riordan (because arms were found on his farm), while Dan Flynn was captured but no evidence was found against him and he was later sent to Spike Island. The Glosters did find a Hotchkiss machine gun, which had been used during the Tureengarriffe and Clonbanin ambushes, together with a revolver, ammunition and some telephone equipment. The British also found Moylan's typewriter, a despatch case and some letters to the commanding officer of the Southern Command as well as a list of secret IRA codes, all more than enough evidence to have Moylan shot. The British also seized a cheque for £115, which was probably made out to pay the men under Moylan's command. The cheque was eventually brought to the bank by the British and the manager was forced to lodge it to one of the army's bank accounts.

* * *

Moylan and thirteen other arrested men were marched several miles before being loaded onto lorries and taken, handcuffed, to Kanturk and placed in cells. He later recalled:

> Small as my wrists were, the handcuffs were still smaller and as I lay all day in my cell I suffered a good deal of pain from my swollen arms. In the evening as the guard was changed, the Orderly officer visited me. He was a small man wearing the ribbons of the MC and Bar. He and I had a conversation for fifteen minutes and then he ordered one of the soldiers who was with him to get me a new pair of handcuffs. These were much more comfortable … and expressed my surprise at his kindness, to which he stated 'I am British.' The term British did not in my experience connote any form of chivalry or fair play and at that time I could not realise that it could mean those things to anybody.
>
> However, there are some British who do play the game.[85]

The following morning, Moylan was brought before the Gloucestershires' commanding officer, Lieutenant Colonel F.C. Nisbet, who had a reputation for toughness and was a decorated First World War hero. Moylan, after his night's sleep, was much more composed and confidently held his own in a robust conversation with the colonel. The exchange was witnessed by Grazebrook who, it is believed, held a Webley revolver in his hand during the interview and, who, in later years, admitted Moylan was a man of intelligence and wit. Moylan recalled the encounter in his witness statement when he said:

> The Colonel told me he wanted to get some information about the reasons for the trouble in Ireland. I asked him what good the supply of such information would do me. He replied that it would do me no good, that I was going to be shot anyway. He said he was really anxious to know something of the reason for Ireland's rebellious attitude. I said that, of course, if he proposed to discuss the matter on that basis I was quite willing. He put a number of questions to me to which I replied. Our question and answer developed into a discussion on English and Irish history. Finally he said, 'I am not anxious to remain here in Ireland. I want to go back home.' I said, 'I am most anxious that you should do so and possibly the whole reason for our attitude is to ensure that every English soldier and official in Ireland should go back to England and cease interfering with matters in this country.' 'Your chief difficulty,' he stated, 'in this country is that you are living in the past. You take no cognisance of modern conditions. You think that the world has not progressed since the days of Wolfe Tone and Emmett and still think in the terms in which those men thought.' I changed the conversation. 'By the way,' I said, 'as I was coming into the office I saw outside a gong with the word "Egypt" on top and the date "1798" in the centre. What does that signify?' 'Oh,' he said, 'that commemorates a great battle which the regiment fought in Egypt in 1798. Surrounded there, our men fought back-to-back to the finish.'
>
> 'You will notice,' he said, 'that there is a badge both in front and back of the caps worn by the men of this regiment. We are not known as the Gloucesters but as the "Fore and Afts".' 'I understand,' I said. 'I assume,' I continued, 'that Regimental

> tradition is a great force.' 'Undoubtedly,' he said. 'And British Regiments,' I said, 'must remember 1798 and Irishmen must forget it.' 'I am afraid,' he said, 'we haven't shot you soon enough.'[86]

After that meeting Moylan was taken back to his cell and, as he recalled, was:

> handed over to a party of soldiers from Buttevant. My handcuffs were removed and a new set supplied. The sadist who locked these on me took care to dig away a portion of the flesh on my wrist as he snapped on the handcuffs. I was then tied hand and foot with a rope, thrown into a lorry. A large convoy of lorries waited outside the barracks to convey me to Buttevant.[87]

The capture and imprisonment of Moylan, while viewed as a coup by the British, was, without doubt, a very severe blow for the IRA and especially for the men in his brigade. The fact that IRA secret codes had also found their way into the enemy's hands only served to compound the situation. Once ensconced in Buttevant the outlook was very bleak for Moylan with the spectre of a court martial and almost certain execution hanging over him. He, his family, comrades and friends could do little more than pray for an unlikely miracle.

Chapter 14

In Custody and Standing Trial

On his arrival at Buttevant military barrack, Moylan was thrown out of the lorry onto the ground, where he laid for an hour or so watching a cricket match that was in progress on the sports ground. He was not particularly impressed by the slowness of the game, especially when he compared it to the pace and excitement of a hurling match. When the stumps were drawn, the general in charge of the troops, whose predecessor General Hanway Cumming had been killed four months earlier at Clonbanin, came across and ordered the removal of the rope that Moylan was tied up with. A sergeant removed it and hung it across his shoulders and, with a file of soldiers, marched Moylan to the provost marshal's quarters. On the way, they were met by the provost sergeant, who made an attempt to strike Moylan with his fist but, thinking the better of it, then drew back and dropped his arm. Moylan was immediately put into a small cell and a few moments later he had a visit from two corporals, who proceeded to give him a good beating. They were of the East Lancashire Regiment, the very same regiment that suffered at the hands of Moylan and his men at Clonbanin.

Moylan was left in his cell for the rest of day without any further attacks made on his person. That night the brigade intelligence officer visited him and questioned him for several hours, without indulging in violence of any kind. Moylan gave him very little information and he had the impression the man was convinced there was only going to be one outcome to the situation Moylan found himself in, his execution. It seemed the officer was so convinced of his conclusion that he imparted to Moylan all the knowledge he had gathered about his brigade and much of the information proved to be very valuable to Moylan over the following months. The following day, Moylan was taken to Victoria Barracks in Cork city and he was immediately struck by the silence in the building. All the prisoners were locked in their cells and he felt the chill air of certain death in the place. He was acutely aware that the first IRA man to be executed in the south of the country, Con Murphy, died in the barracks and Dan O'Brien from Millstreet had been executed in the same place on the very day Moylan was captured.

A friendly Scottish man, a sergeant, took possession of Moylan from the East Lancashire men and asked him to sign the record book. Moylan signed the book in the name of his comrade, Dan O'Brien, and the sergeant asked if had known him. Moylan told him that O'Brien was his comrade and he admired him as a soldier and as a friend. The sergeant then intimated that Moylan would be following his friend to face the execution squad. Moylan, at the time, was in no doubt that he was destined to stand before the firing squad and the sergeant made a very salient point to him, saying even soldiers have to die at some point. The sergeant then offered Moylan the opportunity to take a bath, which he gladly accepted in order to divest himself of the mud he had accumulated from the previous day. Once that was done, Moylan was locked in his cell and the only visitor he had that night was the chaplain, who came to hear his confession.

* * *

During what he believed was his last night in this world, a sense of pragmatism and acceptance took hold of Moylan. He had not asked to see anyone or even requested writing paper to pen his last goodbyes to family and friends. He took the view that as he was unmarried and had no property of any kind, he had fewer reasons than other men to mark his own passing with a sense of sentimentality. His only regret was the Ireland that he had fought for had not yet emerged and he was somewhat unsure that it ever would do so. He made the point in his witness statement that when a man lived like he had for a number of years and had been inspired with grand and worthwhile ideals and had faced disillusionment almost every day it was easy to die. He made it clear that as far as he was concerned there was never any heroism in his actions and went on to say:

> My attitude was quite matter of fact. My time had come and there was no more to be said. I felt sure that that is the attitude of all men in my circumstances. The following morning I was awakened not, to my surprise, to face the firing party but to parade with all other prisoners. For two days this continued. This made all the difference to me. It was easy to die, it was harder to wait for death.[88]

As it transpired, the court martial witness from the East Lancashire Regiment had arrived in Cork to give evidence but Moylan's case did not proceed as planned because of a backlog of cases. Hence his surprise when he woke up that morning and instead of preparing for his trial and probable execution, he found himself biding his time on the parade ground.

On the third day of his incarceration in Cork he demanded to see his solicitor but was told by the sergeant major that he did not need one because he was going to be shot. Moylan still insisted on seeing one, telling the sergeant major that he was fully entitled to see a solicitor so that he might dispose of his private property even though all he possessed were the clothes he stood up in. It seems the sergeant major then consulted his superiors and, that evening, Moylan was brought to an office where there was a notary public and he made a statement to him. Moylan asked to see Mr Barry Sullivan of Mallow, who was a brilliant young lawyer and had been a great help to Sinn Fein in the conducting of republican courts in Cork. He was a committed supporter of the party and had acted for the families of the slain railway men who had been murdered in Mallow by the Black and Tans. He also acted for IRA prisoners who had been charged with having participated in the attack on the Mallow Military Barracks. In Moylan's opinion, Sullivan was the first man in Ireland to pursue the notion of challenging the legality of the military courts and had successfully sought the co-operation of a number of prominent barristers in his efforts to prove them illegal.

According to Aideen Carroll, Sullivan kept a record of his first meeting with Moylan and recalled in a note to himself on 24 May 1921 how:

> On Court adjourning at 5 p.m. I was informed by an officer of the Legal Department of the 6th Division headquarters, that Brigadier Comdt. Sean Moylan TD (Member of Parliament) who had been arrested wished to see me as he had been charged with possession of arms and levying war against the Crown. I stated to the officer that I could not visit the prisoner immediately as I expected to be working most of the night with the court martial.[89]

Sullivan also recorded the officer's reply:

> Moylan will be tried on Thursday morning and as no defence is possible and his record is well known the divisional confirmation will immediately follow and he will be shot on Friday morning.[90]

Sullivan then crossed to the detention barracks and asked to see Moylan, who recalled that first meeting in his witness statement:

> My desire to meet Barry Sullivan was not rooted in any hope to save my own life but I wanted a reliable man to whom I could pass the information I had got from the Intelligence Officer in Buttevant and whom I could inform of the whereabouts of certain documents and arms and ammunition which I had secreted. After some discussion it was agreed that Mr Barry Sullivan would be permitted to see me and the following day he came. I swiftly gave him all the information I had for conveyance to my comrades outside and when I was finished, he asked me 'What about your own case?' I said, 'I have no case they intend to shoot me and it is a waste of time to do anything about it. It is certain that I am to be shot and I may as well go down with flying colours rather than in any way recognise the legal authority of the British.'[91]

Sullivan then informed Moylan that a prominent barrister called Albert Wood who was, at that time, in Cork defending those accused of the Mallow Military Barracks attack, was anxious to speak to him. Moylan agreed to see him on the basis that a discussion with anyone would ease the monotony of a prison day. Sullivan then returned to his hotel and had a conversation with Wood. They quickly drafted an affidavit in support of a writ for habeas corpus, which was basically a command issued by the High Court requiring the authorities to show legal cause for Moylan's incarceration. The affidavit was put on a train leaving Cork for Dublin at 8 a.m. on the morning of 25 May. That same day was a momentous one in Dublin as the Custom House was attacked and burned by the IRA and Moylan's case was hardly major news outside of Cork. In London, the government decided that if the newly elected southern parliament failed to function then martial law would be imposed on all of the twenty-six counties. The government also decided to send a further sixteen battalions of troops to Ireland and an intensification of military activity seemed certain.

The following day Moylan was called into an office where he met Sullivan again, together with another man called Bourke, who was a barrister and a son of the recorder who lived in Banteer. Moylan recalled in his own mind that he had met Bourke a year earlier when he got him out of his bed to get the keys of his car so that he and his men could take the mail they had hijacked back to Banteer. It seemed Bourke did not recognise Moylan and no mention was made of the incident. The third man present, according to Moylan, was:

> A typical Englishman, beautifully dressed and groomed, and with an accent which seemed to me then to be the quintessence of Oxford. This was Albert Wood. Wood proceeded to discuss my case with me and again I pointed out the fact that I didn't have a case and there was no use in taking any legal proceedings. Our discussions went on for over an hour … He then [Wood] said something that amused me. He said that in six weeks time all the fighting would be over … Wood insisted that negotiations were going on and that a Truce was imminent. He said it was very important for many reasons that my case should be defended. It might mean eventually the saving of lives of other men engaged in activities similar to mine. Finally I said that if I am ordered by the IRA Headquarters to defend my case I shall obey orders, but, I said, I must absolutely be permitted to refuse to recognise the British Court. Wood said immediately, 'If we meet your conditions, will you guarantee to say nothing in Court other than the fact that you refuse to recognise the Court?' I agreed and we parted on that note.[92]

Three days later at the High Court in Dublin an application for a writ of habeas corpus was made in the matter of *Moylan J.R v Major General E.P Strickland*. The basis of the writ was that Ireland was not in a state of war, the civil courts were still sitting, therefore the civil courts still prevailed and did not permit trial by a court martial. Justice Powell, who was presiding, was very sceptical and counsel A. Meredith, KC was heard to say how unpleasant it would be for everyone to hear revolver shots. Reluctantly, the judge issued a conditional writ of habeas corpus, pending full argument from both sides. The order was then telegraphed to Major Strickland in Cork, much to the pleasure of Sullivan and Wood, both of whom, at the time, were just wrapping up their defence of the IRA men who were involved in an ambush at Mourne Abbey sometime earlier.

On 30 May 1921, Moylan was given a suit of clothes supplied by a local tailor and brought before a court martial. As far as Moylan was concerned there could be only one ending to his trial and that was an execution sentence. In fact, he later readily admitted that he had very little interest in the trial. He recalled:

> As I walked across the yard to the room where the Court was held I had no fears and no regrets but I was young and it seemed to me that the sky was never so blue or the trees never so beautifully green as they were that May morn and it seemed to me a pity to depart so young from all this earthly beauty. The court was comprised of three officers. I assume that it was in order to emphasise the fact that it was a Court of Justice that there was a loaded revolver in front of the Chairman on the bench. The gallery was crowded with a number of curious onlookers – all British officers and soldiers stood round the chair where I sat with drawn revolvers. The lawyers arrived and the charge was read out to me. As agreed, my statement was a simple refusal to recognise the Court and then the argument started.[93]

The trial itself was a short affair lasting about two hours and, as Moylan had refused to recognise the court, or take part in the trial in any way, there was no cross-examination of the evidence presented and so to this day we have no record of the extent to which Moylan disagreed. However, we do have a record of the court procedure on that day, which is worth recounting here:

> John Moylan of Kiskeam, County Cork, was charged with (1) committing an offence in that he, near Knocknagree, Co Cork, on or about 16 May 1921, did levy war on His Majesty the King, by joining with other persons unknown in an armed attack on a detachment of His Majesty's forces (2) was improperly in possession of arms, ammunition and explosives, namely one revolver, thirteen rounds of revolver ammunition and three Mills pattern bombs.
>
> Mr A.E Wood, KC and Mr J.F Bourke, BL, appeared for the accused.
>
> Counsel for the accused stated that they had no objection to being tried by members of the tribunal individually, but took exception to their jurisdiction.
>
> The court having been duly sworn, the accused was arraigned on both charges. Counsel for the accused pleaded

> in bar and quoted proceedings in the High Court of Justice in Ireland (Chancery Division), in the case of John R. Moylan (plaintiff) and Major General E.P Strickland and the Attorney General for Ireland. Counsel pointed out that the Court of Chancery was the court which formerly issued writs of habeas corpus, for the protection of His Majesty's subjects.
>
> President – Does the accused admit that he is a subject of His Majesty?
>
> Counsel – I make no admission.
>
> Counsel handed in a formal objection marked 'A' signed by the President attached to the proceedings.
>
> The court decided to proceed with the trial.
>
> Both counsel announced that they had decided to withdraw from the trial, and accordingly did so.[94]

The writ was to all intents and purposes a delaying tactic and no one believed it would succeed, but it was designed to cause a rift between the civil courts and the military, thereby causing the trial to be delayed significantly. The strategy failed and the court proceeded to try Moylan. His solicitor, Barry Sullivan, recorded what took place next.

> 30 May – telegram to House of Commons: Military Court is sitting this day at Victoria Barracks to try John R. Moylan, MP for Southern Ireland … Counsel produced an order of a chancery judge dated 28 May ordering the writ of habeas corpus directed to the military governor … The charge is levying war – Penalty – death.[95]

This appeal to the backbenchers at Westminster paid no dividend and there was little in the way of sympathy for Moylan, not helped by the continuing violence in Cork. That week saw the death of Diarmaid Hurley, the commanding officer of the fourth battalion, Cork No. 1 Brigade, in an engagement with the British in Midleton. In Youghal, seven bandsmen of the Hampshire Regiment were killed in a culvert bomb. It was against this background that the trial continued and records show:

> The accused declined to recognise the court and a plea of not guilty was entered in respect of all charges. The accused declined the assistance of an officer in his defence.[96]

Evidence was then given (names of witnesses were usually omitted from records) and Moylan declined to cross-examine each witness. The first witness stated:

> On 16 May 1921, I was on duty with a party of military near Knocknagree and Kiskeam, Co Cork, before daylight. I was a sentry and at about 05.30 hours, we started to close in on an area we had surrounded. I was posted in a small field with Private ----, about 06.45 hours. At about 07.00 hours I noticed about 100 yards away on my right that there was a movement amongst the bushes of a hedge. I went towards the place with ----, I was armed with a revolver and ---- had a rifle. I then saw a man lying on his back who appeared to be asleep. I told ---- to cover him with the rifle, and I told the accused to get up. As he did not get up, I kicked his foot. Before the accused got up, I took hold of the revolver [produced] and a detonated bomb similar to that produced, which the accused held in his right hand. The revolver was loaded in six chambers with the ammunition [produced]. I marched accused back. Accused said to me 'You are a lucky fellow to find me, but you are unlucky to me today.' I was present when ---- searched accused, and I saw him find seven rounds of revolver ammunition [produced] in the right-hand breeches pocket of the accused. The revolver [produced] is a six inch .445 Webley and the ammunition is of the same calibre. The bomb is of Mills pattern and detonated.

A second witness provided exactly the same evidence, while a third witness stated:

> I was with a cycling patrol of my regiment … We advanced across country. Accused was brought to me by the first witness. I proceeded to search the accused and, in his right-hand breeches pocket I found the seven rounds of .45 ammunition. Accused made no statement. In the presence of the accused the first witness showed me the revolver and a Mills bomb. The first witness said he found the accused lying in some gorse with a revolver and bomb in his hand. Accused still said nothing.

A fourth witness took the stand and told the court:

> Parties were dropped at various points. My party consisted of about twenty. We were proceeding on foot up a track … when lots of horns were sounded all around us. We came to a farm, and I skirted it and came to the lane on the other side of it. I went up the lane with a member of the RIC and two men. There were high hedges on each side, and a mud wall at the turning beyond us. My party were fired on by one shot from this mud wall, and the bullet went between me and the RIC man. We replied to the fire, and retired to a bank. Three more men appeared on the bank and rushed up as if to line it. I could not see if they had arms, as the light was still bad. They were twenty yards from me. About two minutes after, I heard a human whistle, which I took to be a signal from the top of the lane. Then I heard ---- challenge someone and then I heard a rifle shot in the lane. I was only three yards from ----, and it was he who fired the shot. Dawn was about 04.30 hours, and we then moved forward. In a farm 150 to 200 yards in advance we found a pair of puttees and two revolver holsters. Then I went about 400 yards from the place I was fired at previously, and there found some of my men around a dugout, which contained a box about four feet high and about two feet sunk into a bank. I saw men pulling out of this a Hotchkiss gun, and some ammunition and some literature. I saw the accused later under escort at a farm 150 yards from where we shot.

The witness went on to confirm they took twelve prisoners that day. And a fifth witness stated:

> Just before 04.00 hours I heard a shot up a lane near a house I was searching. I went up the lane towards where I heard the shot. I got into the lane and a few minutes later I heard a signal whistle from the top end of the lane and it was repeated, then someone walked down the lane towards me, and then I said, 'Halt. Hands up!' I could see that he was wearing an overcoat and a light cap. The man answered, 'All right I have got up.' Then I could see he had his hands above his head. I covered the man with my rifle and told him to

come on. Immediately, he dropped his hands and bolted up the lane. I fired at him with my rifle. At about 4.30 hours we started to search the country and houses. At the top of the lane I saw the bank and then I proceeded to a farm on the right. A greatcoat, Sam Browne belt and a holster were brought to me. The greatcoat was the one the accused is now wearing. Accused was brought into the lane by the first and second witness, and they handed him over to the officer, together with the revolver and the bomb produced. The officer asked the accused if the revolver and the bomb belonged to him and the accused replied , 'Yes.' This reply was quite voluntary … Accused asked me if he could proceed down the lane to find a pair of glasses he had lost. I went down the lane to where I had fired. I had noticed that the accused had on a light cap and spoke like the man I had heard when I fired. So I asked him if anyone had shot at him during the morning. He said, 'Yes' and that it was down the lane. I said it was I who fired at him, and he said, 'It was a pretty near one.' He went down the lane with me and said, 'Where was it that you fired at me?' I showed him and he said, 'I did not think it was so far down as that.' I noticed that accused was searching up one end of the lane. He found nothing there. I saw accused at Buttevant with his glasses, and he told me one of my regiment had found the glasses and given them to him. I asked accused if the greatcoat and Sam Browne belt belonged to him, and he admitted it. Accused put the greatcoat over his shoulders, and said something about me finding more of his equipment if I was lucky. I told the second witness to take me to the place where the accused was found. On arriving at the bank about 150 to 200 yards from the lane I noticed that the grass and bushes were flattened out, as if someone had been lying there, and I saw witness number two pick up a Mills bomb similar to that produced from the top of the bank amongst some gorse bushes and grass. When I first saw accused under arrest, he was wringing the sleeves of his coat, which was very wet. There was a heavy dew that night. Accused had on a light cap. I thought accused seemed glad to be caught. He was white and cold. Accused said he had been in the district about three weeks, and had not been there overnight but had

> evidently arrived at about the same time as us. I asked how many men were with him, and he replied, 'Only two or three but the whole countryside is on the run.'
>
> All statements made by the accused to me or in my presence were quite voluntary … his attitude was friendly towards me and the other soldiers.

The record then shows:

> that Moylan was informed in open court of the finding of not guilty of the first charge.
>
> The President announced that in view of the communications received, which were favourable to the accused, the court wished to give the prosecutor ample opportunity of enquiring into the character of the accused before sentence was passed. And the court adjourned accordingly until 3 June 1921 until sentence was passed.[97]

Moylan's acquittal on the charge of levying war on the Crown was based on the fact that there were many others who might have fired on the military and the absence of firm evidence that Moylan himself shot at the soldiers and police was probably a decisive factor in the court's decision. There is little doubt Moylan's capture eventually became big news and some representations were made on his behalf. It was also known that Moylan acted in an honourable way on many occasions during the independence conflict and that was to his credit in the eyes of some of his adversaries. His case even came up at Westminster, where Captain Wedgwood Benn questioned Sir Hamar Greenwood, chief secretary for Ireland, on 1 June. He asked Greenwood if he was aware that Moylan's execution was due to take place on 4 June and if he would restrain the military from taking action against the prisoner. Hansard recorded the chief secretary's reply:

> John R. Moylan came before a court-martial yesterday at Cork on two charges, one of levying war against the King, and the second of having in his possession improperly one revolver, thirty rounds of revolver ammunition, and two Mills pattern bombs. The trial commenced yesterday … the court now stands adjourned until tomorrow.[98]

Captain Benn then asked if the habeas corpus writ that had been issued would continue to be obeyed by the military court. Greenwood replied that in his opinion it was a very difficult legal question that he could not answer off hand. Captain Wedgwood Benn and a cohort of other backbenchers were often very critical of the government in its handling of Irish affairs. Benn and his colleagues were regarded by the government, the military and certain members of the British establishment as being less than patriotic. The following day, Benn was on his feet again and asked the chief secretary if he had given orders for the writ to be obeyed by the Cork Military Court. Greenwood replied:

> I am informed that the court before which Moylan is being tried has not yet pronounced sentence. If it is ultimately decided that there is power to issue this Writ, it will of course be obeyed.[99]

The real question, of course was, which law should prevail, civilian or military, and who should decide on the answer. Moylan was, by that time, just one of a few men who had sought a habeas corpus writ while awaiting a court martial. The chief secretary continued to sidestep the problem, while Benn continued to pursue him for an answer but, alas, to no avail.

An *Irish Times* report confirmed that Moylan's trial reconvened on 5 June and, on that day, the prosecutor discussed what the court had learned about the character of the accused:

> The case was heard earlier in the week and after finding [conviction], an application was made by the prosecutor for an adjournment which the court granted. At that time certain information concerning the accused had reached the prosecutor. This information the prosecutor wished to investigate and consider. This has now been done and I consider it my duty to lay the information before the court for consideration before passing sentence.
>
> Shortly, the information is as follows. I understand and believe that the accused was in charge of a party of rebels who ambushed a party of police near Kingwilliamstown on 28 January, when Divisional Commissioner Holmes was mortally wounded. Certain of the rebels wanted to shoot some members of the RIC who were lying on the road, but their

Affix
stamp
here

Pen and Sword Books
c/o Casemate Publishers
1950 Lawrence Road
Havertown, PA 19083

> lives were saved by Moylan, who said to his own men, 'If you shoot them, I will shoot you.'
>
> On another occasion, two army deserters were caught by Moylan's gang, who were about to shoot them, when Moylan intervened and sent them on their way saying, 'You have me to thank, or else you would be shot. I don't believe in shooting in cold blood.'[100]

Moylan's chivalry and integrity had impressed the court and the decision was made it should be taken into account before sentence was passed. Sentence, however, was not pronounced at that stage and the following day the Chancery Division of the High Court heard counsel for Moylan in support of an order to make the writ of habeas corpus absolute. After argument, the conditional order was continued pending the outcome of an ongoing similar case, which was set to be announced in due course.

On 9 June the court martial sat again and, in defiance of the writ of habeas corpus, decided to bring matters in relation to Moylan to a conclusion. A sentence of fifteen years' penal servitude was handed down and Moylan's life was spared. It was clear that had he been convicted of the charge of levying war he would most likely have been executed. While conviction on the second charge could also have resulted in execution, the court was influenced by the fact that Moylan was an elected representative to Dáil Éireann and discussions were, at that time, taking place in the background to bring about an end to the independence conflict.

It had been a dramatic and, most probably, a traumatic number of days for Moylan, who, when he was captured and arrested had stoically accepted his fate. He saw no other outcome beyond facing the execution squad and it was only at the insistence of Barry Sullivan that he allowed his legal representatives to pursue his case through the courts. Their expertise and the fact that other powers had started negotiations about a truce coalesced and provided an opening for the courts to shy away from a death sentence that, had it been carried out, would have served no other purpose than to further complicate the quest for a lasting peace.

Chapter 15

Life on Spike Island

Once the court had made its decision and Moylan was no longer in danger of facing the firing squad, he was kept in Cork for several weeks. The detention barracks was a place of rigid discipline and the British soldiers on duty seemed to be consumed by an obvious nervousness and were always on the alert for something untoward happening while they were on duty. Their nerves were so on edge they often fired on their comrades and one soldier was killed by a sentry's bullet. Moylan recalled the barracks as being spotlessly clean and he and his fellow inmates were allowed out from their cells twice daily, in the morning and afternoon. Half of their free time was spent marching aimlessly around the prison yard, while during the other half they were allowed to congregate in a large shed where smokers were given permission to have a cigarette. Each smoker had his own tobacco pouch with his name and prisoner number on it and each pouch was handed out and collected daily by the warders. Prisoners were not allowed newspapers and were forbidden to have any news of the outside world. Despite that restriction, Moylan and his comrades were able to garner information from the constant influx of prisoners, who always brought news of what was happening outside the barracks.

After a few weeks in the barracks, Moylan was awoken one morning about 3 a.m. and paraded with a number of other prisoners on the ground floor. The area was full of British soldiers with rifles and bayonets, while others held revolvers. While Moylan and his comrades paraded, the officer in charge busied himself checking a list. The prisoners were then handcuffed and marched into a yard, where they were loaded onto lorries. They were then driven through the silent streets of Cork city to a quayside, where they were put onto a ship. Moylan recalled he was of the belief they were going to be transported to Dartmoor in England, so he was surprised, two hours later, when they all landed at Spike Island in Cork harbour. He immediately recognised where he was as soon as he came out of the hold of the ship because as he looked across the water he could see the town of Cobh. The prisoners were all marched up the pathway from the pier to the prison, which at that time was called Fort Westmoreland. The yard was occupied by resident prisoners, who were full of curiosity about the new arrivals.

While walking through the barracks gate, Moylan remembered reading John Mitchell's seminal book, *Jail Journal,* as a boy in Kilmallock and remarked to himself he never expected that one day he would be a prisoner detained at the pleasure of the Crown. The new prisoners were all quickly seated around a table in one of the huts and were served breakfast by their new comrades. After the fare they had received every day in Victoria Barracks, what they got that morning, though it was poor enough, seemed like a banquet. The first mug of real tea that morning was like nectar, especially after the bitter cocoa of the previous few weeks. The man in charge of the breakfast was Con Conroy, a big athletic man who exuded an air of soldierly neatness. He was dressed in a spotless white shirt and was a complete contrast to Moylan who, as he admitted, was sartorially in very bad shape. Conroy had been the intelligence officer for the Cork No. 1 Brigade and was at the time serving a fifteen-year sentence. He was later transferred to Kilkenny Prison, where he famously tunnelled his way to freedom and became a very good friend of Moylan.

Moylan quickly realised the prison on Spike Island was run on a different system to that employed in Victoria Barracks. The prisoners were controlled by their own officers and no prisoner accepted an order from the British that did not come to him from his own commandant. There were two prison camps on Spike Island. Moylan was held in one, which housed about 300 sentenced prisoners, and in the other camp there were around 2,000 internees. The accommodation for the sentenced prisoners consisted of a series of huts each housing fifteen to twenty men. The internees were held separately, some in the old fort. There was an exercise yard but no other facilities were provided. The British had little enough contact with the prisoners in Moylan's camp and, apart from general rules that they had imposed, the camp was entirely run by the prisoners themselves. The rule of no smoking was, however, imposed by the British but it did not impact Moylan as a non-smoker. However, it did cause the smokers in his camp no end of annoyance and agitation.

New internees arrived almost daily and many of them showed signs of having been physically beaten, though they were always in good spirits. Security was tight on the island but three prisoners escaped during April and one internee, Patrick White, was shot dead. He had been a captain in the Meelick Company of the East Clare Brigade. An entry in Hansard indicated

White had been reaching through the boundary wire and according to a government spokesman:

> His motive appears to have been innocent, but it had been necessary to instruct sentries to fire immediately on any person attempting to break through or tamper with the wire.[101]

Moylan noticed that prison had different effects on the men. Some, he said, prowled about like caged beasts, straining against their incarceration. Others, he said, just accepted their situation with a certain placidity and were prepared to bide their time. Moylan and his comrades had a daily visit from the medical officer and on one occasion he went to see him because his wounded hand continued to trouble him. The doctor spoke to him with contempt and offered him nothing more than a pill. A few days later another prisoner, Sean Hales TD (Member of Parliament) for West Cork, asked the doctor for some treatment for his eyes, which were bothering him. The doctor, showing the same contempt he had shown Moylan, suggested that Hales rub his own spit into his eyes, obviously to moisten them. Con Conroy was the hospital orderly and the doctor made a remark about Hales to him. Conroy informed the doctor that Hales was a member of Parliament, a fact that shocked the medic. Conroy then informed the doctor that the man who came to see him about his wounded hand was also an MP. The doctor replied:

> 'You mean that ragged chap who was here a few days ago?'
> 'Yes,' said Conroy.[102]

Moylan later recalled:

> The doctor immediately sent for me and asked to see my hand. I told him that I had no further intention of availing myself of his service. 'Well,' he said, 'when you were here a few days ago I didn't know you were an M.P. 'I informed him that there was at one time a person called Hippocrates and that if he did not feel it his duty to treat the wound of a prisoner because he was prisoner he should not propose to treat the wound of the same prisoner because he was an M.P. This man, though he had long service with the British Army, came originally from Youghal. We never saw him in camp again. He was replaced

> by a younger man who had just returned from India and who did not concern himself with the prisoners' political views but treated each man as the need arose with utmost consideration.[103]

It seems that Moylan and Hales were not the only ones to experience the poor quality of care at the hands of the original doctor. Johnny Collins (brother of Michael) lost the use of his right hand due to the lack of proper treatment. Not long after the arrival of the young doctor, Moylan was struck down by illness and collapsed. He was immediately sent to the prison hospital for some weeks. Conroy was in charge of the hospital unit and he nursed Moylan back to a semblance of good health. One fine day, Conroy took Moylan outside and laid him in the sun at the foot of the wall surrounding the camp. As both men chatted, they saw a young soldier in full kit passing back and forth along the wall, which was about 4 or 5ft wide. The weather was exceptionally warm and the soldier was weighted down with a tin helmet, rifle and heavy overcoat. It seems he was undergoing punishment for some offence he committed. Both Moylan and Conroy could see he was suffering badly and he was sweating profusely. He was also licking his lips as if he was suffering from thirst. Moylan sent Conroy back into the hospital to fetch some oranges he had stored away. When Conroy came back with the oranges, he bided his time and when the opportunity presented itself, he laid the oranges on the wall. The soldier stopped and grabbed them as he passed and bit furiously into each one. When he passed again, he dropped a packet of Woodbines down to Moylan and Conroy. Moylan recalled:

> This was the greatest gift that could have fallen into the yard at Spike Island and this was the beginning of a friendship between ourselves and this particular soldier, which had an interesting outcome. The rule against smoking did not affect me. I was a non-smoker but the hunger for tobacco seemed to overshadow every other concern in the minds of the prisoners. Somebody sent me a parcel one day in which there were a few pounds of butter. I asked the Hospital Orderly, a rather innocent young Englishman, if he would like a pound of butter. He was delighted. There was, apparently, no butter ration issued to the British troops. They got margarine. A few days later I gave him a cake which somebody sent me and then I asked him if there was any possibility of his getting some cigarettes from the internees. There was no rule against smoking in the

> internees camp. He arrived that afternoon with linen for the hospital cell. The linen consisted of a pillow case packed full of cigarettes with a few towels laid on top … The dark cloud that floated over Spike Island that afternoon was not caused by any weather conditions but by the smoke arising from the cigarettes in the mouths of 300 prisoners. Everybody smoked. Some, like myself for the first time. From that forward the internees supplied us from their own store and after constant raids and punishment the rule against smoking went into abeyance.[104]

The overall quality of the food on offer to the prisoners was poor and it was Moylan's opinion the contractors who provided the food to the prison had very little in the way of scruples. The prisoners were forever complaining about the food and Con Conroy eventually got his soldier friend to take a letter out to be posted in Cobh on his next leave. The note was sent to a friend of Conroy and it gave the facts in relation to the quality of the food being supplied to the prisoners. The information was then conveyed to the officers of the Cork No. 1 Brigade. Inside a week there was a noticeable improvement in the quality of the food being served up to the prisoners.

Moylan recalled the prisoners had one major bugbear, as he called it, while they were on Spike Island and it was in the form of a sergeant major of the Welsh Fusiliers. The man had served many years in India and he seemed to think he could treat Irishmen in the same manner as he had treated the Indians. According to Moylan, the sergeant major was not averse to using vile language and he spent a lot of time and energy forcing prisoners he did not like to engage in very heavy and often unnecessary work around the prison. Most prisoners were willing to do some work as it got them out in the fresh air close to the sea and with a nice view across to Cobh and the surrounding countryside. However, they resented being engaged in heavy and arduous labour on the whim of the sergeant major, whose abusive language was also bitterly resented.

Moylan and his comrades got to know that the sergeant major's wife and mother-in-law lived in Cobh and that he visited them constantly. Moylan and some of his comrades wrote a letter to him threatening dire consequences for his wife and mother-in-law if he continued his abuse of the prisoners and signed it with the letters, 'I.R.A.' It was given to Conroy's soldier friend, who posted it in Cobh. A few days later an obviously angry sergeant major assembled all the prisoners and proceeded to lecture them on the evil that would befall all of them if anything untoward should happen to his wife and mother-in-law. The vast majority of the prisoners stood in amazement wondering just who he was talking about as none of them had ever heard of their existence. Moylan and Conroy found it very difficult to keep a straight face but finally the angry soldier saw Moylan smiling and pounced on him. He produced the letter and confronted Moylan, who very quickly began to sympathise with him. Moylan then took the opportunity to point out to the sergeant major, that in the opinion of the men, he had done everything in his power to make life difficult for them and went on to say to him:

> 'Even your own soldiers talk about your unjustifiable attitude to the prisoners. It is well known on the mainland what the attitude is. As a prisoner,' I said, 'I cannot offer you any advice but if I could so I would suggest that if you have any concern for your wife and mother-in-law you should immediately mend your ways on the island and treat these men as soldiers and prisoners of war.
>
> Otherwise I am afraid you are merely asking for trouble.'[105]

The incandescent sergeant major continued to fume and swear but, behind all of his bullying bluster, Moylan was of the view that the man was a poltroon. However, from that day onwards life within the confines of the prison became noticeably easier.

Moylan recalled how news from the outside world and especially from the martial law areas was always scarce. However, on occasions a newspaper found its way into the prison from the internees camp and now and then a new prisoner arrived and he brought news with him. Moylan was always keen to have news from North Cork, where his comrades were continuing with the independence fight. He heard of a successful ambush of Auxiliaries, all of whom had been encamped around a big house just west of Millstreet. The newspaper headline of the ambush was large and the account of it was very reassuring to Moylan, and he was glad to know that his boys were still in the ring. He was happy to note the organisation he had been part of since 1916 continued to develop strength in his absence and was refusing to allow the initiative to be taken away from it.

Moylan's brigade was active everywhere and he was happy to hear how the long-planned operation between his men and the West Limerick Brigade had some success in an engagement with the Black and Tans near Abbyfeale. Moylan also read about the large sweeping operations carried out by the British in North Cork and in Kerry. The IRA columns in North Cork had managed to evade the sweep but not without great difficulty. He was very pleased the fight was continuing in his enforced absence. One piece of news did, however, sadden him and it concerned two British Army deserters who had been captured sometime earlier and were suspected by some of Moylan's men of being spies. Moylan saved them from execution and sent them to Kerry to work on farms. During one of the big sweeps, some Volunteers decided the two men knew too much about the Volunteers' activity in the area and executed both of them. Moylan, being the character he was, most likely would not have sanctioned such an action.

Life on Spike Island was acceptable enough for Moylan and he was a resident of Hut No. 17. While the authorities did try to minimise the prisoners' knowledge of and, contact with, the outside world, letters were received by the men and theirs were also sent out by whatever means they could find. Food parcels were gratefully received from home and every so often accounts of social gatherings in the prisoners' home areas trickled through to the men. Those snippets of news were very important and often relieved the boredom of a prison day. They also had the effect of raising spirits but every now and then spirits were dampened when men realised they were missing out on some sporting or social event or other, be it a hurling match or dance. Long-term prisoners and internees were allowed to attend Mass on Sundays, during which the prisoners managed to scrounge some food or tobacco from the internees. During those difficult days of incarceration it was most important for every man to maintain an optimistic outlook and plan for the day when he would be able to walk out through the main gate a free man.

* * *

The last six months of the independence conflict saw attacks and ambushes carried out across the country almost every day. Volunteers took on the Crown forces determined to make life as difficult as possible for them. From the beginning of the year, the IRA carried out attacks on RIC barracks and ambushed military patrols, often bringing about British acts of reprisals against the IRA and the civilian population. As the months passed the pace of violence accelerated and every day brought news of further deaths on both sides. Few parts of the country escaped the chaos and mayhem and countless families were impacted by the killing and suffering. The war attracted attention outside of the country and it was obvious some serious efforts were needed to bring the conflict to an end. Even Pope Benedict XV felt compelled to make his views known and, in May, he issued a letter encouraging the 'English as well as the Irish to calmly consider some means of agreement'. By the last week of June, it was clear that stalemate had set in and there was little chance of either side gaining the upper hand. Public and political opinion in Britain was pressurising the government, led by Lloyd George, to find a solution to the Irish problem, while Michael Collins and those around him in the IRA leadership were becoming increasingly concerned about their ability to continue the war.

On 24 June 1921 the Cabinet in London decided to initiate talks with the leaders of Sinn Fein with a view to finding some common ground upon which to bring about a cessation in the fighting. Lloyd George and his government colleagues had concluded the IRA guerrilla war campaign was set to continue indefinitely. If that was to happen the government would come under increasing financial pressure and would have to deal with further military casualties. In early June, the British made their first move towards a truce when they abandoned the policy of house burnings often carried out as reprisals for IRA ambushes and attacks on Crown forces.

The move towards a truce was given some impetus by the attitude of King George V, who expressed his unhappiness over the conduct of the Black and Tans in Ireland. Lloyd George wrote to Eamon de Valera as 'the chosen leader of the great majority in Southern Ireland' inviting him to talks in London. De Valera had discussions with Southern Unionists to gauge their attitude and when they ended on 8 July he sent a telegram to Lloyd George saying he was ready to negotiate but he did insist on a preliminary cessation of hostilities. The British initially refused the request but Lord Middleton intervened and persuaded Lloyd George to agree to de Valera's request. Jan Smuts, the South African military hero and prime minister, arrived as an emissary to hold discussions with de Valera, during which he cited the compromise that ended the Boer War and how something similar might be applied to the Irish situation. De Valera and Lloyd George agreed to meet and, on 9 July, the terms of the truce were fixed when General Macready, commander of the British forces in Ireland, arrived at the Mansion House in Dublin for discussions, and it came into force two days later. It should be pointed out, however, that many IRA officers around the country were sceptical of the truce and continued to recruit volunteers and train them in anticipation of hostilities resuming at a future date. There was some sporadic violence in the days before and after the truce but in general peace did come to the country, even if it was an uneasy one.

* * *

The opportunity for Moylan to leave Spike Island came quicker than he probably expected because the ending of the independence conflict was officially announced when the truce came into effect on 11 July. Moylan and his comrades had no other choice but to bide their time on Spike Island until everything had been agreed between de Valera and Lloyd George. We know that de Valera was anxious to negotiate the release of all members of the Dáil who were being held in prisons. The British agreed to the release of Moylan and, indeed, Sean Hales, though they initially baulked at allowing Sean MacEoin to walk free. Eventually Lloyd George relented, most likely because he was much more interested in the bigger picture and attaining a lasting agreement. After two and a half years of conflict the country eventually returned to peace and, for the first time ever, the British were brought to the negotiating table by Irish republicans to discuss the question of independence. By then, both sides recognised the stalemate that had set in was unlikely to be broken anytime soon and the more obvious solution to finding a shared consensus about Ireland's future was very likely to be found in negotiations rather than in fighting.

The days after the truce announcement must have been extremely onerous for Moylan as he awaited his release. In a letter to his mother on 7 August 1921, he wrote:

> Dear Mother
> I reckon I've nothing to report. I got Mamie's letter and parcel OK. I also got K.T. Murphy's letter and hope she got mine in reply. Will you get me some stuff when you get this. Butter, some cake and bacon (cooked). Had a note from Dublin notifying me of meeting of An Dáil. I have me doubts about its meaning anything else. Did Joe come home or is he going away on holidays? M.R. wrote to me and she said she had some time at the Truce dances. I didn't get a real account of Freemont concert but from previous experience I can guess what 'twas like. Write me when you have time.
>
> Yours Jack.[106]

Moylan left Spike Island on 8 August 1921, and according to contemporary reports he was dressed more or less in the rags he entered the prison. It seems he was taken to Mrs Martin's house in Cork, where he met up with Sean Hegarty, Michael Leahy and Dominic Sullivan, all fellow Volunteers. Moylan recalled the reunion vividly:

> Sean looked at me sourly and made a few uncomplimentary remarks on my appearance.
>
> He generally greeted his friends with obloquy. It was his way of expressing his genuine welcome, which he emphasised by immediately purchasing a suit of clothes for me.
>
> Jim Gray drove me to Divisional Headquarters where Liam Lynch waited to drive me home.
>
> It seemed an age since we met though scarcely two months had passed and we talked far into the night of plans and hopes for the future. I returned to work the next day.[107]

With the fighting at an end and a peace to be negotiated, a new era was about to dawn for Moylan and his comrades. Hopes were high across the country that those tasked with finding a compromise with the British would be successful in their endeavours. Yet, a certain scepticism prevailed in the IRA and in the wider republican community in relation to the British and their willingness to deliver on a republic. Moylan, though prepared to back the truce and the negotiations process, was not, like many of his comrades, confident of an acceptable outcome.

Chapter 16

From Truce to Treaty

While Moylan was in prison, new arrangements had been put in place with regard to his brigade. It was divided into two, with the eastern half becoming Cork No. 2 Brigade and the western half becoming Cork No. 4. George Power and Paddy O'Brien had been named as respective commanders. When he returned to work, Moylan was named by the divisional Officer Commanding as commander of Cork No. 4, with Paddy O'Brien as his deputy. The Cork No. 4 Brigade covered the Mallow, Kanturk, Charleville, Newmarket and Millstreet areas and O'Brien was happy to stand down in favour of Moylan. As it transpired, the heavier workload in relation to the brigade fell on O'Brien as early as 16 August as Moylan became more immersed in his Second Dáil Éireann duties. Moylan later made the point that the changes and demotions were made in a seamless manner and no one argued against them and, in fact, accepted them as part and parcel of soldiering. Moylan was very grateful to have a deputy like O'Brien because much of his time was spent travelling to and from Dublin; however, he did so safe in the knowledge all was in hand back in Cork.

Moylan was also able to call on his great friend and comrade Sean Nunan, as well as other men like Mick Sullivan, Eugene McCarthy and Michael O'Connell, all of whom were trustworthy, intelligent and committed to the independence cause. Though the truce was in force, they all, to a man, never discounted the possibility that hostilities might resume at any moment. In fact, at times they all felt it was inevitable they would have to take up their guns again. With that in mind, Moylan and his closest officers continued to train, equip and recruit men and instil into them that earnest, aggressive spirit with which they themselves were imbued. The British Army's general staff seemed, at the time, to be of a similar view and did not fully accept the conflict was over. The 6th Division Record of the Rebellion clearly stated that:

> The whole time and energy of everyone during the period 11 July to 5 Dec was devoted to preparing for a possible

> resumption of hostilities. The focus of their preparations lay in intelligence: identifying guerrilla leaders and securing information about the structure of the IRA. Strenuous efforts were made to equip all units with wireless capabilities and to lay down aerodromes in every district.[108]

Because of the truce, conditions for the IRA were soon of an entirely different nature, according to Moylan. A period of relaxation began and the discipline that physical danger always imposes on fighting men disappeared. Moylan and his comrades were quickly confronted with a much more subtle danger. They were, in the eyes of the civilian population, heroes of the independence conflict and had become the targets of a fleeting flattery and adulation. There were a few weeks of joyous abandon among the civilian population across the country, a natural reaction to the strain and tension of the past few years. However, for the fighting men of the IRA there was a consensus that nothing had been settled with the British and the truce might well be nothing more than a mere respite or breathing space. Taking all that into account, Moylan recalled:

> Training camps were re-established and the lessons learned from the experience of 1920–21 formed matter for study additional to the previous routine of such camps.
>
> Workshops and foundries were further developed and every effort was made to produce munitions of war. Trained mechanics and machines not previously obtainable were put to work and since men met more easily ideas and information were more swiftly disseminated. It is true to say that from the Truce to the Treaty those who were the backbone IRA worked more strenuously than ever. And there was reason in this.
>
> Word was passed round from Headquarters in Dublin that the Truce might break at any moment, that the negotiations with London could not succeed and the fight would have to be continued, would be harder and more bitter than before. Knowing that we could not beat the British militarily, we did not believe that a Truce could come; believing that there could be no diminution of the Irish demand, we could not believe in its continuance.[109]

The British Army was cognisant of what the IRA were doing at that time and the 6th Division Records of the Rebellion stated:

> As soon as all chance of immediate fighting was over, the scattered bands of desperados formed themselves into the companies and battalions to which they had always belonged on paper and started to train, practise musketry, hold reviews etc.[110]

Indeed, Moylan was even singled out as someone who was in breach of the Treaty and in a memorandum to the Cabinet in London from General Sir Nevil Macready on 27 September, he said:

> Flagrant breaches of the agreement specifically with regard to a notorious rebel, Moylan by name ... who was seen in Newmarket ... carrying a Thompson machine gun under his coat.[111]

The fact is, of course, both sides breached the Treaty as the IRA briefly kidnapped soldiers and stole arms and ammunition, while some British Army personnel engaged in acts of violence of their own. The IRA leadership in many areas also had to contend with young men who, during the independence conflict, were on the fringes of the Volunteers but were posing as hardened veterans once the truce was called, earning themselves and the IRA a bad reputation. According to Moylan, these renegades posed as veterans of the war in public houses and dance halls and when on the road in so-called 'commandeered' motor cars, they pushed the ordinary decent civilians aside and earned the IRA a reputation for bullying, insobriety and dishonesty that understandably eroded public confidence in the real fighting men. Unfortunately, according to Moylan, the offending men were an evil influence on the young, generous, adventurous boys who, knowing of IRA achievements, also sought an opportunity of proving themselves.

* * *

It proved to be impossible for Moylan and his comrades to deal adequately with the renegades in any given area, mainly because the men who had borne the brunt of the fighting were otherwise engaged in training camps or in workshops and foundries while others had returned home to work on their family farms or whatever other work they could find. Moylan introduced a note of anger or dissent when discussing those very same men, all of whom he maintained were the nation's army. They had been warned, he said, of the probable need to take up arms again in the national defence at any moment, yet hc believed the nation was not making any attempt to provide for them when they most needed help. Moylan was not afraid to ask pertinent questions that might have upset certain people. For example, he wondered out loud if the IRA had been forgotten by the political leaders as they negotiated with the British. He asked if it really was forgetfulness on the part of the Sinn Fein politicians or was it a deliberate omission? He feared those very same Sinn Fein politicians had somehow come to believe that political effort had forced the truce and that same method could conclude the negotiations satisfactorily. Moylan later recalled how Liam Mellows had extolled the virtues of the Volunteers at a meeting of Dáil Éireann on 25 January 1921 when he said:

> 'Were it not for the Volunteer Movement they could not talk of Ireland abroad, and if it were not for the Volunteers they could give up any idea of a Republic.'
>
> No man who knew anything of the matter could have said other. Any man who spoke of the Irish Republican Movement and did not include under the terms both Sinn Fein and the Volunteers, their inter-locking activities and their co-ordinated effort, had failed to group its real significance, composition and purpose. The men of the IRA had served the nation without pay or reward.
>
> Their duty done they would have been content to return to their civilian occupations.[112]

Moylan recalled the early days of August when he and his officers had a visit from Richard Mulcahy, the chief of staff. Moylan had not seen him since 1917 when he was in North Cork working as a Gaelic League organiser. Moylan saw little change in Mulcahy's appearance but did note that he was far better dressed. Mulcahy stressed the need for organisation and training as there was, in his view, the practical certainty that Moylan and his forces would be called upon again to fight. Though the truce was in place, dissent of one kind or another could still be seen in different regions across the country. For example, August saw workers in Bruree in County Limerick take control of the mill they worked in. They raised the Red flag over the building and draped a banner across it proclaiming 'Bruree Workers Soviet Mills – We Make Bread Not Profits'. The protest and the Soviet, which was inspired by the revolution in Russia, lasted until 3 September, when it ended on the intervention of the mayor of Limerick and the local bishop. Unfortunately, sectarian violence continued in Ulster and, on 27 August, a house in Belfast was bombed by Loyalists. Over the following two days two Protestant civilians were shot by republican snipers. The violence escalated over the last two days of the month and eighteen people – nine Protestants and nine Catholics – lost their lives during street battles in Belfast.

* * *

On the political front, Lloyd George and Eamon de Valera continued their dialogue and, in a letter to de Valera dated 7 September, the prime minister indicated there would be real difficulty in persuading people living in Fermanagh and Tyrone to accept their counties were part of Northern Ireland. The partition question again became the source of violence and disagreement among those living in Northern Ireland. The middle of the month saw further riots in Belfast and two Protestants were shot dead by a sniper. On 24 September, Winston Churchill made his views known when, speaking in Dundee, he threatened a resumption of the war if Dáil Éireann refused to accept the British peace proposals. That same day further violence in Belfast saw two people killed and twenty injured when a grenade was thrown at a Loyalist group planning to attack a nationalist area in the city.

October saw the beginning of the Treaty negotiations and on the ninth day of the month the delegation chosen by Dáil Éireann arrived in London. Led by Arthur Griffith and Michael Collins, the delegation was made up of Eamon Duggan, Robert Barton and George Gavan Duffy. Erskine Childers was controversially nominated by de Valera to act as secretary to the delegation. De Valera famously stayed at home, which of course turned out to be one of the most controversial decisions ever made by an Irish political leader. The negotiations began two days later and set the scene for an intensive two months of protracted talks. The Irish delegation was an inexperienced one in the art of negotiating and they were up against probably the best negotiating team in the world led by the 'Welsh Wizard', Lloyd George. The Irish delegation was instructed to demand, a 'thirty-two county independent Ireland', but Lloyd George was only prepared to offer a 'twenty-six county dominion', which included, among other clauses, perpetual free trade between Ireland and Britain.

During the negotiations in London the violence continued in Northern Ireland. Between 21 and 25 November, thirty people were killed in Belfast. The tensions were not eased when, on 28 November, the government in

Westminster decided to transfer the responsibility for local government to the Stormont government. The decision was met with fury by nationalists and Tyrone County Council decided to pledge its allegiance to Dáil Éireann in Dublin. That very same day legislation was introduced in Stormont (which was dominated by the Unionist Party) making it possible for that legislature to dissolve any local authority it wished to. It did not take long for that to happen and on 2 December the offices of Tyrone County Council were raided by the police, who seized all records.

While the delegation was doing its best to get an acceptable deal in London, de Valera travelled around Ireland in the company of Cathal Brugha making speeches and inspecting IRA units. He spent time in Galway, Clare and Limerick and, in a speech on 30 November in Clare, he reminded Volunteers they might still be required to defy the British and their 'savagery'. Just as Mulcahy had indicated to Moylan during his visit to North Cork, de Valera was also clearly hinting that preparations for further hostilities should continue to be made in case the negotiations broke down. In Northern Ireland, the Unionists continued to secure their position and on the same day as de Valera's speech in Clare there was no surprise when James Craig blamed Sinn Fein for the recent violence in the Province. He announced that 700 men were to be recruited as A-Specials, while a further 5,000 men would be enrolled as B-Specials. Ironically, the Unionists, like many in the republican movement, were not inclined to believe the truce would hold and they too began to plan accordingly.

* * *

On 6 December news filtered back to the country that the Anglo-Irish Treaty had been signed in Downing Street between the government and the Irish delegation. For Moylan and, indeed many other republicans, it failed to deliver the republic they had all hoped for. Instead, Lloyd George got his way and a dominion of the Commonwealth based on the twenty-six counties outside of Ulster was agreed. It was clear to Moylan and many of his comrades that the Treaty was set to divide the country and might well be the source of further deaths and suffering. As part of the agreement, the first contingent of IRA prisoners was released on 9 December and preparations were made across the country to welcome them home as heroes. The following day a meeting of the IRB Supreme Council in Belfast approved the Treaty, with eleven members voting for it and four members voting against it. That same day nationalists in the city were fired upon by Loyalist gunmen.

The delegation returned home to a Cabinet, Dáil and a bitterly divided country. The Cabinet discussed the Treaty and, on a vote of four in favour and three against, it was decided that it should be sent to Dáil Éireann for debate. De Valera, Cathal Brugha and Austin Stack opposed sending the Treaty to Dáil Éireann and wanted to repudiate it there and then, but Michael Collins, Arthur Griffith and Robert Barton were in favour of further debate. W.T. Cosgrave broke the deadlock by voting in favour. The Treaty debates began on 14 December in the University College Dublin council chamber at Earlsfort Terrace. The House of Commons debate on the Treaty also began that same day and it was passed on 16 December by a vote of 401 in favour and 58 against. In the House of Lords, it was passed by a vote of 166 in favour and 47 against. Public interest in the Dáil debates proved to be immense and the gallery was full each day as people listened to every deputy who spoke on the issue. From the outset it was clear the following days and weeks were going to be very difficult as each deputy made his or her views known. There was much in the way of vitriol in the chamber and the tension at times was often stretched to the limit.

De Valera opened the debates on 14 December and from the outset made his views on the Treaty very clear when he said:

> It would be ridiculous to think that we could send five men to complete a treaty without the right of ratification by this assembly. That is the only thing that matters.
>
> Therefore, it is agreed that this Treaty is simply an agreement and that it is not binding until the Dáil ratifies it. That is what we are concerned with.[113]

De Valera made it clear in his opening remarks that he felt the delegates had overstepped their authority by signing the Treaty. He did recognise they had full plenipotentiary powers, as given to them by Dáil Éireann, but he also pointed out that he had made it clear to them that nothing was to be agreed with the British until he and the rest of his Cabinet colleagues had been consulted. That assertion was very quickly contradicted by Arthur Griffith, and Michael Collins then pointed out that the delegates:

> did not sign the agreement as a Treaty, but did sign on the understanding that each signatory would recommend it to the Dáil for acceptance.[114]

That early verbal joust between the leading protagonists set the bar for the following weeks and there was to be no real let up in the tension that ensued in the chamber.

Secret Dáil sessions were held between 14 December and 17 December, mainly to keep the sense of bitterness and discord that pervaded the chamber out of the public domain. During these sessions, de Valera produced a redraft of the Treaty that differed little from what had been agreed to in Downing Street by the delegation. Realistically, de Valera's draft would not have been acceptable to the British as the points on which there were differences had already been explored during the negotiation in London. During the debates, de Valera and his supporters continued to maintain the Treaty had been signed under duress because Lloyd George threatened war on the country. De Valera emphasised that point in his speech on 16 December when he said:

> I believe that the document was signed under duress and, though I have a moral feeling that any agreement entered into ought to be faithfully carried out, I have no hesitation in saying that I would not regard it as binding on the Irish nation.[115]

The debates very quickly highlighted the differing views held by TDs in relation to what had happened in the recent past and the direction the country should take in the future. Most speakers focussed their attention on the constitutional options that might be open to them. There was little discussion on how the Treaty, if accepted, might impact on the prevailing economic issues of the day or how it might improve the lives of the majority of the people across the country. It was also very noticeable that the Irish language was rarely used during the debates, even though Sinn Fein had, since 1918, made a great play of preserving the language, seeing it as the ultimate symbol of Ireland's independence. It was also noted by many observers attending the debates how some of the female TDs proved themselves to be of a more militant mind than their male counterparts and were in favour of continuing the war with Britain until a thirty-two county republic was secured.

Personal bitterness was also in evidence and none more so than in the exchanges between two of the delegation members. Arthur Griffith was particularly scathing of Erskine Childers, making it clear to those listening to him that:

> I will not reply to any damned Englishman in this Assembly.[116]

A particularly incensed and agitated Cathal Brugha went out of his way to remind the Dáil that Michael Collins's position in the IRA was technically inferior to his, not that Collins ever paid much attention to what Brugha thought. Unfortunately, the spectre of civil war hung over the debates as early as 17 December, when Liam Mellows repudiated the right of the Dáil, or indeed of anybody, to accept the Treaty when he said:

> We who stand by the Republic still will I presume rebel against the new government that would be set up if this Treaty was passed.[117]

Collins adamantly stood by the Treaty and during one particularly heated argument when he was accused of being a traitor to the republic, he fired back at his accusers saying:

> I have been called a traitor … If I am a traitor, let the people of Ireland decide it or not.[118]

Colins was not for turning during the debates and he famously reiterated his support for the Treaty when he said:

> it gives us the freedom, not the ultimate freedom that all nations desire and develop to, but the freedom to achieve it.[119]

The debates continued right up until the Dáil took its Christmas break and, while the initial reaction of the chamber was one of rejection of the Treaty, it seemed possible, as the deputies left for home, that the tide might well be turning in favour of acceptance. Moylan rose to speak on the Treaty a number of times during the debates and his first telling contribution came on 17 December when he told the chamber:

> There is a little for me to say. As one who has made up his mind about the Treaty and who has since he came up to this meeting heard nothing that would make him change his views, I would like to say a few words. Most of the soldier members of the Dáil who have spoken at all have been more or less favourable to the Treaty …
>
> Now I will vote against this Treaty … [120]

However, without doubt his most telling contribution came just prior to the Christmas break on 22 December:

> What I say is this: Hands off the Republic. And I am to be told this is a declaration of war on England? No English statesman will take it so. It is a definition of our rights, and Lloyd George, if he wants war will have to declare war. If he is giving us freedom he can do so without declaring war.
>
> All we ask of Lloyd George is to allow us carry on. There is just one point more.
>
> It is this. As I said we have been fighting for the extermination of British interests in Ireland. We are told we have it. I don't believe we have it. If there is a war of extermination waged on us, that war will also exterminate British interest in Ireland; because if they want a war of extermination on us, I may not see it finished, but by God, no loyalist in North Cork will see its finish, and it is about time that somebody told Lloyd George that. The terms of reference must be interpreted in their broadest, and not in their narrowest, sense. For our Republic we are offered (1) An Oath of Allegiance; (2) A Governor General: (3) A New Pale; (4) An army entrenched on our flank; (5) Independence, internal independence; (6) The Treaty to preserve and consolidate British interests in our midst.[121]

It is generally accepted that had a vote been taken on the Treaty prior to the Dáil's Christmas break it most probably would have been rejected. However, the vote was adjourned until after the Christmas break when the deputies returned to their constituencies. Moylan, most likely, took the train back to Millstreet for the holidays and it seems he had a personal reason for doing so as well as to meet with his constituents and IRA comrades to discuss the Treaty. For some time he had been corresponding with a young lady called Nora Murphy and seemingly the relationship was blossoming into something of a serious nature. Nora was the daughter of Annie and Dan Murphy, who owned the Shamrock House in Kiskeam. Nora was a teacher in the North of England and accounts describe her as a self-possessed young woman blessed with very good looks. The story goes, according to Aideen Carroll, that Nora's parents invited her to meet Moylan, who was visiting the household. She is said to have swept into the front room but was not much impressed by the rather thin and forlorn Moylan. He did manage to engage in some banter with her on the question of whether she might marry him and is reported to have replied 'We will have to see.'

The Newmarket of Christmas 1921 was a complete contrast to that of the previous year when Moylan was in town on Christmas Eve for a meeting with Con Moylan and Con Flynn at the home of Liam Moylan's parents. That was a dark night in every sense with the town blacked out and everyone indoors. It was made no better by the death of local man John Murphy, who was shot dead by British troops when he took his Christmas candle to his bedroom window. However, the Christmas of 1921 brought a lighter atmosphere with less fear and more hope. The signing of the Treaty had brought a renewed sense of hope across the country for a brighter future. Though not the result most people wanted from the negotiations with the British, the Treaty was viewed by the majority of the people as the basis for the way forward for the country. While the Treaty did not deliver a thirty-two county republic, so gallantly fought for during the Easter Rising and the War of Independence, it did represent a real stepping stone to peace for many people, not only in Newmarket, but also across the country and hence the prevailing upbeat mood. There was much evidence to suggest the majority of the people had put their trust in the Irish delegation during the Treaty negotiations. They viewed it as a vehicle for peace and stability, which had been lacking across the country for so long. It was then, with a certain amount of hope, the people of Ireland enjoyed Christmas and welcomed the new year with a full expectation that normal life was about to return after many years of tragedy, suffering and loss, and who could blame them for not doing so?

When the deputies returned to the Dáil just after the New Year, the mood had clearly changed in the chamber. They had all availed of the opportunity over the holidays to sound out their constituents and many of them had been left in no doubt by those they met that the Treaty was to be embraced as it offered the chance of peace. During the hiatus the powerful Catholic Church weighed in on the Treaty and backed it wholeheartedly. The Treaty also found favour with most of the national and local press and many public bodies across the country also threw their weight behind it. As far as the civilian population was concerned, the possibility of peace was not something to be discarded lightly.

* * *

That view was further entrenched when people read statements purporting to come from British politicians like Churchill and Lord Birkenhead threatening a return to war and an even more fearsome one than had just ended. Many citizens saw the Treaty as real progress and though it may not have delivered on all that they wished for, they were inclined to agree with Collins's general view that it was a major stepping stone on the road to an eventual republic. Some commentators were also keen to point out that Dominion status offered a greater degree of independence than the Home Rule Act of 1914 and it put the country on a par with the likes of Canada, New Zealand and Australia. That view, it seems, resonated positively with much of the ordinary citizenry, all of whom just wanted a peaceful future for their country.

Taking public and other opinion into account, it really should have come as no surprise to the Dáil deputies that a new dynamic had suddenly been introduced when they resumed the Treaty debates in the early days of January 1922. The reconvening of the debates saw an intense few days in Dublin and indeed around the country, where people watched and waited for an outcome to the deliberations. Moylan became engaged to Nora over the Christmas break and she, together with her sister Mary, travelled to Dublin to sit in the public gallery to watch the debates. As soon as the debates resumed on Tuesday, 3 January 1922 it was clear the views and voting intentions of some TDs had changed dramatically. The Treaty was eventually ratified on 7 January by 64 votes to 57. When the final vote was announced there were some moments of silence in the chamber as deputies took in the enormity of their decision. It seemed the whole chamber was suspended in time as no one moved or said a word, or even cheered the result. Moylan, it was later reported, was said to have broken down in tears. Two of the members of the Treaty delegation, Robert Barton and Erskine Childers, voted against the agreement that they had signed with the British (maintaining they had done so under duress) and de Valera led a symbolic protest walkout of his supporters from the floor of the Dáil. The narrowness of the Dáil majority probably did not reflect the extent of support for the Treaty in the country but the new Free State was intended to be built on the principles of democracy and the majority in the chamber were in favour of accepting the agreement. On 9 January, Arthur Griffith was elected president of the Provisional Government set up under the terms of the Treaty, defeating Eamon de Valera by 60 votes to 58, with Michael Collins appointed as minister for finance.

The early days of January 1922 proved to be defining ones in Irish history. The Treaty divided the country and the republican leadership to the point where old friends and comrades were forced to forsake each other. Moylan naturally foresaw that scenario and it undoubtedly cut him to his very core. The bitterness, so evident in the debates, eventually manifested itself in a conflict that had a profound and lasting impact on the country for much of the twentieth century. Brothers and friends who fought on the same side in the Rising and the War of Independence were soon pitted against each other during the months following the ratification of the Treaty in what turned out to be a vicious and bloody conflict that came to be known as the Civil War.

Chapter 17

An Uneasy Peace

When Michael Collins took possession of Dublin Castle from the British on 16 January 1922 it marked the end of 700 years of domination in Ireland by the Crown. Collins was late for the handover ceremony and was taken to task by a pompous British official, who chided him for being seven minutes late. Collins is reported to have made the point that seven minutes hardly mattered in the greater scale of things considering the British had been subjugating Ireland and her people for seven hundred years. Collins took over from the very same people who only a few months earlier would have executed him for treason. The handover marked the end of British rule in Ireland and from that day on the country's destiny was firmly placed in the hands of the Irish people. Over the following weeks similar scenes were enacted across the country and in December 1922 the last British troops left Ireland. The Treaty allowed for a twelve-month transition period to 6 December 1922, during which the British would hand the running of the country over to a provisional government headed by Arthur Griffith. It eventually fell upon the new government to set up institutions like a new police force called the Garda Síochána in 1923, as well as a new National Army in January 1922, under the direction of Richard Mulcahy, who was also appointed minister for defence. The army was made up of pro-Treaty IRA men and Irishmen who had military experience serving in the British Army.

As a result of the Treaty and the divisions that emerged because of it, many senior men in the IRA demanded the convening of a convention. They had sworn an oath to the republic and to Dáil Éireann and believed the Treaty placed them in a very difficult position not of their own making. They then demanded the IRA revert once again to a Volunteer organisation ruled by an executive. The suggestion was bound to bring the anti-Treaty faction of the IRA into conflict with the Provisional Government and all the indications were that if it was pursued there could only be one extreme and unsavoury outcome. Ernie O'Malley and the 2nd Southern Division's refusal to recognise the authority of GHQ exacerbated what was already a very challenging situation. This was a very serious development that only served to heighten the obvious tension that existed across the country. While all of this was taking place, recruitment to the Irish National Army continued at a rapid pace. As for the request to hold an IRA convention, the minister for defence, Richard Mulcahy, confirmed it would take place at a future date.

* * *

At the time of the handover, popular support for the Treaty extended across the country, though it was undoubtedly greater in the east than in the west. The *Cork Examiner* was the only newspaper to declare against the Treaty, claiming that:

> The flowing tide in favour of ratification of the Peace Treaty is submerging all opposition in its course.[122]

On the other hand, *The Irish Times* affirmed:

> the whole Nationalist Press and, as we believe, the vast majority of Southern Irishmen have accepted it with joy … Now, Mr de Valera steps between Ireland and her hopes.[123]

It was also noted that some 328 statutory public bodies declared in favour of the Treaty. Others to give their backing included farmer and labour organisations as well as church leaders like the Archbishop of Cashel, who said:

> The people of Ireland, by a vast majority, are in favour of the Treaty, and in a democratic country the will of the people is the final court of appeal.[124]

Despite the obvious support for the Treaty across the country, there was still an undercurrent of dissent and it was becoming more vociferous and concerning. The barrister Albert Wood, writing from the Four Courts to Moylan, said:

> Great rumours reach the courts each day of impending changes and still the Liffey flows by unrippled.[125]

Michael Collins ensured the new state was quickly into its stride and he chaired the first meeting of the committee charged with drafting the new constitution on 30 January 1922. The following day the first edition of *Iris Oifigiúil*, the newspaper of record of the state, was published and on 1 February the British military began its withdrawal with the formal handing over of Beggar's Bush Barracks. The Treaty split the IRA, with most of the headquarters staff following Collins and Mulcahy and a minority, including Liam Mellows and Rory O'Connor, taking the anti-Treaty viewpoint. As it transpired the Cabinet, by this stage, had recognised most IRA men were actually taking a stand against the Treaty and rowed back on its decision to allow a convention to take place. Despite the Cabinet's order banning the convention, it did go ahead on 26 March as the chasm between pro and anti-Treaty forces continued to widen at a rapid rate. Indeed, a number of violent stand-offs took place, notably in Limerick, where both factions clashed over taking possession of former British Army barracks. The convention re-affirmed the IRA's allegiance to the republic and decided that the organisation would once again be controlled by an executive. It was agreed to draw up a new constitution and have it ready for a second convention set for 9 April 1922.

* * *

The convention also repudiated the authority of the Dáil and set up a sixteen-man executive and declared the minister for defence and chief of staff no longer had any control over the IRA. The convention also demanded an immediate end to the new National Army recruiting campaign. Afterwards, Rory O'Connor was asked by a reporter if he acknowledged any other government in Ireland apart from the IRA Executive and he replied in the negative. He was then asked:

> whether there was to be a military dictatorship.[126]

He famously replied:

> You can take it that way if you like.[127]

The anti-Treaty faction also demonstrated its disdain for the agreement when a number of its men destroyed the offices of the pro-Treaty *Freeman's*

Journal on 29 March 1922. The die of confrontation had been cast and the Free State was clearly hurtling towards internal conflict. As all of this was unfolding, Moylan was busy with speaking engagements at rallies around the country, including Dublin's O'Connell Street. He was also occupied with his IRA duties and, when the convention reassembled on 9 April, he, together with all those present, agreed to adopt the new republican constitution, which vested control of the organisation in an elected executive. Liam Lynch was elected chief of staff and Moylan was, naturally enough, elected on to the executive, together with other notables such as Liam Mellows, Rory O'Connor and Ernie O'Malley.

It seems that Moylan and Lynch had a close working relationship at that time, though Moylan was always prepared to speak with those on the pro-Treaty side. He spoke with Richard Mulcahy during April in an effort to find a compromise. In his notes on the meeting, Mulcahy noted Moylan was not particularly worried about his own safety if the violence restarted but he was worried about the innocent being caught up in the shooting. However, it was very clear Moylan was extremely concerned about any return to violence and Peadar O'Donnell recalled how he came upon him in tears after his meeting with Mulcahy. With the prospect of a civil war becoming increasingly likely and the split in the IRA growing with every passing day, Moylan spent much of his time travelling between Cork and Dublin and, in late April, the *Irish Independent* reported that both he and Rory O'Connor had been involved in a car accident near Carrick-on-Suir. Ironically, those who came to their aid and offered accommodation and new transport were members of the local pro-Treaty forces. Though the country seemed to be hurtling towards a civil war, friendships and goodwill continued to endure between men on both sides of the divide.

As part of the Treaty process, the British began to withdraw their troops from the many garrison towns and relocated them to Dublin and the Curragh in anticipation of a final withdrawal from the country. In North Cork, the Gloucestershire Regiment moved out of the Old Workhouse in Kanturk during the first few days of February. As the British Army, the Black and Tans and the Auxiliaries took their leave of the regions, the RIC remained confined to barracks for the most part. The creation of an authority vacuum allowed for certain people to carry out robberies of post offices or banks and some of them, it has to be said, were carried out by unscrupulous anti-Treaty men, all of whom saw a chance to enrich themselves. The lawlessness led to some confrontations between pro and anti-Treaty factions, all of which only added to the general tension prevalent across the country.

* * *

Some notable incidents took place during the months after the Treaty ratification that cast the fledgling Free State in a very poor light. For example, on 26 April three British intelligence officers and their driver were taken prisoner in Macroom and subsequently shot dead. However, one of the most high-profile incidents took place at the end of April and became known as the Dunmanway Massacre. Some thirteen Protestant civilians lost their lives at the hands of various IRA men in a killing frenzy sparked by what was essentially a most innocuous event. A group of IRA men led by Michael O'Neill attempted to commandeer a car belonging to a man called Thomas Hornibrook in Ballygroman. Hornibrook was no friend of the republican movement and, anticipating a visit to his home by the IRA, he deliberately disabled his car. The IRA men entered the Hornibrook home through a window and, when they did so, O'Neill was shot dead by Hornibrook's son-in-law. What then transpired was a litany of killings in the district between 26 and 28 April and among the dead were two sixteen-year-old boys and a local curate. Fourteen males lost their lives in the killing frenzy, which resulted in many Protestants leaving the area in a self-preservation exodus.

Some historians and commentators have, over time, maintained that the killings in Dunmanway were essentially sectarian in nature and that the undercurrent of sectarianism, which they argued was evident during the independence conflict in Cork, was still there in the early months of 1922. As we know, Moylan very conspicuously alluded to the 'Loyalists of North Cork' with a certain contempt in one of his contributions to the Treaty debates but one could surely put that inflammatory rhetoric down to the heat of the verbal battle that was being fought out in the Dáil chamber. However, to their credit, Moylan and other prominent local leaders like Tom Barry and Liam Deasy condemned outright the killings and, according to Meda Ryan in her book *Tom Barry, Freedom Fighter*, they ordered armed guards to be placed at the homes of individuals known to be loyal to the British. As for those who carried out the killings, they were never apprehended so to this day we have no real knowledge of their motives for taking such drastic action.

One objection of the anti-Treaty side to the agreement was the failure to solve the problem of Ulster or Northern Ireland, as it was by then known.

Those opposing the Treaty, including Moylan, claimed it had abandoned the nationalist community in the Province. In the early months of 1922, there was consternation in the Free State that Catholics were still being driven from their homes and their jobs in Ulster. Evidence emerged that the police were either involved in the attacks or were taking no action to stop them. In an effort to protect the nationalist community, Collins held three meetings with the Northern Ireland prime minister, James Craig, between January and March. Collins agreed to end the Free State boycott of Northern Ireland produce in return for Craig's promise to end the persecution and discrimination against nationalists. The IRA convention took the opposite view to the boycott and Moylan and his comrades demanded its continuation. However, Craig was unable to stop the discrimination and the violence being perpetrated against the nationalist community continued unabated.

* * *

While Arthur Griffith and Michael Collins nailed their colours firmly to the pro-Treaty mast, the attitude of the other great political icon of the time, Eamon de Valera, was very much the opposite. He formed the anti-Treaty Cumann na Poblachta party on 15 March and it was basically made up of anti-Treaty Sinn Fein personnel. In a number of speeches, de Valera made it very clear that those who wished to complete the work of republicans over the past four years would have to wade through blood to do so. Many on the pro-Treaty side felt that type of language was incendiary and only served to fuel the tension in the country. De Valera met a delegation from the Labour Party on one occasion and in response to their appeal for peace he is reputed to have intimated that, in his view, the majority of the people in the country had no right to repudiate the republic. This, of course, left him open to charges of being undemocratic and of inciting violence, which he vehemently denied.

The cessation of hostilities left the men of the IRA in something of a hiatus and unsure of their future. As well as being at a loose end, they were not receiving any remuneration and Moylan was becoming increasingly concerned about comrades he valued so highly. He felt, as their leader and commander, the onus was on him to make sure the men continued to be the recipients of some remuneration. Many of them had returned to their homesteads, some to farming, others in the hope they might pick up work in the labour market, but there is little doubt very many of them were beginning to struggle financially. He was so concerned about the situation he made a speech in the Dáil on 28 April, during which he castigated the politicians for not addressing the IRA men's financial situation and their general well-being. It was a forceful and resolute Moylan who made it clear that he was determined to take matters into his own hands irrespective of any concerns the government might have had:

> During the war, the British enemy called me the leader of a murder gang. My hands are free from murder. The Minister for Defence, in his report yesterday called me the leader of a robber gang. I am as free from the crime of robbery as I am from the crime of murder … We unfortunate, plain soldiers, not being used to legal quibbles and legal methods of speaking, were easily gulled by the politicians here in the Dáil. Everywhere we were told that the Truce was a breathing space to give us a chance to organise to carry on the fight for the Republic. And we did organise. We took men away from their employments. We drilled them and trained and armed them and got them ready to fight. And they were ready to fight. These men have been out of employment, without a smoke, ill-shod, badly clad and – we are not all pussyfooters – in want of a drink too. That is the fault of the men who told us the Truce was a breathing space. We were guaranteed payment for those men, funds for the maintenance of those men. We did not get it. I have always seized every opportunity I could get to try and get comforts for my men – to clothe them, to put shoes on them, and to feed them. In February last, I issued an order in my area, seeing that no other action was taken by the Dáil, that the dog tax in the area should be paid to me. During the war, my word went in north Cork. In spite of any terms that would be applied to me today, my word goes there yet … I put up a notice on Friday evening that I would come to the parish on Sunday to collect the dog tax. I did, and I collected £47, and the people willingly paid me … That is the extent of my robbery. I am not ashamed of it …[128]

An obviously very emotional Moylan could not hide his sense of bitterness and disappointment at being let down by the politicians, many of whom, he believed, failed to grasp the enormity of the fighting men's financial and social problems. On the other hand, the fact that Moylan took matters into his own hands and filled a vacuum left by the lack of civilian government authority highlighted how the IRA continued to play a dominant role in many communities. Moylan and his comrades on the anti-Treaty side continued to apply compulsory levies in areas where they could get away with doing so, while post offices were raided for funds. Besides looking for ways to accumulate even more funds, the anti-Treaty IRA also disrupted the distribution of newspapers and train services.

By early March 1922 it was clear to both pro and anti-Treaty leaders that the country was moving closer to a catastrophic civil war and Collins was warning almost every day of how dire the situation was. Sean MacEntee told the Dáil in April:

> We are now upon the verge of Civil War in Ireland. Let there be no mistake about that.[129]

The Labour Party organised a peace conference in the Mansion House between 26 and 29 April when it proposed a return to the Dáil's sovereignty, the unification of the army, the establishment of a police force under civilian control and a revised electoral register. Unfortunately, everything collapsed on Collins's insistence on holding a plebiscite on the Treaty. Yet, despite that setback it was clear most of the important players in the drama, Moylan included, wanted to avoid war. On 1 May, army and political unity talks began when influential officers from both sides of the military divide met to look for a compromise. Among those who took part in the talks were Collins, Richard Mulcahy, Eoin O'Duffy, Dan Breen, Florrie O'Donoghue, Sean Hales and Moylan. They produced a document calling for unity based on their belief that the majority of the civilian population wanted peace and were prepared to give the Treaty a chance to work. They did, however, also warn ominously that if a compromise was not found, a major conflict was sure to ensue that:

> Would be the greatest calamity in Irish history and would leave Ireland broken for generations.[130]

The document called for an acceptance of the Treaty as the basis for army unity as well as the holding of a non-contested election. It also envisaged a coalition government following the election. The document was signed by Sean Hegarty, Dan Breen, Humphrey Murphy, Florrie O'Donoghue, Tom Hales and Sean Boylan. Moylan did not sign the document as he and Liam

Lynch did not see how the Treaty could bring about a lasting peace. During the meeting, Moylan expressed his fears for the future of the country. He claimed he was not worried by what might happen to him personally should a conflict break out. He was, however, very concerned that many people would die in the fight and that he might have to shoot men for whom he had the highest regard. He was clearly, at that stage, a conflicted man full of foreboding. The document was published without the authority of the Army Executive, which quickly denounced it. On 3 May, Sean Hegarty, the architect of the document, was permitted to present it to the Dáil, even though he was not a member of that body. He told the chamber there was little choice for all concerned but to accept the Treaty because, in his view, civil war would not produce a republic. In fact, he was of the opinion that such a conflict would only have one outcome: a return of British rule in Ireland. Moylan listened to Hegarty's presentation before rising to his feet to address the chamber:

> I was a member of the Conference from which this statement has come. I was the only army officer there who did not sign it. Every thinking Republican views with horror the possibility of strife between comrades. To myself, personally, the idea of fighting the men who fought with me is particularly abhorrent and I was willing to explore every avenue to peace. It was for that purpose I went to the Conference.
>
> I went there and said to the other side that one of my great failings was that I found it difficult to believe evil of anybody and they all the time said they are as good republicans as we are. I am willing to meet any man who is a republican, because a republican can only work for the Republic. I am not a politician. I am simply a soldier of the Republic and I will serve no other government but a republican government; but I am very anxious to accept, if possible, an assurance that the Treaty can be made a step to the Republic, that the Constitution, when drafted, will prove that this assurance is correct. I and the men I represent will anxiously await that. But in the light of the knowledge I have at present, and in the highest interest of the country as I conceive them, the men who are republicans, like myself, cannot agree, much as we want peace, with the document that has been presented here. We must stand by, or act to preserve the Republic.[131]

The outcome of the document presentation and the ensuing debate saw the Dáil set up a committee to work on political peace proposals while army unity talks took place independently. Moylan was appointed to the political committee along with other notables such as Liam Mellows, Harry Boland, Sean MacEoin and Mrs Tom Clarke. A Joint Army Committee was set up, to which Moylan was also appointed, and its remit was to bring IRA factions together. Liam Lynch was also appointed to this committee as were, among others, Liam Mellows, Rory O'Connor, Michael Collins and Richard Mulcahy. It was agreed to release prisoners on both sides who were not being held on criminal charges and public buildings occupied by anti-Treaty men, with the exception of the Four Courts that had been taken over on 14 April, would be evacuated. The political committee continued to look for a compromise until 10 May but failed to come to any agreement. On the other hand, the Army Committee produced drafts and counter-drafts of an agreement, and a document initiated by Moylan that sought to find an acceptable compromise to unify the army seemed to command some agreement among the members. Unfortunately, like so many of the proposals and counter-proposals that surfaced during that time, it went by the wayside.

Ever mindful that a civil war was looming, Michael Collins, always the compromiser, proposed an electoral pact between himself and de Valera for the upcoming general election that had been called for 16 June. Collins suggested that both sides of the Treaty divide take part in a coalition government after the election in the hope of bringing about some political stability. The proposal did not meet with the approval of Griffith and others in the Provisional Government, all of whom viewed it as undemocratic because it denied the right of the people to have a choice of who to vote for in the election. The British were also furious over the suggestion and forcefully made their point of view known to Collins.

At the end of May, both Collins and Griffith travelled to London with a draft of the new Free State Constitution. Collins, fearing the anti-Treaty side would disrupt the election, deliberately omitted any reference to the Oath of Allegiance and the king in the draft. When Lloyd George noticed Collins's sleight of hand he angrily rejected the draft as it stood. Collins and Griffith had no option but to revise the draft to include references to the oath and the monarch. When he returned home, Collins called off the pact with de Valera and, much to the annoyance of the anti-Treaty faction across the country, the new constitution was only published on the morning of the election.

The result of the general election was a major win for the pro-Treaty side, while those who opposed the Treaty vowed to continue their opposition to the agreement with the British. Having won just thirty-five seats in the election, the anti-Treaty side could not bring itself to accept the legitimacy of the Treaty and the status of the Provisional Government. Moylan was returned to the Dáil, having secured 4,585 first-preference votes, and took the seventh of the eight seats on offer in a constituency dominated by Collins, who secured a massive 17,106 first-preference votes. The result of the election confirmed the existing political division in the country over the Treaty and, within days, the Irish people divided along military lines and faced into a conflict that had the most terrible of consequences.

Chapter 18

The Civil War

By April of 1922 the leaderships of the pro-Treaty and anti-Treaty factions were aware the fledgling Free State was moving steadily towards a destructive and bloody civil war. Even the British became concerned at the turn of events in Ireland and Winston Churchill implied there might come a time when the British would be forced to intervene. The nation held its breath as it waited for one side or the other to take the decisive action that would ignite the flames of conflict. There were definite signs that it was on the way as early as spring 1922 when the anti-Treaty forces had some spectacular successes in the procurement of arms and ammunition. They captured and raided the naval vessel *Upnor* on 29 March as it made its way from Haulbowline to Portsmouth. A cache consisting of 400 rifles and 25,000 rounds of ammunition was taken from the ship when it was intercepted by another vessel, the *Warrior*, under the command of the local IRA leader Sean Hegarty at Queenstown (Cobh). The arms were brought to Ballycotton, where they were taken away by a fleet of lorries. The anti-Treaty forces had already raided Clonmel RIC Barracks in February and the *Upnor* raid served to heighten the growing concern in London, where the Cabinet was told the captured arms and ammunition had given the anti-Treaty forces a significant advantage over the National Army.

Across the country various incidents took place, all of which increased the cause for concern. On the night of 13 April anti-Treaty forces led by Rory O'Connor, Liam Mellows and Ernie O'Malley took possession of the Four Courts in Dublin. While the Provisional Government took no immediate action, the occupied building eventually became the focal point of the first action of the Civil War in June. Pro-Treaty and anti-Treaty forces clashed in Athlone and the pro-Treaty General Adamson of Custume Barracks was shot on the night of 25 April after a tense stand-off at the Royal Hotel in the town. Other confrontations came in Dublin and in Mullingar but the largest and final one before the start of the Civil War came in Kilkenny in early May. Supported by men from South Tipperary, the anti-Treaty forces in Kilkenny took over various buildings in the city, including the castle. The Provisional Government rushed some 200 troops by train from Dublin and after two days of much shooting they gained the upper hand and reclaimed the buildings. An extraordinary peace deal was struck in Dublin whereby both sides in the conflict agreed to share the military barracks in the city.

The anti-Treaty side also disrupted political meetings around the country, most especially when they were addressed by Michael Collins and Arthur Griffith. Collins was so vexed by their antics he complained bitterly about them in a letter to Clan na Gael's Joe McGarrity, saying:

> The opposition policy is making it almost impossible for us to hold useful meetings.
>
> The crowds assemble alright, but 20 or 30 or 40 interrupters succeed in most places in preventing the speakers from being heard. That apparently is the official policy accompanied by blocked roads and torn up railways to prevent the excursion trains from bringing the people to our meetings.[132]

Undaunted by the anti-Treaty faction's tactics, Collins continued to address people across the country. In March, he addressed, by his own calculation, a crowd of around 50,000 people in Cork. Shots were fired that day, which caused a certain amount of panic in the crowd. In April, he was prevented from speaking in Dungarvan when the train from which he was to address the crowd was driven off and he had to transfer to a local hotel balcony. He met with further anti-Treaty opposition when he addressed meetings in Castlebar, Killarney and Tralee. Arthur Griffith was also forced to contend with anti-Treaty obstruction in the run-up to the outbreak of the Civil War when he addressed public meetings. He had a particularly difficult time on Easter Sunday in Sligo when anti-Treaty forces took over some buildings in the town. Responding to the developing situation, the Provisional Government sent National Army troops from Athlone to deal with it, under the command of Sean MacEoin. They took possession of the jail and were later joined by more troops led by J.J. O'Connell. In the end no shots were fired and the tension in the town abated, with the whole affair seen as a victory for the National Army troops.

The assassination of Sir Henry Wilson in London by two IRA men on 22 June exacerbated an already precarious situation and the British reaction to the killing increased pressure on the Provisional Government to put an end to not only the occupation of the Four Courts, but all the activities of the anti-Treaty forces. Collins did not want to be seen to take action against the men in the Four Courts, many of whom he had fought with in the Easter Rising and worked with during the War of Independence. However, his hand was forced when his deputy chief of staff, J.J. O'Connell, was captured by the Four Courts garrison. Collins issued an ultimatum to Rory O'Connor to end the occupation of the building or face grave consequences. The ultimatum was ignored and the following day, 28 June, Collins, using field guns borrowed from the British, ordered the shelling of the Four Courts. His attempts at conciliation and compromise over the previous months had come to nothing and the Civil War was unleashed on a fearful populace.

Once the bombardment of the Four Courts began, members of the anti-Treaty faction of the IRA came together. Liam Lynch called a meeting of senior officers and they met in Dublin's Clarence Hotel. They quickly agreed to lend their support to the men under siege in the Four Courts. Lynch proceeded to draw up a proclamation and it was signed by the attending officers, including Moylan, Liam Mellows, Rory O'Connor, Liam Deasy and Ernie O'Malley. It was agreed the senior officers not in the Four Courts should leave Dublin and join their respective brigades. Moylan left for Kingsbridge railway station with Lynch, Deasy and Moss Twomey in two jaunting cars and they were joined by Con Moylan and Sean Culhane. They caught a train to Newbridge, where they split up and travelled along back roads to Mallow, arriving there in the early hours of the morning on 29 June.

While Moylan and his fellow officers in Munster were in the process of getting their brigades up to speed, the Dublin No. 1 Brigade of the anti-Treaty forces set up their headquarters in Barry's Hotel, which was on the north side of the city and hardly an ideal position to launch any attempts to relieve the men occupying the Four Courts. Under the command of Oscar Traynor, some anti-Treaty forces took over the Hammam and Gresham Hotels on the east side of O'Connell Street, which also made communications with the Four Courts very difficult to sustain. In fact, any communication between O'Connell Street and the Four Courts during the week of fighting was largely dependent on the women of Cumann na mBan and, in particular, Maire Comerford, who cycled between the two points carrying messages.

* * *

The military men were joined at various stages of the fighting by anti-Treaty politicians like Robert Barton, Eamon de Valera, Austin Stack and Cathal Brugha. Sean T. O'Kelly also arrived at one stage and the sight of him armed with nothing more than an umbrella must have amused the fighting men. De Valera decided to rejoin his old battalion as a private and he gave his public support to the anti-Treaty forces in a press release in which he claimed:

> England's threat of war, that, and that alone, is responsible for the present situation.
>
> In the face of England's threat of war some of our men yielded. The men who are being attacked by the forces of the Provisional Government are those who refuse to obey the order to yield – preferring to die. They are the best and bravest of our nation.[133]

However, this view was not a universal one and *The Irish Times* believed de Valera had:

> associated himself with the men who are firing on Irish homes … What does he expect to gain? His political cause is hopeless.[134]

Privately, it seems de Valera was sceptical of the tactics used by the anti-Treaty forces in Dublin and when the fighting ended he was forced to backtrack on his earlier support for the Dublin No. 1 Brigade men, maintaining they got themselves into a foolish type of battle. He then suggested they should, in future, carry out operations more suited to their training and the equipment they had in their possession. From a military point of view, the anti-Treaty occupation of the eastern side of O'Connell Street was as pointless as the occupation of the Four Courts. Many of the anti-Treaty men were very frustrated by the fact that nothing much had been achieved by their stand in Dublin and by 2 July nearly all of their strongholds in the south of the city had been captured. As a result, most attention centred on O'Connell Street, where the occupied hotels had been linked up by smashing through their connecting walls. The National Army opened its attack on the anti-Treaty strongholds in O'Connell Street with a barrage of heavy rifle and machine gun fire that proved to be less than effective. It was decided by the officers in command to bring up armoured cars with artillery and launch an even more ferocious offensive, which forced the anti-Treaty men to evacuate the buildings under siege. Very quickly the situation became a hopeless one for the anti-Treaty forces and on 5 July they hoisted the white flag of surrender above the Hammam Hotel.

The defeat of the anti-Treaty forces in Dublin and their surrender of the Four Courts had a major impact on the republican leadership. Rory O'Connor and Liam Mellows were sent to Mountjoy Jail, where they remained until their very controversial execution some months later. Tom Barry was arrested as he entered the Four Courts disguised as a woman and was held prisoner until his escape the following August. The arrests weakened the republican leadership even before the main action of the conflict got under way. Outside of Dublin, Lynch's strategy centred on the creation of what he termed a 'Munster Republic' along a line from Limerick to Waterford. Moylan was appointed director of operations and rather bizarrely, de Valera, a man with almost no military expertise, was appointed as his adjutant. The most pressing problem Lynch and his senior officers had to contend with was the management of large numbers of men in a conventional war. They were all experienced in guerrilla warfare but they were now faced with a completely separate set of circumstances and they had to adapt to them very quickly.

The National Army, from the very outset of the conflict, had a number of advantages, most especially in the area of arms, ammunition and armoured cars, much of it supplied by the British. For example, when General Prout and his National Army forces eventually took possession of Waterford city from the anti-Treaty forces, he used an 18-pounder gun to pummel his way to a decisive victory. Most of the anti-Treaty men in Waterford had no experience of shellfire and the effects it had on them left many of them reeling in shock. Waterford became a precursor to many other encounters between the anti-Treaty forces and the National Army troops, especially in places like Limerick, Cork and Kilmallock. Not only was the National Army in the ascendancy in terms of firepower but also in the numbers of men. Recruitment was going along at a pace and by July the numbers in the National Army stood at more than 14,000 men. The conventional warfare phase of the war was also marked by National Army sea landings carried out in Cork and Kerry. The innovative landings, devised and commanded by Emmet Dalton, were highly successful and hastened the end of that stage of the conflict.

In early July anti-Treaty forces were comprehensively routed in Wicklow and Ernie O'Malley and a contingent of Tipperary men headed for Wexford and quickly captured Enniscorthy. Moylan decided to take a force of around 230 men to New Ross and his intention was to link up with O'Malley in Wexford Town. The taking of Enniscorthy and New Ross by the anti-Treaty forces was part of a proposed offensive campaign that they hoped would see them move up the east coast. Moylan initially intended to divide his men into three groups and advance on Wexford town, where he proposed to link up with O'Malley and his men. Their intention was then to move up the coast and advance on Dublin in an attempt to recapture it from the National Army. Moylan notified O'Malley of his intention in a note he sent to him, saying:

> Have arrived here in New Ross with 230 men, propose dividing them into 3 columns and advancing towards Wexford. Suggest that you advance and try to get your column into touch with mine … I believe that our job is to finish this Beggars' Bush Column here in Wexford before tackling anything else.[135]

The plan never materialised because of poor organisation and communication. While they were in Wexford, the anti-Treaty men made themselves very unpopular among the civilian population in the county. During their couple of days in New Ross, for example, they commandeered almost anything they could. They received little assistance from the local anti-Treaty men and Moylan, in a note to O'Malley, confirmed his disappointment when he wrote:

> We are without a base, transport, food or intelligence. The local Volunteers seem to be practically non-existent and the few men we've met have been of very little assistance to us.[136]

Moylan then concluded there was little point in maintaining his men in the Wexford area to carry out his original military strategy, and proposed to O'Malley that:

> the only method of successfully combatting the Free State here is by guerrilla tactics, small columns of snipers and obstructionists.[137]

In effect, Moylan was proposing to revert to the tactics he employed successfully with his Active Service Unit against the British during the independence conflict. He went on to announce he was taking his men back to concentrate on:

> Thurles, Nenagh and perhaps Kilkenny … I hate leaving here but I can see no use in having a column here which has no

> knowledge of the country, and which would be blind and useless.[138]

Moylan's actions in Wexford were not only derided by his opponents but also by some of his own comrades, including Pax Whelan, the Officer Commanding of the Waterford Brigade, who said:

> He marched them to New Ross. And he marched them down again … Moylan's army didn't march. They went up and down by special train.[139]

The New Ross and the county Wexford debacle in general was symbolic of the disarray and lack of cohesion within the anti-Treaty leadership. It seemed as if individual leaders, and Moylan must be included among them, were incapable of working effectively outside their own localities. By 8 July the anti-Treaty forces had evacuated Wexford town, Enniscorthy and New Ross, leaving them to the National Army, while a report later surfaced claiming O'Malley and his men left the area in cars to travel towards Carlow. A military report prepared for the Provisional Government on the events in Wexford contained a less than complimentary opinion about the enemy. The report stated:

> They are forming Flying Columns. We have no intention of bothering about these, for of all the crowds in Ireland, the Wexford Brigade are most assuredly the most pitiful and helpless.[140]

It was not all negative for Moylan because his next action was more successful when he led a raid to capture the National Army barracks at Caherconlish around 11 July. Even the *New York Times* described the raid, saying:

> The barracks was captured after stiff engagement. Generals Hayes and Connolly and five staff officers were taken prisoner.[141]

After that success Moylan returned to Limerick, where the anti-Treaty leadership saw the taking of the city as a vital element in its overall strategy to isolate National Army troops in Clare, Galway and Athlone while at the same time providing a springboard to launch another attack on Dublin. By that stage the number of anti-Treaty troops in Limerick city had risen to seven hundred, which considerably outnumbered the four hundred National Army troops. Such was the importance placed on Limerick that Liam Lynch set up his headquarters in the city's New Barracks and surrounded himself with an experienced staff, which included trusted men such as Moylan and Liam Deasy.

* * *

Sporadic fighting broke out in Limerick on 11 July and over the following days anti-Treaty prisoners were taken by the National Army. On 15 July a National Army 18-pounder gun opened fire on the Strand Barracks occupied by anti-Treaty troops. Some thirty shells were fired at the barracks, followed by the storming of the building by National Army troops to capture it. General Eoin O'Duffy later remarked that the storming of the Strand Barracks was probably the finest operation of the war up to that time. The anti-Treaty forces burned other barracks in the city before retreating from it and the fighting was over by 21 July. It was reported that the National Army suffered the loss of eight men, while the anti-Treaty forces lost around twenty-five. Other than the barracks there was little damage to property in the city and the only negative aspect for the National Army was that it failed to stop the anti-Treaty force of around 1,000 men from escaping to rural Limerick.

According to Aideen Carroll, little is known about Moylan's activities after the Wexford debacle and the defeat in Limerick but she surmised he was most probably in the vicinity of Newmarket. After a couple of days of fighting, the National Army took control of Bruree on 30 July, which left Kilmallock outflanked on two sides. The anti-Treaty defence of Kilmallock was not helped by the landing from the sea in Kerry of a strong National Army force and many of that county's Volunteers were ordered home to confront the enemy there. The republicans in Kilmallock were outnumbered by the 2,000 National Army troops who flooded into the area around the town. The troops were backed up by artillery and armoured cars, which gave them an even greater advantage. On 4 August many of the anti-Treaty men began to slip away from Kilmallock under the cover of a stout rearguard action by the Cork brigades. On Saturday, 5 August the town of Kilmallock fell to the National Army. It proved to be one of the more defining events of the Civil War and marked the end of the road for many of the anti-Treaty fighters, all of whom simply went home and stayed there.

The month of August saw the deaths of two of the most influential individuals in the country with the sudden passing of Arthur Griffith in Dublin and the killing of Michael Collins in Beal na mBlath. Undoubtedly, the deaths of the two iconic national figures were huge blows to the pro-Treaty side, both in the political and military sense. However, their deaths served to galvanise those left behind on the pro-Treaty side, all of whom pursued the establishment of the Free State with an even greater vigour than before. By the end of August it was clear the conventional phase of the war was over and the republicans could not compete with the vastly superior National Army in the field. It was time for a change in strategy and Moylan, together with his fellow senior officers, had no option but to revert to the tried and trusted guerrilla warfare tactics they employed successfully in the war against the British.

The whereabouts of Moylan continued to exercise some minds and two reports of his capture during August and September proved to be very wide of the mark. He was, though, back in Knockavorrheen in mid-September because Jim Riordan later recalled Moylan lending him his old Spanish revolver when he went to Knocknagree fair. It was as well he did because Riordan was forced to shoot his way out of the place after being surrounded by National Army troops. September 1922 was a stark month for the anti-Treaty side as the number of men who lost their lives mounted. Twelve were shot dead in custody and ten others were shot dead outside it, despite being unarmed, while six men, revered as the Noble Six, died on Ben Bulben in Sligo in a much-publicised and often criticised operation carried out by National Army troops.

* * *

Around that time Moylan, together with some other officers, signed a declaration issued by the Republican Army Executive reaffirming their determination to continue the war against the Free State. On 25 October he and a number of leading republican Dáil deputies came together in a secret Dublin location and affirmed themselves as the 'Second Dáil Éireann'. They appointed a Council of State that included Moylan himself as well as, among others, Austin Stack, Robert Barton, Sean T. O'Kelly and Count Plunkett. What they hoped to achieve was not clear to most observers but many saw the move as just another act of defiance. On 26 September the Provisional Government, in the guise of Richard Mulcahy, introduced an amendment to the Emergency Powers Act allowing for military courts to impose the death sentence on civilians for the possession of guns. It also provided for the internment of anti-Treaty men but it also offered an amnesty if they surrendered to the National Army by 15 October.

Undeterred by setbacks in the field and the loss of men, the anti-Treaty forces continued to take the fight to the National Army in the south and west of the country. The return to guerrilla warfare tactics meant bridges were once again blown up and roads were blocked and trenched. Ambushes became a major tactic and, as a result, National Army troops were often confined to barracks. Moylan led an ambush against the National Army troops in early November near Millstreet. He and his men placed a felled tree across a road blocking the path of troops, who immediately sent for reinforcements out of Macroom. Moylan's unit ambushed the reinforcements and during the engagement the National Army suffered a number of casualties. On 9 November *The Irish Times* reported on a:

> concentration of republicans in Carriganimmy between Macroom and Millstreet under the command of Sean Moylan MP … after two hours of fighting the republicans retreated across the country.[142]

It seems Moylan disappeared from the scene in Cork on the following day and, some days later, he turned up in America, sent there by Liam Lynch to raise money and buy arms. It is probably as well that he did travel as he was by that stage a wanted man at home and was increasingly targeted by the Provisional Government for capture and probable execution. Aideen Carroll, in her book, claims Moylan was picked up by a fishing boat off the Kerry coast. He then travelled to Rawtenstall in Lancashire, where on 2 December he married Nora Murphy, his fiancée from Kiskeam. A small Volunteer outfit based in Manchester and Salford took him in hand and organised a false passport for him in the name of John Morris. He was described as a motor mechanic and the passport was stamped by the British Foreign Office on 28 November 1922. Moylan and Nora spent a few days in London together before she returned to her teaching post in the North of England and he left for America from Southampton. His passport was stamped at the American consulate office on 6 December, which was, of course, the very same day that legislation was passed in Westminster bringing the Irish Free State into existence.

* * *

While Moylan was settling himself in America, the situation at home was becoming even more fraught, not helped by the killing of Sean Hales TD on the streets of Dublin and the decision by the government to execute four prominent anti-Treaty men as a reprisal the following day. All the executions that blighted the Civil War landscape merit mention but the deaths of the four anti-Treaty men on 8 December 1922 had a particular significance for the new nation as a whole. The men in question – Rory O'Connor, Liam Mellows, Richard Barrett and Joe McKelvey – were well known across the country and all four had been captured when Michael Collins ordered the storming of the Four Courts the previous June. While a number of other men, including Erskine Childers, had already been executed, the Provisional Government made a very definitive statement when it carried out these particular executions. It was making it clear to all concerned that those who chose to undermine the state, especially through the use of violence, ran the risk of being convicted of treason, which was punishable by death. The government viewed the previous day's killing of Sean Hales TD as a treasonable crime, and while the four men chosen for execution did not carry out the murder, it was decided that an example should be made of them. If the Provisional Government felt justified in taking this action and, many in the country were in agreement, the deaths of the men shook the country to its core. More than any other of the executions, the killing of the four men brought about a realisation that the Civil War was tearing the new state apart even before it had become established. What made the executions even more repulsive for so many people, irrespective of the side they supported, was that the men were killed for no apparent reason other than revenge.

As well as Moylan, the anti-Treaty leadership sent a number of other people across to America to bring its message to the Irish-American Community. Mick Leahy joined Moylan as representatives of the army while J.J. O'Kelly and Joseph O'Doherty travelled to represent the political side. Laurence Ginnell was appointed by de Valera in December 1922 to be the anti-Treaty envoy to Washington. Unfortunately, Ginnell was to die suddenly in the American capital the following April. These representatives were supplemented at various times by the likes of Muriel MacSwiney, Austin Stack, Father Flanagan and the Countess Markievicz.

However, it did not take long for divisions to emerge between the military men, especially Moylan, and the political representatives. Indeed, tensions also surfaced within the political representatives themselves. Moylan was particularly scathing of the political representatives and accused them of interfering in his work and of spending unnecessary amounts of money. He was very critical of Ginnell and famously called him 'a damn nuisance', and on the political side, Ginnell and MacSwiney became embroiled in many arguments with their fellow representatives. Everything was going so badly even de Valera began to lose patience with them and, in a letter to O'Kelly, he wrote:

> there are five or six of you over there, and America is a big place. Surely, it should have been possible to secure harmonious working.[143]

De Valera became so concerned at the infighting he sent O'Kelly and Father Flanagan to Australia to continue their fundraising there.

* * *

Moylan seemed to get even more angry the longer he remained in the country and, in a letter home, which was intercepted by the British, he bemoaned the situation he was faced with. He wrote:

> the trouble here seems to be that there are 32 Irelands in America and you'd need a man from every county to make a really successful appeal.[144]

He went to say that he only had faith in the reorganised Clan na Gael and that everyone else simply did not come up to scratch. He concluded his letter by saying:

> The story about this being the land of the flowing gold is all rot. I'm always on the run and I shall be under the necessity of holding up a bank if the fellows here don't come across with a more plentiful supply of cash in the near future.[145]

Despite all his problems, Moylan did make progress and became almost expert in acquiring fake passports as well as using false addresses. He learned how to correspond via safe houses, he moved men and money across frontiers and he involved himself in finalising arms deals. He was aware that letters he wrote were being intercepted by the British Intelligence Service, was conscious informants were watching his every move and at times he felt his life was in danger. He was right to be concerned about his letters home. Correspondence between himself and Liam Lynch passing through a safe house in London was intercepted regularly by British intelligence and passed on to the Provisional Government in Dublin.

In some of his letters, Lynch regularly displayed his impatience in relation to the flow of arms and funds coming from America and increasingly made more and more demands on Moylan. The situation in the field was gradually deteriorating for the anti-Treaty side and the correspondence between Moylan, Lynch and Joe McGarrity, the leading Clan na Gael fundraiser in America, seemed to ignore the realities on the ground. The general theme of the letters indicated all was going well for the republican forces and it was only a matter of time before they would claim a complete victory. The fact was, of course, the National Army was very much in the ascendancy and were in complete control of cities and major towns. The lack of arms and ammunition meant the republican forces were reduced to carrying out just a few ambushes and attacks and were relying mainly on sniping and acts of sabotage to inflict damage on the enemy.

According to Aideen Carroll, her grandfather was in Germany in early April 1923 and his false passport had been stamped in Hamburg on the fourth of that month. Moylan, in a letter to Joe McGarrity, indicated he was involved in negotiating an arms deal. He most likely went to Germany to ensure what was being bought was of good quality. However, while in Germany, it is clear Moylan received news from home indicating that all was not well and that the end was in sight for the republicans. In a letter to Joe McGarrity it is obvious Moylan feared the worst but still remained somewhat defiant:

> Your man arrived and delivered his stuff all right. We have made … practically complete arrangements for securing our stuff and exporting it but owing to press reports and the apparent slump in our stock we decided it was better not to close the deal until we found out if our people could handle … I trust all will be well but we certainly have had severe reverses during the past few weeks … I feel I ought to be at home. If our fellas have got to take the gruel, I want to be with them … all will yet be well and we'll pull a victory out of the fire in spite of fate.[146]

A few days later Liam Lynch was shot by National Army troops in an engagement on the Knockmealdown Mountains and he died later that evening in Clonmel. On hearing the news Moylan wrote to Pa Murray, the republican Officer Commanding in Britain, saying:

> I am sorry about his death. I'm damn glad he went down fighting.[147]

Two weeks later he wrote again extolling the virtues of his former chief of staff, saying he was:

> wonderful, brave and generous without any trace of materialism … he was a good comrade and a brave soldier.[148]

Moylan cut an isolated figure in Germany and Nora was increasingly concerned about him. The fact that she had only spent a total of five days with her new husband since the wedding certainly added to her unhappiness. Moylan did ask her to join him in Germany but when news came of the offensive operation's suspension, the arms deal was abandoned and it seemed pointless for Nora to travel. The end of the hostilities came as a bitter blow to Moylan and most likely caused him no end of agonising. He had given so much to the cause of independence and the republic and all he could do was watch from afar as his and his comrades' endeavours came to an ignominious end. He had lost good and decent friends and witnessed suffering and death on an unimaginable scale. He never wanted a civil war and, from the outset, felt it would not only take the lives of many good people on both sides of the conflict but it would also tear the country apart and leave a long and bitter legacy.

A joint meeting of the republican government and army was held on 13–14 May and Frank Aitken, who had replaced Lynch as chief of staff, was instructed to issue an order to ceasefire and dump arms. The order was issued on 24 May and included a plea from Aitken urging his men to work towards developing a vibrant Gaelic civilisation and to participate in the Sinn Fein organisation. On the same day, de Valera issued a proclamation to the army, which declared:

> Further sacrifice on your part would now be in vain and continuance of the struggle in arms unwise in the national interest. Military victory must be allowed to rest for the moment with those who have destroyed the Republic.[149]

After eleven months of fighting in many areas across the country, the Civil War was over. The conflict ended without a negotiated peace. Neither side conceded ground on the political and constitutional beliefs that had set them apart. In the long term the spectre of the Civil War continued to haunt the political system in the country for at least the next half century. However, in the short term, the emotional, physical and economic cost had to be managed by an inexperienced government that did not have the support of all the people.

For both sides the immediate aftermath of the ceasefire was a time of reflection. Leading men on the republican side concluded the military tactics that had been adopted during the war proved to be a failure. Aitken held the opinion they had greatly underestimated the Free State's determination to put down the republicans' resistance to the Treaty. Ernie O'Malley took the view their tactics had been too defensive and they should have carried the fight to the National Army troops in a more offensive manner. Aitken concurred with this view and pointed out that:

> if we have to fight another war with the Staters, it will have to be short and sweet, and our units will need to be trained in taking the offensive in large bodies.[150]

He also pointed out that if a further conflict should break out, they would need a greater support from the general public that, given the attitude of the majority in the country at that time, was probably fanciful thinking on his part.

Moylan arrived back in Cork in December 1923 and, according to Aideen Carroll, both he and Nora were in poor health. On 27 December the couple were issued with false passports in the names of John and Nora Harrison and their visas were stamped in Southampton on 2 January 1924 prior to their return to America on another fundraising trip. While Moylan was happy to bide his time living in Brooklyn and continue with his fund-raising activities, it seems Nora was less enamoured by the place. She had become pregnant and missed her family back home. Taking Nora's wishes into account, the couple arrived back in Kiskeam in early September 1924 just weeks before the birth of their first child, Peig. Moylan's return to Ireland did not please his superior officers in the IRA and by the end of the year he had been demoted to the ranks. Aideen Carroll suggested he had defied an order to remain in America but whatever the reason it was a sad and ignominious end to an outstanding military career.

Chapter 19

Civilian Life and the Call to Politics

With the Civil War at an end, Moylan had to make plans for the rest of his life. After six or so years living as a military man with much of his time spent moving from one location to another in order to avoid the enemy it was time to settle down. Now a married man with a child, he was in the unusual situation of having to look after a family and not just himself. The Moylans found a home for the next few years at Shamrock House in Kiskeam, which was the homestead of Nora's parents. Moylan went back to the carpentry and building business but he found it tough to make a decent living for a number of reasons. First of all the economy, both on a national and local level, was struggling in the aftermath of civil war conflict. The Free State was by then an independent entity devoid of the traditional economic supports that were available while the country was under the British regime. The only industrialised region on the island was in the north-east of Northern Ireland and of no economic value to the fledgling Free State. It was clear from very early on that the Free State had some economically difficult few years ahead of it and Moylan joined the ranks of those who endeavoured to make the best of any work opportunities that came their way.

Those early months as a civilian were very tough for Moylan as he eked out a living on the few construction and repair jobs that he was offered. His plight was not helped by the fact that those who fought on the anti-Treaty side in the Civil War were often discriminated against in the area of employment and across society in general. Aideen Carroll claimed he was reduced to house renovations and the repair of a bridge that, most probably he and his unit destroyed during his military career. With everything looking bleak on the job front, he was given a lifeline right out of the blue when a substantial building and maintenance contract came his way courtesy of a community of nuns based in Drishane near Millstreet. The contract helped put his finances on a much sounder footing and it seems the nuns, under the stewardship of Mother Anthony from Bandon, had republican sympathies and connections, especially through Terence MacSwiney's family, and were more than happy to help out one of their heroes.

Though not at that time directly involved in politics, Moylan kept himself abreast of all that was happening and was unhappy with Sinn Fein's continued abstention from Dáil Éireann. He was particularly concerned the party was abdicating its responsibilities to those citizens who had supported it over the previous decade. He vented his feelings in January 1925 in a letter to Joe McGarrity when he said:

> I think we'd do more towards the ultimate realisation of our ideals if we tried to help our people economically or rather showed them by precept or example how they might help themselves … I believe money could be usefully spent on commissions of inquiry into fisheries and agriculture and co-operative societies and co-operative working brought along the lines of the findings of these commissions.
>
> This would be, to my mind, peaceful penetration as opposed to what I call the stone wall-butting as presently practised.[151]

In further correspondence with McGarrity it was clear Moylan was thinking deeply about politics and the direction the Free State was going in. He railed against money being wasted on political action that he felt was paying little in the way of dividends. He was particularly scathing about the Oath of Allegiance to the British monarch and the requirement that it had to be taken by all who wished to sit in Dáil Éireann. He claimed the oath was never likely to be removed and that it was being used by Cumann na nGaedheal to maintain control of the political system by insisting that every candidate swear allegiance before his or her name could be placed on the ballot sheet. Though Moylan had distanced himself in many ways from his military past, he wasn't totally isolated from Sinn Fein or the IRA. He did maintain contact with some notable and hard-line republicans like Peadar O'Donnell, Austin Stack and Mary MacSwiney, as well as Constance Markievicz. Though he was invited to attend the Sinn Fein Ard Fheis in November 1925, he did not travel.

Eamon de Valera finally cut his ties with the Sinn Fein party in 1926 and went on to found Fianna Fáil. He invited Moylan to join the party and stand for election to Dáil Éireann but once again, he showed no inclination to get involved in the party or allow his name to go forward for election. The result of the general election in June 1927 saw the new party win a total of forty-four seats. De Valera and his successful party candidates took their seats in Dáil Éireann on 12 August after taking the much-loathed oath. The presence of Fianna Fáil ended Cumann na nGaedheal's working majority and Cosgrave was forced into leading a minority government. Another election took place in September 1927 and Fianna Fáil returned with a very creditable fifty-seven seats. However, Cumann na nGaedheal also increased its seat numbers by fourteen, leaving it with a final total of sixty-two. The government party was the beneficiary of a sympathy vote after the assassination of Kevin O'Higgins, the Minister for Home Affairs and vice-president of the Executive Council, the previous July. The Labour Party was the big loser as it saw its number of seats decline by nine, leaving it with a final total of thirteen. De Valera persisted in his pursuit of Moylan who, in 1928, received further correspondence from the Fianna Fáil party leader that included an official notification of his selection for Seanad Éireann. Moylan once again resisted the overture, leaving de Valera not only perplexed but disappointed.

While the Civil War was over, certain people still harboured grudges and Moylan was subjected to verbal and physical abuse as he went about his own business. Some who had fallen foul of the republican courts in the years prior to the Treaty were determined to exact revenge on those who had passed judgement on them. On one occasion Moylan was challenged by five or six men who surrounded him while he was cycling not far from Kiskeam. They knocked him from his bicycle but he drew his old Spanish revolver and shot the ring leader through the shoulder. That was the end of the matter and Moylan was not asked to account for his action by anyone in authority. On the other hand, he was prepared to stand up for anyone who had played an honourable part in the revolutionary era. One man he defended was Edward Drew, who lived local to Moylan. Drew was a good and loyal soldier during the War of Independence but opted to support the Treaty. He, together with some of his brothers, joined the Civic Guards after the Civil War. Some local republicans did not take kindly to that decision and promptly shot at the Drew family home. Moylan made it clear those responsible for the shooting would be answerable to him if they continued with their action. The men in question did not have to be told twice to desist and the Drew family were left in peace.

Moylan also took a keen interest in the pensions issue that was exercising the minds of so many during the years after all hostilities had ended. The Military Service Pension Acts from 1924 onwards were intended to compensate soldiers of the republic. Senior officers like Moylan were asked to confirm the service record of those who served under them, and though the pension amounts were small, no officer ever wanted to be in the position where he had to exclude the applicant from the scheme. The pension scheme was operated by the Department of Defence and it seems those who oversaw the payments were not always sympathetic to the applicant. Public money was in short supply at the time and the civil servants often looked for an excuse not to pay out the monies that the applicants felt they were due. Despite all the difficulties surrounding the pension issue, Moylan felt it was his duty to pursue applications for his men and it was not uncommon for him to be still doing so well into the 1930s.

It may well be that one of the reasons why the Free State government was so miserly in paying out pensions was because it had little money to run the country with. As well as the human suffering, the Civil War was also the cause of much economic hardship. It has been recently estimated that the damage caused to property came to around £50 million, with many administrative buildings and businesses destroyed. That figure is equivalent to somewhere in the region of 2.1 billion to 2.4 billion euros in modern-day values. A huge amount of damage was also inflicted on the country's railway and road infrastructure. This all impacted on business and the transportation of foodstuffs, building materials and machinery. Initially, the Free State government estimated the cost of prosecuting the war was somewhere in the region of £17 million, which is equivalent to about 883 million euros today, but, by September 1923, it had revised the figure up to £50 million. As a result of the war, the government ended 1923 with a budget deficit of around £4 million, equivalent to about 196 million euros today. It was no surprise the government attempted to keep its expenses as low as possible and making it difficult for ex-IRA men or their dependents to claim a pension during a very difficult time economically was just one way of doing so.

Near the end of the 1920s Moylan's employment situation improved again when he won a contract to build the new parish church in Kiskeam. It was consecrated in 1930 by the Bishop of Kerry, Dr O'Brien, and it became Moylan's house of worship. Aideen Carroll, in her book, tells of a incident that took place in the church on one occasion while the parish priest was delivering a sermon laced with political opinion not to Moylan's liking. To the amusement of the congregation, he interrupted the priest and urged him to quit his politicking and stick to the Gospel. In 1930, Moylan began to build a house on a site adjacent to his in-laws' home using stones from the ruins of an old local church. By that time he and Nora had five children, one son, Rick and four daughters, Peig, Mary, Stephanie and Carmel. Tragically, Mary, died in 1932 from septicaemia following a perforated appendix, which left her parents heartbroken. However, joy returned to their lives in 1934 when their youngest child, Eileen, was born.

As the country moved into the new decade of the 1930s, it seems Moylan was taking a greater interest in politics and was drawn more and more to Fianna Fáil. His past relationship with de Valera was, most likely, a factor in his decision to support the party but clearly the policies it was pursuing in relation to the Treaty and the gradual dismantling of it made it a natural political home for him. He was also drawn to the party by its social and economic policies, many of which advocated reforms designed to provide a better and a more acceptable standard of living for all citizens of the state. By the early years of the 1930s, Fianna Fáil was the party of the urban working class, the small farmer and the rural labourer, all members of society Moylan easily and comfortably identified with. It was, in hindsight, a natural progression that Moylan should eventually find his way into the party and onto the political stage.

* * *

More overtures came from the party asking Moylan to stand for election, though he was reluctant to run against Dan Corkery, a lifelong friend and military comrade. Corkery, from Macroom, was a sitting independent republican TD and was a much-respected and admired public representative who had served gallantly during the War of Independence. Eventually, Moylan gave in to the pressure and consented to run in the February 1932 general election. It came as no surprise, of course, that he was duly elected as a member for the North Cork constituency, topping the poll with 6,238 votes. For the first time in its history, Fianna Fáil took power in the country, albeit in a minority capacity with the tacit support of the Labour Party. De Valera's party also attracted support because it promised to initiate a policy of public spending designed to stimulate a struggling economy and bring about an increase in employment opportunities for working-class people all across the country. The party also indicated it would introduce a strong house-building programme and initiate social welfare reforms to help the unemployed, sick and elderly. During the election campaign it also promised to withhold paying the much-detested land annuities to the British government, a move applauded by every small to medium farmer in the country. In essence, Fianna Fáil planned to be a much more socially caring party in government with an emphasis on public spending policies instead of the monetarist polices employed by Cumann na nGaedheal over the previous decade. By standing for election as a Fianna Fáil candidate, Moylan readily bought in to the new politics the party was offering to the people of the Free State. In 1932, after some years of soul searching, he found a political home he could be comfortable in and one he was more than happy to reside in for the rest of his life.

The coming to power of Fianna Fáil in 1932 marked the beginning of a new era in Irish politics and the party was set to dominate the political landscape for many decades. During that time the party developed a legendary name for itself because of its impressive organisational ability. Every nook and cranny across the country could boast Fianna Fáil members, all of whom were loyal to de Valera during his time as leader and when he departed the scene they demonstrated an unflinching loyalty to the party itself. According to Aideen Carroll, the first meeting of the parliamentary party in 1932 was a tempestuous affair as those in attendance struggled to identify the most important policies to be pursued. De Valera quickly showed his obsession with dismantling the Anglo-Irish Treaty and seemed to place rather less emphasis on the many economic and social problems that were besetting the country at the time.

During that first meeting, de Valera talked about removing the Oath of Allegiance as well as the position of governor general, the king's representative in Ireland. He was determined to dismantle the Treaty in stages and essentially remove all traces of British rule in Ireland. That was all very well but, in Moylan's mind, there were many other and more pressing problems to be solved like alleviating the obvious poverty that existed in the country and exploring ways to increase employment. At the end of his speech, a self-satisfied de Valera looked down at Moylan and Dan Breen and asked them what they thought of his ideas. Breen sat stoney faced and uttered not a word while Moylan, as forceful and direct as ever, replied in an explosive manner using language that could only be described as unprintable. He, along with Breen, were much more interested in hearing about what was going to be done to find work for men and how food was going to be put on families' tables. It was clear then as the meeting ended that de Valera and Moylan were poles apart when it came to settling on the most immediate aims of the fledgling party.

De Valera called a snap general election for January 1933 in the hope of winning enough seats to form a majority government. Moylan was returned in his North Cork constituency with 7,463 first-preference votes, taking the second seat on offer. His old friend and comrade Daniel Corkery took a second seat for Fianna Fáil in the three-seat constituency. During the campaign Moylan continued to place an emphasis on economic and social issues rather than those centred around the Treaty. He was also at pains to point out that he saw no reason for the country to return to the violence of the past few years. The time for fighting, be it against the British or even among themselves, was well and truly over and the only way forward for the country was through the art of politics. He made that view very clear on addressing a meeting in Tralee on 17 December 1932 when he said:

> I come here among friends, among old comrades with whom I have tramped the roads of Kerry, and with whom I have lain beside in Kerry ditches. I do myself the honour of coupling my name with de Valera when we faced the music of the enemy's guns, and the policy he adopted, and the reason for our coming to Kerry is to prevent the women and children, aye and the young manhood, of hearing ever again the guns of the enemy of the nation in Kerry.[152]

Moylan had transitioned from a military man to a politician but not everyone was happy to see that very public transformation. He had become a mainstream politician consumed by a need to help his poverty-stricken people attain even a modicum of economic and social dignity. Some former republican colleagues did not take kindly to the transformation and five of them arrived in Kiskeam one day in search of Moylan with the intention of assassinating him. Having searched the Moylan home and terrified his wife and children, they failed to locate their target. They then retired to the pub next door to await Moylan's return to the village. However, they failed to realise the pub was owned by Moylan's brother-in-law and were unaware a message had been sent out across the district detailing what was afoot. Very soon the pub was surrounded by two dozen members of Moylan's old flying column, all armed with rifles. Their presence soon put a stop to the incident, which was never repeated. It was clear from that incident there was still a great deal of suspicion and unease across the country and that it would only take one misstep to ignite the underlying and simmering volatility.

Despite the criticism coming from some of his old republican comrades, Moylan continued to transform himself into a mainstream politician. In fact, he became even more entrenched in his economic and social views and demanded that the Fianna Fáil government pursue policies designed to make society much more equitable. He demanded a better and fairer pension system, not only for those who gave military service but also for the aged as well as widows and orphans. Moylan was proving himself to be something of an idealist and his views brought him very close to being a raging socialist in the eyes of many who worked with him, both in and out of parliament. On the other hand, he had every right to legitimately claim his views were simply those of a man who had given exemplary and unstinting military service and had experienced the misery of poverty and personal deprivation during the years he was fighting for his country.

Moylan was also a fair employer, and as it turned out, probably too generous. Together with his work in Dáil Éireann, he continued to keep his building contracting business running, albeit with some difficulty. He paid his workmen above the average rate of pay; however, his business suffered because of his political commitments and he eventually lost it all. He was left with so much debt that rumours emerged of his pending resignation from politics. On Saturday, 23 March 1935 the *Southern Star* newspaper even published his political obituary, reporting that he was about to resign due to ill health. As it transpired, many friends came to his aid and bailed him out financially and got him back to some semblance of solvency, which averted a resignation. Moylan, with a wife and a family of five children to look after, was never to be financially comfortable during his lifetime and even when he was earning money a proportion of it was set aside to pay off his debts. In fact, he did not own a car during the first twelve years of his political career, travelled from Cork to Dublin by train and lived in digs when Dáil Éireann was in session.

While Moylan was known by all and sundry to be an enigmatic character who could be difficult and intransigent with a penchant for saying something off the cuff, he became much more measured as the years passed. His time spent in the Dáil chamber undoubtedly had a major impact on the development of his political character. He became a much more polished and well-informed politician capable of holding his own in any debate. His development did not go unnoticed and, in 1937, he was appointed by de Valera as a parliamentary secretary at the Department of Industry and Commerce. In essence, the legendary military leader and hero had transitioned successfully to an establishment politician. His elevation coincided with major diminutions to the Anglo-Irish Treaty with the dispensation of the Oath of Allegiance and the introduction of a new constitution, Bunreacht na hÉireann, in December 1937.

Moylan's elevation up the ranks was confirmed in 1937 when he was chosen by Sean Lemass, the Tánaiste and Minister for Industry and Commerce, to chair an inter-departmental Commission tasked with looking into seasonal migration, most especially from the west of the country. The decision to set up the Commission was the result of a heart-breaking tragedy involving ten young men from Achill. On Saturday, 16 September 1937 they were burned to death in a bothy (hut) while working as potato pickers in a remote Scottish village called Kirkintilloch in Dunbartonshire. On the night of the fire, the door of the bothy was locked from the outside and the windows were covered with wire netting. When the fire started the ill-fated young men had no means of escape and what resulted was a scene of unimaginable horror.

The Commission was asked to examine the problem of seasonal migration to Britain from congested districts, mainly in the West of Ireland. It was also asked to make recommendations on how to improve the conditions under which the migrants were recruited and employed in order to prevent any future abuses. The Commission met around seventeen times before it issued a report about a year after the tragedy. Moylan was anxious from the outset to widen the terms of reference to incorporate a much more comprehensive review of the abject poverty that blighted the West of Ireland at that time. Taking everything into account, the Commission could not deny one simple fact: the widespread economic hardship that was so prevalent in the region left many people with little choice but to look for seasonal work in Britain. That, of course, often meant they were vulnerable to extreme exploitation by employers who cared little for the well-being of their workers.

The first part of the Commission's report accepted the government was not in a position to prevent people from travelling to Britain as it would amount to a denial of their liberty. The report also concluded there was little the government could do to improve the working and living conditions of the workers while in Britain. Any improvements in living and working conditions had to be negotiated by the workers themselves. These conclusions naturally led to certain members of Dáil Éireann questioning why the Commission was even set up if, as it transpired, the government had little in the way of power to improve the seasonal migration issue. The second part of the report did put forward a number of suggestions designed to keep the workers at home and gainfully employed. One such suggestion was the setting up of a power generating station that could burn peat, an abundance of which was readily available in the region. There were other recommendations, such as introducing a programme of resettlement for the congested areas of the West of Ireland. It was also proposed that a reclamation programme of waste land and cutaway bogs should begin, as well as the development of the tourism industry and the introduction of new, but unspecified, industries.

Like all reports, there were diverse views in relation to its findings and many commentators were sceptical that improvements would be introduced to enhance the lives of those living on the western seaboard as well as in other poverty-stricken regions across the country. In fact, even before the report was made public, the government had already let itself down by a decision it had taken some two weeks after the tragedy. It closed down the Achill railway line for both passengers and goods, which effectively cut the area off from the rest of country. It was a crass decision that hardly augured well for any proposed regeneration of the West of the country.

The Kirkintilloch tragedy only served to highlight the problem of poverty in the West of the country and the Commission's report and proposals did little to address the problem. The whole sorry saga reflected badly on the Free State as a whole and the fact that a cohort of its citizens had to leave the country to find employment in order to alleviate their poverty did not bode well for its future. One can only imagine how Moylan, who had always envisaged a new Ireland based on economic and social equity, must have felt. This was clearly not the country he fought so long and hard for. It was no surprise then that he spent the rest of his political career working towards a better deal for all the people of Ireland.

Chapter 20

Becoming a National Figure

Once he was appointed as a parliamentary secretary in 1937, a new era in Moylan's life began and he became a better-known figure on the national political stage. Essentially, he was forced to leave his rural Cork comfort zone where he was a confident and self-assured leader of his own people and a man almost every individual looked up to and admired. He found himself spending more and more time in the capital away from his family and he had to adjust to a different kind of limelight than he was used to. It wasn't long before many new responsibilities came his way, offering him new opportunities to make a contribution to the development of the country both at home and abroad.

During the summer of 1939, the World Fair took place in New York at a time of rising tension in Europe. The theme of the fair was 'the World of Tomorrow', which knowing now what transpired over the following six years was hardly appropriate. However, during that last summer of peace no one could be blamed for adopting an optimistic outlook for the world at large. The government in Dublin decided to take the opportunity to portray Eire as a new and ambitious country determined to make its mark on the modern world. Moylan was given the task by Sean Lemass to oversee the construction and development of the Irish pavilion at the fair and, in April 1939, he set sail on the SS *President Roosevelt* on a very familiar voyage across the Atlantic. Just prior to docking in New York on 23 April, he wrote to Nora and indicated a certain unease about world affairs when he made an indirect reference to what was taking place in Germany. He wrote:

> Dear Nora,
> We are only 370 miles from New York and land DV (Deo Volante) about midday tomorrow … The deck is like the ground floor of the Tower of Babel with the mixture of tongues. Quite a number of those on board can speak no English.
>
> One German girl told me that coming out of Germany she was allowed to bring only forty dollars. This is to carry her to

> Frisco. She doesn't look or act in any way Jewish but there must be some strain otherwise she would not have to leave … I shall write at once when I land.
>
> Love to you and the gang.
>
> Sean.[153]

The initial government idea was that the pavilion should have a distinctly Irish character and its architect, Michael Scott, designed a shamrock-shaped internal floor plan, much to the delight of those who visited it over the course of the fair. The pavilion was opened on 13 May 1939 and it proved to be a memorable occasion with a nineteen-gun salute fired as the Irish dignitaries arrived. For many Irish-Americans, the pavilion in one sense represented a step back to the old homestead but in another sense it was a major source of pride in just how far the relatively young state had progressed since attaining its independence. When it was first mooted that Eire should take part in the fair it was suggested the pavilion site would be incorporated into that of the British Empire. This, of course, was the source of much consternation in Dublin and de Valera insisted on the country having a prime location of its own, signifying its status as an independent state. The political posturing paid dividends and de Valera got his wish.

Around that time the IRA bombings in Britain were becoming a major problem for the Dublin government. The worsening political situation in Europe only served to increase international tension and de Valera decided to forego his planned trip to New York. He appointed the Tánaiste, Sean T. O'Kelly, to make the trip and he set sail from Cobh on 13 May 1939. The trip to New York offered Moylan a chance to revisit all the places he was familiar with. He did not, however, make contact with his old friend Joe McGarrity, a man he relied upon so much during his time in the city sixteen years earlier. Both men had grown apart when Moylan took his leave of the IRA and Sinn Fein during the 1920s, and the rift was cemented permanently when de Valera marched his Fianna Fáil deputies into Dáil Éireann in 1927. McGarrity never reconciled himself to the fact that republicans had put down their guns to pursue a political path.

The World Fair proved to be a successful venture and Moylan returned home during that summer. The outlook for Europe was becoming more uncertain as the spectre of war loomed ever darker on the horizon. When war was declared, Eamon de Valera rose to address Dáil Éireann on 2 September and announced his government's decision to remain neutral in the conflict. He justified this policy with the following words:

> It is not as representing the sentiments or feelings of our people that the government stands before you with this policy. It stands before as the guardian of the interests of our people, and it is to guard these interests as best we can that we are proposing to follow the policy.[154]

The Dáil then declared a state of emergency, giving the government extensive powers to deal with any problems that might arise during the war. In general, the decision to remain neutral was popular and many saw neutrality as the ultimate expression of Irish independence. It was also hoped that neutrality would keep the country immune from all the horrors and suffering the fighting would inevitably bring. Having been given a 'blank cheque' by the Dáil, the government quickly set about making plans to see the country through the conflict.

The decision to remain neutral was, of course, not a surprising one as de Valera had for some years signalled his intention to follow that policy in the event of a war. The threat of conflict had been escalating ever since Hitler's march into the Rhineland in 1936 and his subsequent march through Austria, the Sudetenland, Czechoslovakia and finally Poland plunged the continent of Europe into the abyss by September 1939. As if he had inside information on what was about to transpire, de Valera insisted during the 1938 Anglo-Irish Treaty negotiations that the ports of Cobh, Berehaven and Lough Swilly be returned by the British to the control of the government in Dublin. To have left control of these ports in the hands of the British would have, in de Valera's mind, compromised Ireland's neutral stance in the event of war. If we go back as far as July 1936 and examine de Valera's speech to the League of Nations in Geneva we can get an indication of his intentions in relation to Ireland's position in any future European conflict. In the speech he told the assembly that:

> Peace is dependent on the will of the great states and all the small states can do, if the statesmen of the great fail in their duty, is resolutely determine that they will not become the tools of any great power and that they will resist with whatever strength that they may possess every attempt to force them into a war against their will.[155]

So when war did eventually break out in September 1939, de Valera and his Fianna Fáil government put into action their plan to keep Ireland out of the war. The fact that they succeeded in doing so, despite bouts of intolerable pressure from Britain and indeed from America, should, even to this day, draw a sense of admiration. However, in hindsight and given the sense of international isolation the country endured in the decade following the war, one could certainly be justified in questioning whether the policy of neutrality was the correct one to follow. However, that is a question for another day.

When Moylan returned from New York he was obliged to attend to family and constituency matters. He and the family managed to go on holidays in August to Dunquin on the Dingle Peninsula but he had to cut it short when de Valera recalled him to Dublin. Moylan was appointed to head up the Air Raid Protection (ARP) service while, at the same time, continue with his roles as parliamentary private secretary for the Ministries of Defence and of Industry and Commerce. In his new role it was envisaged that he would oversee the setting up of an air raid protection system for the country's cities. The government was also primarily concerned with making sure it could deal with any threat to the country's citizens, most especially if there was widespread bombing from the air. It was also concerned with minimising any possibility of the country being accidently drawn into the conflict. All in all, it was a very busy time for Moylan and it was clear de Valera saw him as a trustworthy and dependable foot soldier and ally. There was, by this time, every indication that Moylan's political career was destined to develop into one of real substance.

Moylan was diligent in his duties and attended many ARP wardens meetings and gave outstanding support to all of those involved in the service. By the end of 1940, some 4,500 wardens had been appointed and Moylan made sure the fire and hospital services were ready for any eventuality. By the time everything was in place the first German bombs had dropped on Ireland. The first horror took place in Campile, a rural village in County Wexford, on the afternoon of 26 August 1940 when a German bomber dropped its payload on the local creamery. Three girls, Kitty and Mary Kent and Kathleen Hurley, died in the incident, which seriously damaged the creamery and some other buildings. By all accounts it was a horrific scene never to be forgotten by the local people.

Two days after the bombing, *The Irish Times* devoted its editorial to the incident, saying:

> A German plane released bombs over Wexford on Monday afternoon and through this dreadful happening, Ireland has experienced for the first time the meaning in all its horror of

> an aerial bombardment; no accusations were made against those responsible, but the poignant consequences were a stark reminder that it might have been Dublin and Cork and the number of dead might not be three but 300.[156]

The taking of three young lives brought the war to Eire's shores and a sense of shock and terror rippled across the country. At first the reason for the bombing was unclear but some historians later concluded that it was a deliberate act designed to warn Ireland off exporting foodstuffs to Britain. It was a callous and uncalled for act and the £9,000 compensation paid by the German government in 1943 can only be seen as derisory.

That year saw other bombing incidents when on 20 December two bombs fell in Sandycove, injuring three people, and one other near Carrickmacross in County Monaghan, injuring one person. Despite Ireland's declaration of neutrality, it seemed at the time that German bombs paid little attention to boundaries. The New Year started with more terror dropping from the skies when, on 1 January, between five and eight bombs fell on Duleek and Julianstown in County Meath, where no injuries were recorded. Three bombs were also reported to have fallen on Ballymurrin in Wexford, causing no damage or injuries, while incendiary bombs fell on the Curragh racecourse. The most serious incident occurred in County Carlow when three members of the Shannon family lost their lives in Knockroe, near Borris, after a bomb fell on their house. Mary Ellen and Bridget Shannon and their sixteen-year-old niece Kathleen were killed. Michael and James Shannon were badly injured.

At 6 a.m. on 2 January, two bombs fell on Terenure in County Dublin. The first did little damage but the second destroyed two houses and damaged many others. Two other bombs fell close to the Kimmage Crossroads, injuring one person and damaging two houses. The following day a bomb fell on the South Circular Road area of Dublin, destroying three houses and damaging around fifty others. There was also damage to a Presbyterian Church and school as well as a Jewish synagogue. No deaths occurred but twenty people were injured during the incident. The Dublin bombings, the first to be endured in the city, shocked Dubliners but it was just a taste of what was to come later in the year.

* * *

Many theories were put forward as to why the bombs were dropped on the country and some were suspicious that the bombings may have been the deliberate actions of one or more of the belligerents. The German Legation in Ireland had been refused permission by the Irish government to bring in extra staff prior to the New Year and there was speculation the bombings were carried out in retaliation for that decision. Others put forward the more fanciful notion that the bombs had been captured from the Germans by the British, who then dropped them on Ireland in an attempt to force the country into the war. However, the explanation offered by the German government that their aircraft had mistaken the east coast of Ireland for the west coast of Britain seems the more plausible reason for the bombings.

At midnight on Friday, 30 May 1941 army search lights around Dublin began to scan the skies above the city. There had been a number of reports during the evening of aircraft overflying the eastern coast of the country as well as reports of explosions out to sea. Soon the familiar drone of German aircraft was heard over the city. Some eyewitness put the number of planes at around thirty flying in formation. The army fired three flares each of green, white and orange to warn the German pilots that they were over Irish airspace. A red flare was then fired to warn that defensive action would be taken if the aircraft did not leave immediately. When they continued, anti-aircraft fire began and the war had come to Dublin. Strangely, there was little in the way of panic and the city did not even have an air raid siren network to warn the people of any impending danger.

The city was essentially unprepared that Whit weekend with no blackout being enforced. The general holiday atmosphere in the city was shattered around 1.30 a.m. when a bomb fell on the junction of North Circular Road and North Richmond Street, startling the area's residents. Many of them ran up Summerhill to a barber shop, where people had gathered to say the rosary. Other bombs fell on Ballybough, demolishing two houses in Summerhill Park, injuring many but there were no fatalities. Another bomb also fell near the zoo in the Phoenix Park. There were no casualties but damage was done to Áras an Uachtaráin. Just after 2 a.m. a low whistle signalling an incoming bomb could be heard. What experts would later describe as the 'perfect bomb' landed between the tram tracks on the North Strand near Newcomen Bridge. It was a 500lb landmine more commonly used against heavily fortified military targets. Its massive explosion shattered everything around it and the subsequent implosion did even greater damage. The entire city shook on impact, timed at 2.05 a.m. when the clock outside Corcoran's shop on the North Strand stopped, and the shockwave was felt in places as far away as Enniskerry and Mullingar. It is estimated that approximately 2,500 houses suffered bomb damage of varying degrees with around 300 completely destroyed, leaving 400 people homeless. The bombings galvanised the ARP wardens into action and twenty-eight people were reported to have died instantly in the incident, while scores of people were injured. Some more people died during the following days from their injuries, bringing the known total of deaths to thirty-four. Moylan's lodgings had its front door blown in, which of course brought the magnitude of the incident very close to him.

The bombing not only stunned the city but the country has a whole and left many people wondering why the Eire should be targeted. In a speech to Dáil Éireann, de Valera tendered an expression of sympathy on behalf of the government to the families of the bereaved and injured. Reasons put forward at the time for the bombings ranged from navigational error to a deliberate attack in retaliation for Dublin's assistance to Belfast. In an article written in 1999 for *The Independent* newspaper in London, the late Robert Fisk reminds us that after the bombing some people recalled how Lord Haw Haw, in one of his radio broadcasts, had warned that Dublin's Amiens Street railway station would be bombed. This was backed up by those who witnessed the lone German aircraft flying around the area for at least a half an hour before the bombing, giving the impression the pilot was looking for a specific target. It was into this station that many Belfast refugees, fleeing the bombing in that city, had arrived and it is no coincidence the station stands only a few hundred yards from the North Strand. Fisk's article also quoted a German pilot who was one of the pathfinders on the raid and he maintained that navigational error was the cause of the bombing. This may well be the obvious answer and post-war West Germany's payment of £344,000 in compensation for more than 2,000 claims by 1958 would seem to vindicate that. Two further German raids were reported in 1941, one on 2 June when bombs were dropped near Arklow and 24 July on Dundalk. Both incidents caused only minor damage and no casualties.

Dublin Corporation led the response to the bombing on the North Strand by purchasing 800 mattresses and 2,400 blankets from the ARP Department of Defence stores. Moylan was anxious that everything possible should be done for those impacted by the tragedy and in one letter on 13 June to the city manager he made it clear that:

> Public morale demands that this matter should be dealt with swiftly and efficiently. I visited the North Strand on the twelfth instant and to say that I was amazed and shocked at the lack of progress is to put it lightly.[157]

It took some months for the repairs to be carried out in the area, much to Moylan's annoyance, but on the first anniversary of the bombing the ARP held a parade to commemorate the tragedy and all of those who died in it. A clearly mollified Moylan took the salute and in his address he recalled how:

> On this day, exactly a year ago, a number of citizens were hurled into eternity and a larger number received injuries, the marks of which they would carry all their lives … when the bombs began to fall there were no grievances in the allied organisations that tackled the work of rescue, healing and restoration, only a desire to carry out their duties.[158]

Moylan, in his speech, showed his high regard for all the volunteers who readily came together to help alleviate the suffering of their fellow citizens in a tragedy that would never be forgotten. Though he would not have wanted it to have panned out as it did, his ARP duties and his leadership of the response to the Dublin bombings were instrumental in bringing him to the notice of a wider public. Moylan had, in every sense, become a fully fledged national politician and it was only a matter of time before his boss, de Valera, would entrust upon him a greater role in government.

Chapter 21

Ministerial Recognition and Death

Moylan topped the poll with 6,456 first-preference votes in the four-seater North Cork constituency in the June 1943 general election and de Valera appointed him as Minister for Lands. This was his first Cabinet post and he remained in it for the next five years. His new post required him to be based in Dublin and he had no option but to leave Kiskeam and move his family to the capital, where they rented a house in Clontarf. It was to be the Moylan family home for the rest of his life and by all accounts it proved to be a happy one where learning and debate were encouraged. It was a home packed full of books and Moylan was at his happiest spending an evening in his library winding down after his many busy days as a government minister. Though he accepted he and his family had to live in Dublin, he never lost touch with Newmarket, where we can be sure his heart remained.

His ministerial post was a very important one as the land continued to be at the heart of so much life in Ireland. The government was determined to redistribute the land that had been purchased under various Land Acts during the 1920s as a means of alleviating poverty and congestion. The Land Commission was tasked with administering the programme and was answerable to Moylan as the relevant government minister. He ruffled some feathers in September 1943 when, in a letter to de Valera, he questioned the whole process of land distribution. In Moylan's view the practice of giving land away was creating a culture of dependency and he maintained those who were in receipt of land were often not competent enough in farming to make good use of it. He was also of the view that the policy of distributing the land only served to create economically unviable small holdings that were not conducive to modern farming initiatives or methods and were not generating much in the way of wealth for the nation. Considering that agriculture was the nation's greatest industry and underpinned the economy, Moylan's lack of confidence in the policy of land distribution was somewhat controversial but in hindsight one cannot argue that his assessment of the situation was accurate.

Every day until the war ended and, even in the years up to the general election of 1948, the de Valera government was forced to contend with enormous economic difficulties, many of which were the result of decisions made in London and Washington. The role of the government was essentially to look after the well-being of the people in the face of the terrible adversity that the whole world was experiencing as well as maintaining the country's security. The lack of essential supplies was a pressing problem during the war years and in the years directly after hostilities ended in 1945. Throughout the war years the government had to take matters into its own hands in order to maintain some semblance of normality across the country. Moylan readily bought into the notion of Cabinet collective responsibility and became part of a government that diligently held the line of neutrality. The country survived the conflict intact because of de Valera and his administration's determination that it should remain neutral despite the intense pressure applied by powerful external forces. In general, across the political divide and among the ordinary people neutrality was viewed as a test of the country's independence and when hostilities ceased in 1945 everyone, including Moylan, could safely claim the test had been passed. The war years were a triumph for Fianna Fáil and politically nothing much changed. There was no real downturn in the party's popularity until the general election of 1948, when rumblings of discontent began to emerge. People were not seeing any improvement in their standard of living since the end of the war and the economic restrictions applied during the conflict were largely still in place.

* * *

Throughout his term as a government minister, Moylan maintained a social conscience and tried to improve life across the country wherever he could. One of his last acts as Minister for Lands came just before the 1948 general election when he initiated a report into the lives of the few people still living on the Blasket Islands. The islanders eked out a living through lobster fishing and sheep farming and were often cut off from the mainland. They lived in appalling conditions and by 1947 the population had declined to just fifty-one islanders, all of whom were happy to be resettled on the mainland. While the report was a positive one and set out a constructive resettlement strategy, it unfortunately fell by the wayside once a general election was called.

De Valera called a general election for Wednesday, 4 February and he was most probably very confident of being returned as the leader of a new Fianna Fáil administration. Moylan returned to Cork and to his constituency to begin his own campaign for re-election. By that time he was well known for his oratory and he once again proved to be a powerful speaker on the stump. He came across as passionate about politics and he could work a crowd, enthralling all those who were listening to him. Aideen Carroll tells a story in her book about a campaign meeting during a 1946 by-election in Cork when Jack Lynch was campaigning for the Fianna Fáil candidate Pa McGrath. The meeting was not going as planned; in fact it was going so badly that even the hecklers had lost interest. Moylan, as Director of Elections, rearranged the speaking order and stepped up to the podium to speak. By the time he was finished, after having thrown in a few quips about hurling, he had the crowd completely engaged and interested in what he was saying.

Moylan had cut his teeth in public speaking while addressing crowds in Newmarket from a wall or the back of a lorry. During one campaign Moylan believed a certain speaker was taking up too much time and, to the amusement of the listening crowd, he edged slowly across the tailgate until the speaker was tipped off the side. In his later years he recalled an amusing anecdote from the 1948 general election when he had been on the stump at Ballylanders in County Limerick. After the meeting the crowd and speakers adjourned to the local public house. Moylan was introduced to the lady of the house and he referred to the big turnout for the meeting and also asked her why the kitchen door was shut. The lady replied that she always locked the door when a crowd from Kilmallock was in town. She went on to say the Kilmallock people stole a pig's head from her in 1904. Moylan then recalled privately the day that he, as a fifteen-year-old boy, had gone to the feis in Ballylanders with the Kilmallock Brass Band. While he never admitted to being much of a musician he was given the cymbals to play that day. After the feis the band retired to the very same pub, where Moylan and his friends made themselves comfortable in the kitchen. One of the band members looked into the pot hanging over the fire and found the aforementioned pig's head. The bandsmen slipped it into the head of the biggest of their instruments and played their way out of the village. Once they were a safe distance down the road, the very hungry musicians, including the young Moylan, sat by the side of the road and devoured their booty.

* * *

Moylan was re-elected in the general election of 1948, having been returned with 7,624 first-preference votes, which saw him top the poll once again. Fianna Fáil did not have enough seats to form a government and power passed to the first inter-party administration in the history of the state. Out of ministerial office, Moylan had time to bask in some family successes and happiness as he watched his son, Rick, complete his law degree and also welcomed his first grandchild into the world. During this time in opposition, Moylan set about putting down on paper his memories of the revolutionary era and it all evolved into his wide-ranging and fascinating witness statement to the Bureau of Military History. It is a statement this author has examined and analysed in great detail and written extensively about elsewhere. It is, without any shadow of doubt, one of the most important documents ever compiled in relation to the quest for Ireland's independence.

In the general election of 1951, Fianna Fáil was returned to power as a minority single-party government and Moylan was re-elected in his constituency with 5,269 first-preference votes. He did not top the poll and took the last of the three seats available, with his two Fianna Fáil running mates failing to get elected. Back in the Cabinet, Moylan was appointed as Minister for Education, which was probably a surprise to many observers and most likely to himself. When Moylan addressed the senior civil servants in the department for the first time, he displayed his sense of humour when he said:

> There are many mistaken beliefs current about Eamon de Valera, one of them being that he is a man totally lacking in a sense of humour. But the fact that I stand here before you as Minister for Education is testimony to his sense of humour.[159]

While many might have been surprised to see Moylan in the Department of Education, it should be remembered that he was a very well-read and articulate individual, so much so that Jack Lynch once described him as:

> One of the most widely read men that ever graced Irish public life.[160]

Moylan quickly made his own mark in the Department of Education and one of his main objectives was to improve and accelerate the school rebuilding programme. The school building situation all across the country and, most especially in rural areas, was appalling and was an embarrassment to the country. At the time it was estimated that around ten per cent of the country's primary schools were structurally defective almost to the point of being derelict and were obviously in need of immediate replacement. Moylan, with the backing of his Cabinet colleagues, decided to double the building target to one hundred new primary schools per year, which was a very ambitious target. Aideen Carroll tells the story of Moylan's visit to a school in Listowel and how, in the presence of the headmaster, he took a penknife from his pocket and thrust the blade into the window frame right up to the hilt. The timber was rotten and it disintegrated. A smiling Moylan turned to the headmaster and asked him if wished to have a library in his new school. As usual, Moylan, was proving that he was a man of action rather than a man of words and platitudes. According to Kevin Devlin in his 1952 *Sunday Press* article on the minister, Moylan was not an education professional but he gained the admiration of his department's civil servants as well as the teaching profession, all of whom:

> Responded to the quickening of a new spirit … an educational idealism built on the rock of uncommon common sense.[161]

A carpenter by trade, it was no surprise that Moylan interested himself in vocational education. The Vocational Education Act of 1931 was intended to advance the education of children who were more suited to trades than professions and was to be free of the religious influence prevalent in primary and secondary schools. Moylan made a real impression in this area of education during his time as minister. He oversaw the building of thirty-two vocational schools during a two-year period and was anxious to see young people attain qualifications in craft trades. He believed, that while academic education was most important, the needs of young people not inclined towards an academic or professional way of life also needed to be addressed. He wanted to draw out the best in every child and one suspects he drew on his own experiences as he developed this policy. He was also eager for teachers to broaden the scope of their teaching and go beyond the curriculum with their students, and he encouraged them to implement a 'hobbies half-day' into their teaching week. This was just another example of the progressive thinking for which Moylan was increasingly becoming noted.

For all his outstanding work as Minister for Education, we cannot ignore the fact that Moylan's tenure did finish on a rather sour note. The problem came to light on the day the Fourteenth Dáil was dissolved and it concerned a young boy who was physically beaten in an incident at the

Artane Industrial School and sustained a broken arm. It seems the boy, who was fourteen years old, had been punished for misbehaviour following an altercation with another boy and a number of slaps from the punishment leather was administered to him. The boy resented his punishment and was ordered to submit to further slaps on the hand from the edge of the strap. He, naturally enough, refused to submit to the punishment and the Christian brother administering the punishment sent for another brother to assist him in carrying out the cruel action. It seems the second brother snatched a sweeping brush and struck the boy a number of times on the head, back and arm. The boy was taken to hospital two days later and had his arm set in plaster. His mother was not informed of the incident and was prevented from seeing her son for more than a week. She contacted Peadar Cowen, TD, and he made representations in the Dáil on her behalf asking for an investigation into the distressing incident.

Cowen rose to ask Moylan that an investigation into the incident be initiated and give an assurance to the House that such an action would not be allowed to happen again in the school. Moylan replied, saying he would share Cowen's fears if he thought the incident was anything other than an isolated one and it might even be called an accident. One can imagine how this remark might have caused some consternation because the act of taking up a sweeping brush and hitting the young boy repeatedly cannot, in any manner, be construed as an accident. Moylan did go on to say that he would not tolerate any acts of cruelty to any child in the school or any other institution. He then, however, somewhat muddied the waters when he said:

> I cannot conceive any deliberate ill-treatment of boys by a community motivated by the ideals of its founder. I cannot conceive any sadism emanating from the men who were trained to a life of sacrifice and of austerity. They are also trained to have great devotion to a very high purpose. The point is that accidents will happen in the best-regulated families and in this family there are about 800 boys. Many of them were sent to Artane because of the difficulties of their character and because of a good deal of unruliness of conduct. These boys are difficult to control at times. Maybe it essential that now and again that children should be punished.[162]

Moylan's defence of the Christian brothers would seem in this day and age to be almost unforgiveable considering what has emerged in recent decades concerning that particular religious organisation. The Catholic Church and its affiliated teaching organisations wielded great power at the time and one can get the sense that Moylan found himself in a situation where he was reluctant to criticise them. The only real mitigation that might be applied is that he was the minister in charge at a time when corporal punishment was accepted as a normal response in society to what was perceived as bad behaviour. His did say, however, that he appreciated the concern of the boy's mother and that he deeply regretted that the incident ever took place. We must also look at Moylan's response to the incident in the context of the time he lived in but, very obviously, through our modern-day eyes it was, in every sense, a pitiful and regrettable response to what was essentially an act of violence visited upon a child by an unfeeling and sadistic adult.

During the adjournment debate, Moylan made it very clear that he wished to see conditions in industrial schools and, indeed all schools, improved but it would, he said, have to be done by increased funds from the public purse. The problem, of course, was that the government was hardly awash with money at a time when the economy was struggling very badly. Moylan undoubtedly had the interests of all school children at heart while he was the Minister of Education but, like all of his Cabinet colleagues, he was constrained in what he could achieve by the unrelenting lack of funds. He was, without doubt, a compassionate and caring man and he probably showed a certain naivety when he dealt with the Artane incident having never been a past pupil of any Christian brothers school and consequently unfamiliar with what took place in them. It was an unfortunate note to end his tenure in the Department of Education on but it should in no way overshadow the progressive and forward-thinking work he carried out while he was at the helm.

The Dáil was dissolved on 24 April 1954 at the request of de Valera and a general election was called for Tuesday, 15 May. Moylan was once again re-elected in his North Cork constituency with a first-preference vote of 7,461 that saw him top the poll. However, his personal success was tempered by the fact that Fianna Fáil once again found itself removed from office and a period in opposition beckoned. Moylan and his Fianna Fáil colleagues occupied the opposition benches until 1957 and watched with a growing sense of frustration as the second inter-party minority government stumbled from one crisis to another. Moylan during that time did serve as an Irish representative to the Council of Europe in Strasbourg and attended an assembly meeting during the last weeks of 1956 just prior to the general election of 1957.

The election was held on 5 March and it was to be Moylan's last campaign. Polling 5,960 first-preference votes, he sensationally lost his seat. Fianna Fáil pursued a strategy designed to deliver the party two of the three seats on offer. The plan backfired spectacularly and while Batt Donegan was elected, Moylan lost out. Being the man he was, Moylan was magnanimous in defeat as he addressed the crowd at the count saying:

> I have no complaint, no grievance. We men who came into Irish politics in the revolutionary period took victory with humility and defeat with good grace.
>
> I have the very good consolation in my personal defeat of being replaced by a man of high honour and principle and in whom the people will have confidence, and who will, I believe, represent them as diligently as I tried to do. Naturally it would be hypocrisy on my part if I did not tell you that I must feel a certain sense of personal disappointment but, after all, the Fianna Fáil vote is really the majority vote in this constituency still.[163]

Having lost his seat, Moylan had time for his family and spent some of it in Mallow with his daughter Stephanie and her husband. He had time to reflect on his life and all that he had achieved. He was in the autumn of his life and had lost his brother, Ned, during the previous year. He reflected on how many of the men he fought with during the War of Independence had already passed away, including some of his fellow officers in the 1st Southern Division. The passing of his old comrade, Ernie O'Malley, had a profound impact on Moylan and during his graveside oration in honour of his friend he spoke fondly of their ancient comradeship. He went on to say O'Malley was a soldier:

> who carried the gospel of national freedom into every corner of the country, inspiring men by his example and steeling their courage by his contempt of danger.[164]

Until the end of his days, Moylan always extolled the virtues of the Volunteers he fought with and described them as the most courageous of men who were prepared to lay down their lives for a cause they firmly believed in. He once wrote of those very same men, saying:

> They were neither adventurers nor professional soldiers to whom revolution was the breath of life, they were men who left their peaceful avocation in a patriotic desire to serve their country, they expected neither reward or recognition … whatever capacity they displayed in the difficult and unusual conditions which their country's history had thrust upon them, they were almost wholly simple men, of no political experience or knowledge, no familiarity with historical facts that might have guided them.[165]

Though he never wanted to see the Civil War break out, he fully understood why it did and refused to lay the blame at the feet of those who rejected the Treaty with the British. He maintained they were all honourable men who:

> found it difficult to accept anything less than the full recognition of that for which they fought … it is difficult to expect that they shall be satisfied with a bargain which leaves their country in a state of subservience with a territorial division, the justice of which has not been and cannot be recognised.[166]

What a pity it is that Moylan never got the chance to write his memoir of the Civil War and leave for posterity his view of the conflict and a greater justification for it.

After his general election defeat it looked like Moylan's political career was at an end but de Valera thought otherwise and co-opted him to Seanad Éireann. He then nominated Moylan to the post of Minister for Agriculture and he was the first government minister to be appointed from the Seanad. This, of course, caused some consternation in the Dáil, where the constitutionality of the appointment was debated. The appointment was opposed by some deputies but it was overwhelmingly approved by the House without the necessity of a vote. Whatever his party politics, Moylan remained a very popular and much-respected member of the Oireachtas who came across to many of his colleagues as a thoughtful, introspective and quietly humorous man far removed from the hardened freedom fighter of his earlier days.

The appointment as Minister for Agriculture must have pleased Moylan greatly as his love for the land never waned throughout his life. Living in Dublin had become a necessity once he accepted high public office but his heart still remained in Newmarket and the rural landscape he grew up in.

Being Minister for Agriculture was a kind of crowning glory for Moylan and befitted a man so inextricably tied to the land. T.P. Kilfeather, in an article for the *Sunday Independent* in March 1957, claimed the agriculture minister was as rugged as a boulder of Irish granite, and went on to write:

> His voice with its rasping quality … has never been known to call a spade an agricultural implement … this is the blunt Sean Moylan to whom de Valera has given the task of directing the efforts of those engaged in the biggest industry in the country and if there is one man who is not dismayed by the responsibility which has been given to him, he is Sean Moylan, book-lover and straight-talking man of dynamic action.[167]

Moylan, being the man he was, threw himself wholeheartedly into the role as minister for agriculture, seeing it as the pinnacle of his political career. He was so enthusiastic it caused de Valera to wonder if he made the right choice, not because he doubted Moylan's ability to do the job but that he might become all consumed by it to the detriment of his notoriously fragile health. During the Dáil debate on the nomination of his ministers, de Valera expressed only one reservation about his appointment of Moylan, saying that:

> the man should not overwork himself and kill himself because it is a very difficult task.[168]

In his first speech as Minister for Agriculture, Moylan made it clear how he saw the industry fitting into the wider spectrum of Irish life. He was at pains to point out that Irish agriculture was a national resource to be nurtured but he was also aware that the industry needed to be able to compete with international competitors. He believed reform of the agriculture industry could only be achieved by the application of science and research. He claimed the industry, even in the middle of the twentieth century, had to remove its insular and often outdated attitudes in order to succeed and, consequently, Moylan was determined to oversee a programme of modernisation during his time in office. He made numerous appearances across the country, turning up at cattle marts, ploughing and sheep-shearing competitions alike. He wanted to be visible and in his conversations with many of those involved in the industry he emphasised the necessity to improve production processes and marketing techniques. He maintained the agricultural industry was the mainstay of the economy and, as such, it was incumbent upon it to strive constantly for excellence. In a speech at the Bandon and Fermoy Mart in June 1957 he said:

> The marketing conditions of a former age were entirely unsuitable for the trade of the present day where changes in production methods had brought competition in the international markets to the keenest edge … Government can make laws to ensure that only completely disease-free animals are placed on the market. But legislation does not formulate public taste.[169]

In essence, Moylan wanted Irish agriculture to be a world leader and made it clear that every single product needed to be in the very best condition with quality guaranteed. He believed that, once agriculture had its own house in order, it would contribute in a very positive manner to the economy as a whole and indeed cement its position as the mainstay of it.

* * *

Unfortunately, Moylan never got to see his vision for the Irish agriculture industry come to fruition because he died suddenly at his Clontarf home on 16 November 1957 at the age of sixty-seven. His death came as huge shock, not only to his political colleagues but to the country itself. Once the sad news had sunk in, the correct decision was made to offer a state funeral. The funeral cortège travelled from Dublin to the village of Kiskeam, which is not far from his old brigade headquarters at Riordan's of Knockavorheen. The cortège paused for a few moments in Cahir where it was met by veterans of the War of Independence including Moylan's old friend, Dan Breen. As the funeral proceeded through the rural hinterland of Munster, old comrades stood to attention and saluted one of their own. The cortège travelled through Mitchelstown, Mallow, Kanturk and, of course, Newmarket; all towns where Moylan was admired and revered as the hero and fighting man that he undoubtedly was. In all the towns he passed through, the people stood silently as they paid their respects in a sad farewell to a man who had fought gallantly to give them their independence. At the burial ,the small village of Kiskeam was thronged with thousands of mourners, including de Valera, who reminded all those listening that Moylan had been a man of the highest integrity.

In my own examination of Sean Moylan's life through his wonderful witness statement I have concluded that he was indeed a complex and very single-minded man. He may, at times, have been a very difficult individual to get on with, and he often displayed a stubborn streak, but he was, at all times, a man of principle and honesty who always looked out for and stood by the men he commanded. He was a man who was always courteous to the ordinary people of Ireland he met on a daily basis. Yet, he could be a brusque man when his mood dictated, and he was often extremely forthright when expressing his views and never attempted to court political popularity. He had the ability to hold an audience even from a young age but, most especially, in his later years as a politician, and could comfortably hold his own in any debate.

Moylan was respected by friend and foe alike both in his political career and in his military life. Tom Barry once said:

> He was a brave and able field commander, a tireless military worker for the Republic and a wise counsellor at Brigade, Divisional and Executive meetings, who never hesitated to take his own line and speak out his mind. He had a hatred of sham and slogans which obscured realities. His sense of humour was the strongest of all the Volunteers I met.[170]

Even his military enemy, the Gloucestershire Regiment of the British Army, took time to mark the passing of a respected foe in their regimental magazine *Back Badge* in December 1957. During his confrontations with this enemy, Moylan always fought by the accepted military rules of engagement and on every occasion he treated all of his prisoners humanely and with courtesy. It was an approach that the British regiment came to respect and seemingly never forgot.

* * *

For a man who achieved so much in his life it is somewhat perplexing to me as a historian and a writer on Irish modern history how Moylan has, over the decades since his death, faded from the nation's memory. Here was a man who made his mark during the War of Independence as probably the greatest of all IRA military strategists and who inflicted very telling damage on the enemy without losing any of the men he commanded. He was, without doubt, a soldier and commander possessed of immeasurable courage who never asked any of his men to undertake a task he was not prepared to do himself. His actions in the field during the independence conflict earned him the unwavering respect of all of his men and, very uniquely, the respect of those he fought.

Having made a huge contribution to eventually bringing the British to the negotiating table, Moylan could not, in all conscience, accept the Anglo-Irish Treaty because it did not deliver the republic he had fought for. Though he never wanted the Civil War to take place and did all in his power to prevent it, he stood by his convictions and became a powerful influence on the republican side during the conflict. There was no one more relieved than Moylan when the dreadful hostilities of the Civil War came to an end because he could see the endless possibilities for the new and emerging Ireland once peace had descended across the land. Leaving behind a gallant and glittering military career, Moylan, after a hiatus of some years given over to his family and personal life, eventually answered de Valera's call and returned to serve his country in a political capacity. He, not unsurprisingly, became a visionary politician of immense ability and intellect and put in place many programmes and policies that greatly enhanced the lives of all those he represented. The pity of it all is that his political career was cut short at a time when he looked destined to make an even greater and long-lasting contribution to the development of the country he loved.

Moylan was an outstanding individual who now deserves to be remembered by modern Ireland on the same level as some of his more well-known revolutionary contemporaries such as Michael Collins and Liam Lynch as well as political contemporaries including de Valera, Lemass and Jack Lynch. Indeed, one can make a sound argument that he achieved as much, if not more, in his life than his illustrious colleagues did and for that reason he deserves the same modern-day recognition. I wrote this book with just one aim in mind and that was to reintroduce to the modern generation of Irishmen and women a man who played a hugely significant role in ensuring they now live in a free and independent Ireland. Sean Moylan was a unique man who lived through turbulent times in Ireland's history but never lost sight of the vision he had for his country. He was, in every sense, a truly remarkable man, a committed IRA revolutionary and a visionary national politician who somehow managed to live what can only be described as a most extraordinary life.

Chapter 22

Men of the South

The Story of Sean Keating's Iconic Painting

Sean Moylan provided the Bureau of Military History with a very comprehensive and enthralling witness statement detailing his time as an IRA commander during the War of Independence. However, Moylan took time in 1957, just seven months before his untimely death, to provide the archive with one other fascinating statement in relation to Sean Keating's iconic War of Independence painting, *Men of the South*. The painting itself epitomises the fighting men who bravely took on the might of the Crown forces during that tumultuous time in order that Ireland could become a free and independent nation. It depicts the six men in all their ruggedness and it is a remarkable testament to the many men all across Ireland who were committed to the independence ideal during that momentous time. The six men depicted in the painting were all loyal comrades of Moylan and have a real sense of the heroic about them as they gaze into the distance awaiting a call into action. The painting is now a national treasure and an outstanding reminder to modern generations of Irishmen and women that their freedom is due entirely to the men of the south and all other fighting men like them who bravely put their lives on the line for the country they loved.

The story of the painting begins with a visit to Cork in 1921 by Albert E. Wood, who was one of the mainstays of the Irish Bar. Wood was being briefed at the time by a solicitor in Mallow called Barry Sullivan as he prepared to defend a number of IRA men who were being court martialled for their part in the capture of the Mallow Military Barracks in 1920. Wood's arrival in Cork coincided with Moylan's capture by the British, after which he was brought to the military prison in Cork city. While Moylan was incarcerated, Sullivan brought Wood into the prison to see him. Their intention was to persuade Moylan to make and defend a case before his court martial. Moylan was less than willing to do so because he was of the opinion that all the charges brought against him were true and he felt that any defence might be regarded as an apology for his actions, and it would also be detrimental to the general morale of the IRA. In essence, Moylan was resigned to his fate and was prepared to face his execution safe in the knowledge that he had done all that he could to achieve his country's independence from the British.

However, as it transpired, both Wood and Sullivan were persuasive individuals and eventually they managed to convince Moylan to change his mind. He agreed to put up a defence after insisting on certain conditions being put in place and the eventual outcome of the court martial process saw Moylan, by means of an amazing set of circumstances, avoid the execution firing squad. One of the reasons for Moylan changing his mind was because Wood told him that, in his view, the fighting was coming to an end and he had every chance of avoiding execution. In fact, Wood's prophecy was correct and the fighting was over six weeks later. Wood was an Englishman of fine breeding and an unlikely champion of the independence and IRA cause. Though initially unfamiliar with the character of the men he was defending, he came to admire their courage and sincerity.

* * *

With the truce in place and Moylan released from his incarceration, he travelled to Dublin on 16 August 1921 to attend a meeting of Dáil Éireann. That evening he was invited to dinner in the Gresham Hotel by Hugh Harold, a Mallow businessman and a brother to one of those who were court martialled for taking part in the attack on the Mallow Barracks. They were joined for the meal by John McLoughlin from Donegal, who later became a Senator and a man known to Moylan since 1918. After dinner they sat at the table chatting and were joined by Albert Wood and their discussion continued. Wood, it seems, suggested to Moylan that he should visit the National Gallery while he was in the capital and a few days later both men took the time to do so. Wood was a great admirer of art and sculpture, in contrast to Moylan, who had never been in the National Gallery. They spent a pleasant afternoon in the gallery, which Moylan found both interesting and informative. The following day Wood mentioned that he would like to have a painting done of Moylan wearing the clothes he had on while in the dock during his trial in Cork and he suggested that Sean Keating might be the right man to carry out the commission. Moylan readily agreed to sit for the painting and Wood set the wheels in motion. Keating, a Limerick man, eventually became one of Ireland's best political painters. He trained under the great William Orpen at the Dublin Metropolitan School of Art from 1911. The school was a hive of political activity and was frequented by the likes of the Pearse brothers and Constance Markievicz.

When Moylan sat for the painting, Wood often visited to watch Keating's progress and during their various conversations it was agreed that a painting of some of Moylan's men who had participated in the War of Independence with him would be a project of real historical significance. Moylan was enthusiastic about the proposal and agreed to bring some of his men to Dublin. The story goes that when the men arrived at the door of the school, pandemonium ensued. It was opened by a porter who was confronted by men with Cork accents carrying guns and demanding to see Keating. In a blind panic, the porter ran up the stairs to Keating's studio to tell him he was going to be shot. Keating put the man at his ease and told him to see the Cork men up to his studio.

The painting of the picture was not a straightforward operation and Keating later mentioned that he encountered some difficulties in getting his work under way. A series of photographs of the men were taken as they posed with their rifles. Eventually, preliminary sketches of the men were made at Keating's studio and later developed into pictures. They were exhibited in the Academy in 1921 and eventually sold to various individuals. Keating actually produced two paintings of the men together, the first of which now hangs in Áras an Uachtaráin, the home of the Irish President. This version includes Moylan (standing) together with Jim Riordan, Denis Mullane, Jim Cashman, Michael O' Sullivan, John Jones, Roger Kiely and Dan Browne. The other more famous version, which was done some months later, does not include Moylan or O'Sullivan and is now on display in Cork's Crawford Gallery. In the second picture the man in a standing pose is Jim Cashman. The exclusion of Moylan and Sullivan from the second picture is due to one simple fact: they were still wanted men and there was no guarantee that the peace negotiations would conclude with an agreement, so there was always the possibility of a return to hostilities. Moylan feared that if they were included in the picture they would become even more recognisable to the British. In his later years, Moylan saw the reason for his omission in the second picture as a poor one and I suspect he rather regretted his self-imposed absence.

Moylan confirmed in his witness statement that the picture now hanging in Áras an Uachtaráin was, for many years, in an outhouse at Keating's premises in Rathfarnham. Though Keating offered it to Moylan a number of times, he refused it because he believed it was too valuable a gift to accept. The painting, which was entitled, *An I.R.A. Flying Column, 1920*, was eventually acquired by Dr Douglas Hyde, the then President of Ireland, in 1944 as part of his campaign to establish a national collection to be housed in the Áras. Keating was always apt to making his views known and on a number of occasions he told Moylan that he believed the men who were the subject of the paintings had been very badly treated by the Free State and not given the due recognition they all deserved. Moylan saw no real need for Keating's expressions of concern or sympathy and made the point that the men in question had willingly accepted the difficulties they were forced to endure during the independence conflict. He also claimed some of the men had to eventually leave the country to make a living, a fact they readily accepted. Revolutionaries, he believed, by their very mentality, were precluded from living comfortable lives. Soft living, he said, would have made them uncomfortable but, as it was, his comrades could look back on their lives as a great adventure pursued successfully. Moylan believed the men's characters had developed under the pressure of adverse circumstances and, as a result, they had a tremendous advantage in life over those who had chosen a more comfortable and safer existence during the revolutionary era.

Moylan pointed out that Keating sometimes referred to the men as members of a West Cork Column; they were in fact, all North Cork men and most of them were Duhallow men. In his statement, Moylan provided his own character assessment of the men depicted in the picture and all of them are portrayed as people who were deeply committed to the ideal of Ireland's independence. Keating was particularly taken by **Roger Kiely**, who was a school teacher and he later described him as about the best man he ever knew. Moylan, for some reason, saw Kiely, who was an intelligence officer with the Millstreet Battalion, as being somewhat different to the rest of the men and was not an obvious fighting man. However, like his comrades, Kiely was imbued with the tradition of resistance to British rule having come, just like the rest of the men, from a deeply republican family. He went on in later life to become principal of the Boys National School in Cullen while his wife, Hanoria, was the principal of the girls' school. Roger Kiely had a fine interest in the Irish language as well as in Irish music and he died in April 1967.

Denis Mullane came from a family immersed in the ideal of Fenianism and it was no surprise then that Denis was deeply committed to the republican ideal. Moylan went on to point out that four graves existed on Mullane's farm in Freemount and they were the graves of four O'Sullivan Bere soldiers who were killed at a nearby fort during the famous march to Leitrim in the aftermath of the Battle of Kinsale in 1601, when the English finally defeated Gaelic Ireland. Moylan mused in his statement that the story of O'Sullivan Bere's epic march, part of which went through the Cork countryside, might well have influenced the young mind of Denis Mullane.

Moylan remembered **James Riordan** as a big man who was involved in all of the fighting in North Cork during the War of Independence. The Riordans came originally from the North as Galloglasses (elite mercenary soldiers of the thirteenth to sixteenth century) and James displayed all the fighting capabilities of his forefathers. Yet, according to Moylan, the man was gentle and disciplined but capable of a real fierceness when it was time to fight the enemy. **Dan Browne** was a good soldier in Moylan's view and a man who always seemed to have a grim face. He was a clerical student and became a parish priest. Moylan was of the opinion that he developed the characteristics of a parish priest during his days as a freedom fighter.

James Cashman was, in essence, only a boy and a very fine athlete. He was a very enthusiastic Volunteer and was a first cousin of Moylan's wife, Nora. The final individual in the picture is another young man called **John Jones**, who had his first encounter with the enemy as a sixteen-year-old. Jones emigrated to Oregon in the United States after the Civil War but later returned to his native county to take up farming. Another comrade, **Michael O'Sullivan**, was depicted in the first painting that hangs in the Áras but was, like Moylan, omitted from the second painting. However, in Moylan's view, O'Sullivan was one of the most outstanding fighters in all of Cork during the War of Independence. He characterised O'Sullivan as a nervous, gentle and imaginative man who quickly crushed any fears he might have had at the beginning of the conflict and turned himself into the most fearless fighter Moylan ever knew. Like his comrades, O'Sullivan was imbued in the ideal of nationalism and his father was a captain of a local Moonlighter group that agitated against landlords for fairer rents back in the nineteenth century. Michael O'Sullivan was, like his father, a gentle unselfish type who was entirely sincere and was committed to seeing an end to British rule in Ireland.

The men depicted in Keating's picture were individuals in their own right and each contributed in no small way to the cause of their country's independence. While they are six in number in the painting, they, as a group, represent all the fighting men of the IRA across the country during that tumultuous time in Ireland's history. The decision to create the painting was an inspired one, not just in terms of its artistic value, but it also went on to provide modern Ireland with iconic visible evidence of the bravery, commitment and determination of all the fearless fighters who secured the country's much-longed-for independence ably led by Sean Moylan and the much-vaunted men of the South.

Appendix

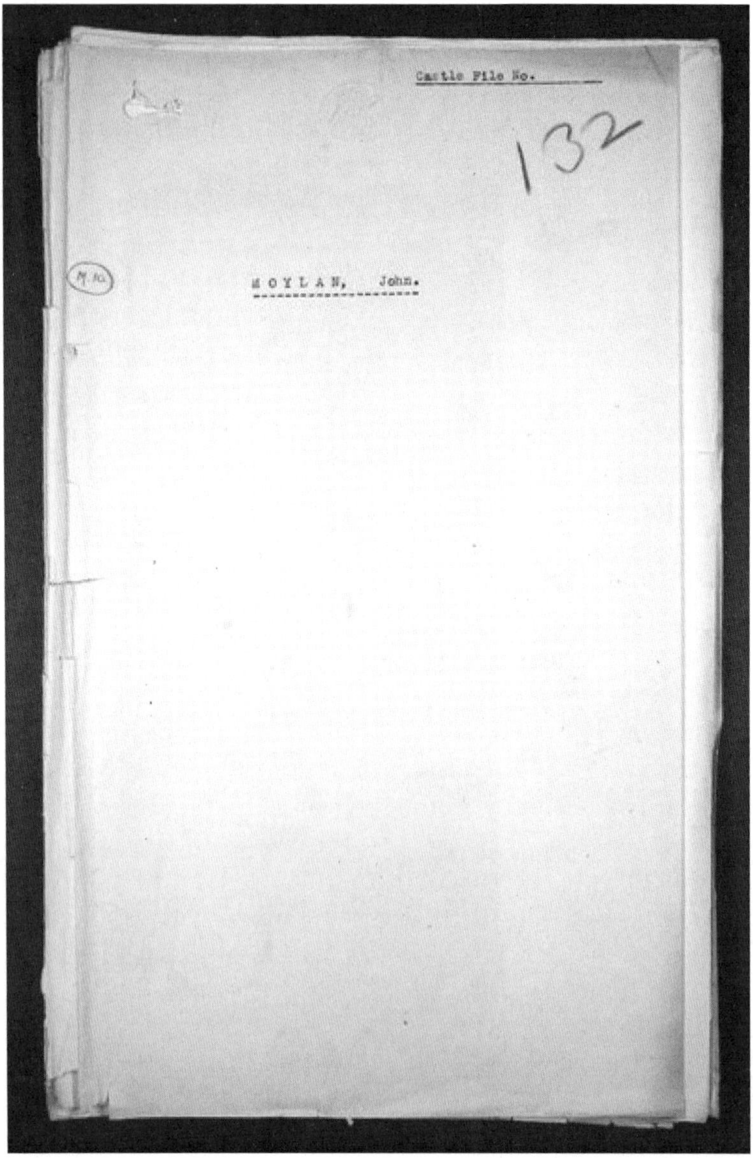

VIEWED FROM BROADWAY

Sean Moylan Writes To "O.C., Britain"

SPLIT IN U.S.A.

Mr. Laurence Ginnell And "His Fool Stunts"

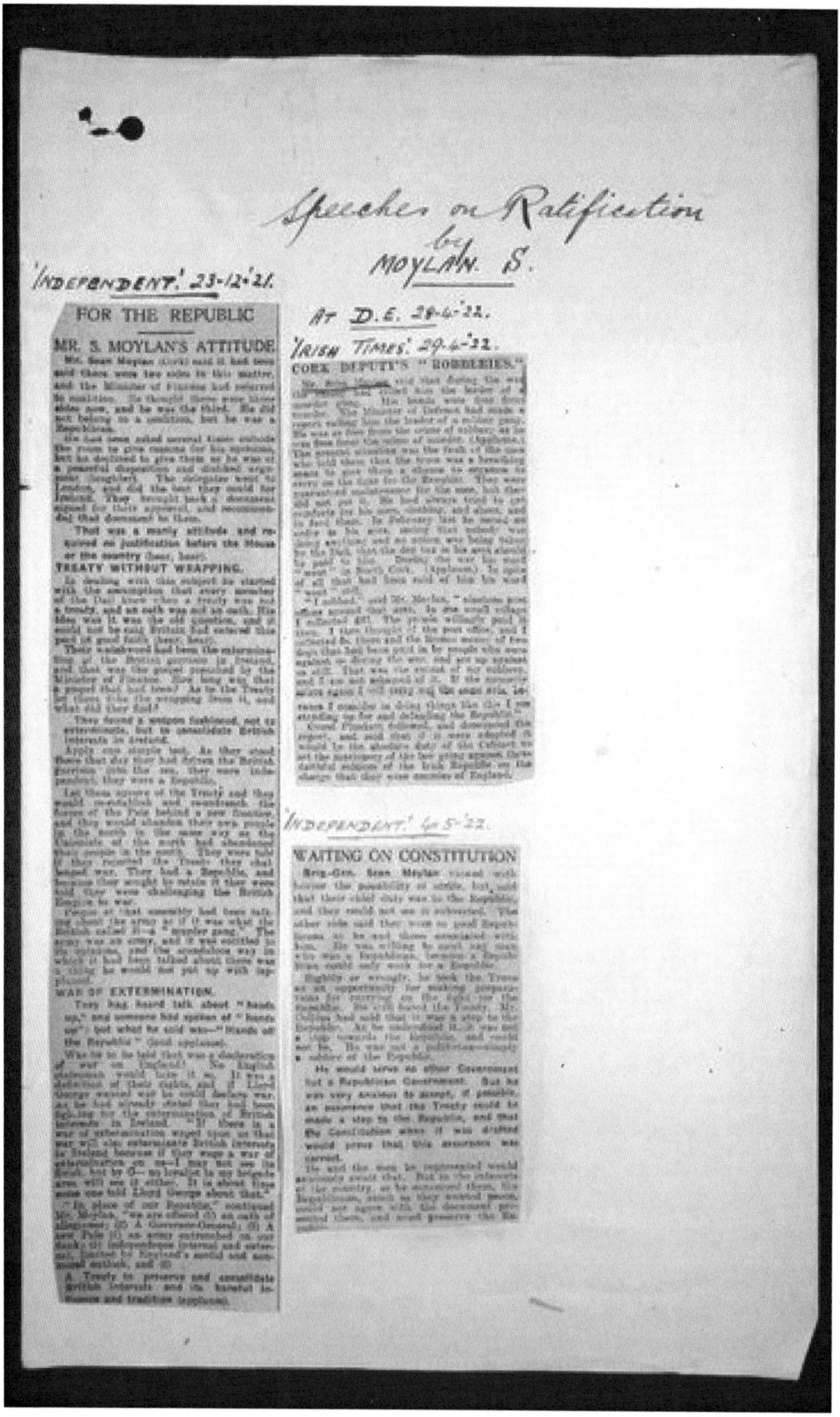
Speeches on Ratification
by
MOYLAN. S.
'INDEPENDENT.' 23-12-'21.
FOR THE REPUBLIC
MR. S. MOYLAN'S ATTITUDE
TREATY WITHOUT WRAPPING.
WAR OF EXTERMINATION.
AT D.E. 28-4-'22.
'IRISH TIMES.' 29-4-'22.
CORK DEPUTY'S "ROBBERIES."
'INDEPENDENT.' 6-5-'22.
WAITING ON CONSTITUTION

EXTRACT FROM "REPUBLICAN WAR NEWS No: 2" dated JUNE 29th.

P R O C L A M A T I O N.

FELLOW CITIZENS OF THE IRISH REPUBLIC.

The fateful hour has come. At the dictation of our hereditary enemy our rightful cause is being treacherously assailed by recreant Irishmen. The crash of arms and the boom of artillery reverberate in this supreme test of the Nation's destiny.

Gallant soldiers of the Irish Republic stand vigorously firm in its defence and worthily uphold their noblest traditions. The sacred spirits of the Illustrious Dead are with us in this great struggle. "Death before Dishonour" being an unchangeable principle of our national faith as it of theirs, still inspires us to emulate their glorious effort.

We, therefore, appeal to all citizens who have withstood unflinchingly the oppression of the enemy during the past six years to rally to the support of the Republic and recognise that the resistance now being offered is but the continuance of the struggle that was suspended by the truce with the British. We especially appeal to our former comrades of the Irish Republic to return to that allegiance and thus guard the Nation's honour from the infamous stigma that her sons aided her foes in retaining a hateful domination over her.

Confident of victory and of maintaining Ireland's Independence this appeal is issued by the Army Executive on behalf of the Irish Republican Army.

(Signed). Comdt. Gen. LIAM MELLOWES. Comdt. Gen. Rory O'CONNOR.
Comdt. Gen. JOE. McKELVEY. Comdt. Gen. EARNAN O'MAILLE.
Comdt. Gen. SEUMAS ROBINSON. Comdt. Gen. SEAN MOYLAN.
Comdt. Gen. MICHAEL KILROY. Comdt. Gen. FRANK BARRETT.
Comdt. Gen. THOMAS DERRIG. Comdt. T. BARRY, Col. Comdt.
F.O.'FAOLAIN, Brig. Gen. J. O'CONNOR, Gen. LIAM LYNCH.
Comdt. Gen. LIAM DEASY. Comdt. PEADAR O'DONNELL.
P. RUTLEDGE.

29th. JUNE, 1922.

Irish Times 27/10

A RIVAL DAIL PROCLAIMED.

<u>REPUBLICANS' SECRET SESSION.</u>

<u>MR. DE VALERA AGAIN "PRESIDENT."</u>

The daily bulletin issued by the irregulars makes the following announcement under Thursday's date:-

"DAIL EIREANN, the Parliament and Government of the Republic, met yesterday in secret session - the former Deputy Speaker presiding.

"A Clerk of the House was appointed, and the following resolutions passed:-

"1. WHEREAS the Speaker (Ceann Comhairle) and the other appointed Executive Officers, in disregard of their duty, and in open disobedience to the <u>mandamus</u> of the Supreme Court, have refused to summon Dail Eireann, the duly elected Parliament and Government of the Republic;

"AND WHEREAS, notwithstanding their oaths and public pledges to maintain the Republic, these officers, abetted by other members of Dail Eireann, have in this, and divers other ways, endeavoured, illegally and unconstitutionally, to subvert the Republic and its Government, Dail Eireann; and with foreign aid have joined in a traitorous conspiracy and armed revolt with that intent, pretending to establish a so-called Free State and a Provisional (Partition) Parliament, the creatures and subordinates of an alien Legislature, and purposing thus to destroy the independent sovereignty of the nation and the integrity of its ancient territory:

TWO Rival Dail.

"THEREFORE, we, the faithful Deputies of Dail Eireann, assembled to maintain the Republic and to secure the continuity of independent government for the whole of Ireland, in the name of all loyal citizens of the Republic, and by the express wish of the soldiers fighting in its defence, call upon the former President, Eamonn de Valera, to resume the Presidency, and to nominate a Council of State and Executive Ministers to assist him in carrying on the Government until such time as the Parliament of the Republic is allowed freely to assemble or the people are allowed by a free election to decide how they shall be governed.

"2. That Eamonn de Valera be hereby appointed President of the Republic and Chief Executive of the State.

"3. That the following, nominated by the President, be hereby appointed the Council of State:-

The President.

Austin Stack, T.D.	Sean O'Mahony, T.D.
Robert Barton, T.D.	Mrs O'Callaghan, T.D.
Count Plunkett, T.D.	Mary MacSwiney, T.D.
J.J. O'Kelly, T.D.	P.J. Ruttledge, T.D.
Laurence Ginnell, T.D.	Sean Moylan, T.D. ✓
Sean T. O'Kelly, T.D.	M.P. Colivet, T.D.

"4. That, pending the next meeting of the Dail, we hereby empower the Council of State to sanction such Ministers and Executive Officers of State as the President may nominate and may have the Council's approval.

<u>NOTE</u>. Reports indicate that about the last week in October, 1922, considerable activity was noticeable near the residence of De VALERA, at "Glenvar", Blackrock, and it is possible that Sean MOYLAN took the opportunity of using the safe conduct reported to have been issued to him by Maj-Gen.DALTON of the F.S.Forces to interview De VALERA and other Republican Leaders with the result shown above.

PROCLAMATION BY THE I.R.A.

"TO MAINTAIN THE REPUBLIC."

THE GOVERNMENT ATTACKED.

Last night the Irish Times received the following document:-

IRISH REPUBLICAN ARMY.
PROCLAMATION.

Last December certain representatives of the nation, yielding to English threats of war, violated their pledges and their oaths, and entered into an agreement subversive of the independence of the nation and destructive of its territorial integrity.

Since that time these representatives and their adherents have been engaged in corrupting and seducing soldiers and citizens of the Republic from their allegiance, and, in violation of the Constitution, of a special decree of Dail Eireann, and of their own express undertakings to maintain the Republic, have suppressed the legitimate Parliament and Judiciary, usurped the Government of the State, and now, by the instigation of the English and with English aid, are endeavouring traitorously to destroy the Republic by force of arms, waging illegal war upon it, and proclaiming death, exile, or imprisonment to all its faithful citizens, though they are aware, as everyone in Ireland is aware, that the people desire the continuance of the Republic, and that, given a free choice, they would vote for it in an overwhelming majority.

In these circumstances, in order to preserve the continuity of independent Irish Government, and the better to organise the resources of the Republic in its defence, we, on behalf of the soldiers of the Republic, acting in the spirit of our oath as the final custodians of the Republic, and interpreting the desire of all true citizens of the Republic, have called upon the former President, Eamonn de Valera, and the faithful members of Dail Eireann, to form a Government, which they have done.

Accordingly, in the name of the Army, we hereby proclaim Eamonn de Valera to be President of the Republic, with

Austin Stack, T.D.	Sean O'Mahoney, T.D.
Robert Barton, T.D.	Mrs O'Callaghan, T.D.
Count Plunkett, T.D.	Mary MacSwiney, T.D.
J.J. O'Kelly, T.D.	P.J. Ruttledge, T.D.
Laurence Ginnell, T.D.	Sean Moylan, T.D.
Sean T. O'Kelly, T.D.	M.P. Colivet, T.D.:

as Council of State, and declare such Cabinet as they shall appoint to be temporarily the Supreme Executive of the Republic and the State, until such time as the elected Parliament of the Republic can freely assemble, or the people, being rid of external aggression, are at liberty to decide freely how they are to be governed, and what shall be their political relations with other countries.

On behalf of the Army, we pledge to that Executive our allegiance and our support in all its legitimate efforts to maintain and defend the Republic, and we call upon all our comrades and loyal fellow-citizens, and upon our kin throughout the world, to join with us in reasserting our ancient right to be a free people and a free nation, owning allegiance to no foreign authority whatever.

Signed on behalf of the Army of the Republic:

Liam Lynch, Chief of Staff;	Frank Barrett, O/C.1st Western Div.
Liam Deasy, Deputy Chief of Staff.	Seumas Robinson, " 2nd Southern Div.
	Tom Barry, Operations Staff.
E.O'Maille, Assistant Chief of Staff.	Sean Moylan, O/C.Cork No.3 Brigade.
	P.Whelan, O/C.Waterford Brigade.
Con Moloney, Adjutant General.	Joe O'Connor, O/C. 3rd Bn.,
Tom Derrig, Asst.Adjt.General.	Dublin 1st Brigade.
Sean Lehane, O/C.1st & 2nd Northern Div.	
Frank Aiken, O/C.4th Northern Div.	

MOYLAN. John. Main Street, Newmarket, Co. Cork.
Kiskean, Newmarket, Co. Cork.

Age, 40. (1921).

Occupation, Carpenter.

Description:- Height 5'9". Light brown hair. Grey eyes. Sallow complexion. Sturdy built. Wears pinc-nez.

Elected Sinn Fein M.P. for N. M. W. S. and S-E. Cork, May 1921.

Prior to May 1921 Election, was a Member of Agricultural Loan Bank Committee, Dail Eireann.

Member of Inner Circle I.R.A. (Information from D.I. personally).

Arbitrator for An Dail Labour Department ("Irish Indpdt" 22-11-21).

Commandant, 6th Newmarket Battalion, 2nd Cork Brigade, I.R.A. from the time of its formation.

Sentenced to 12 months imprisonment on the 15th August 1918 for being in possession of seditious documents.

Escaped from Cork Lunatic Asylum May 21st 1919. (IX/0150).

<u>Took part in the following outrages:-</u>

Meelin Ambush, 4th January 1921.
Kingwilliamstown Ambush, 28th January 1921.
Cloonbannin Ambush, 5th March 1921.
Millstreet Ambush.

Arrested 16th May 1921 near Kiskean for having in his possession a revolver, a rifle, and two bombs, and for firing at Crown Forces. He also had documents in his possession. (File No.649 A).
He was identified as the leader in the Kingwilliamstown Ambush when Major HOLMES, D.C. was killed. (W.I.S.15-3-21).
Tried by Court Martial 4th June 1921 at Cork and sentenced to 15 years Penal Servitude. (It was disclosed at the Court Martial that MOYLAN had saved wounded R.I.C. men from being shot by the I.R.A.)
(Ext. "Irish Times" dated 8th June 1921).

Released 8th August 1921 as a T.D. to attend the Peace Conference at the Mansion House, Dublin. (Casualty Return G/234/1).

Delivered a hostile speech at Charleville. (IX/0038 dated 30-9-21).

Inspected the I.R.A. Course of Instruction at Boherboy, Co. Cork for rebels of the Nad District during week ending 8th October 1921, and expressed dissatisfaction at their progress. (IX/0207)14-10-21.

Has resumed Command of No. 2. (N) Cork Brigade, I.R.A. at Nad. (IX/0173 dated 10-10-21).

Is at present living in the house of a man named Collins somewhere between Mallow and Buttevant where a Course of Instruction is being held, possibly at Twopothouse Cross Roads. (IX/0173 dated 10-10-21).

/Attended

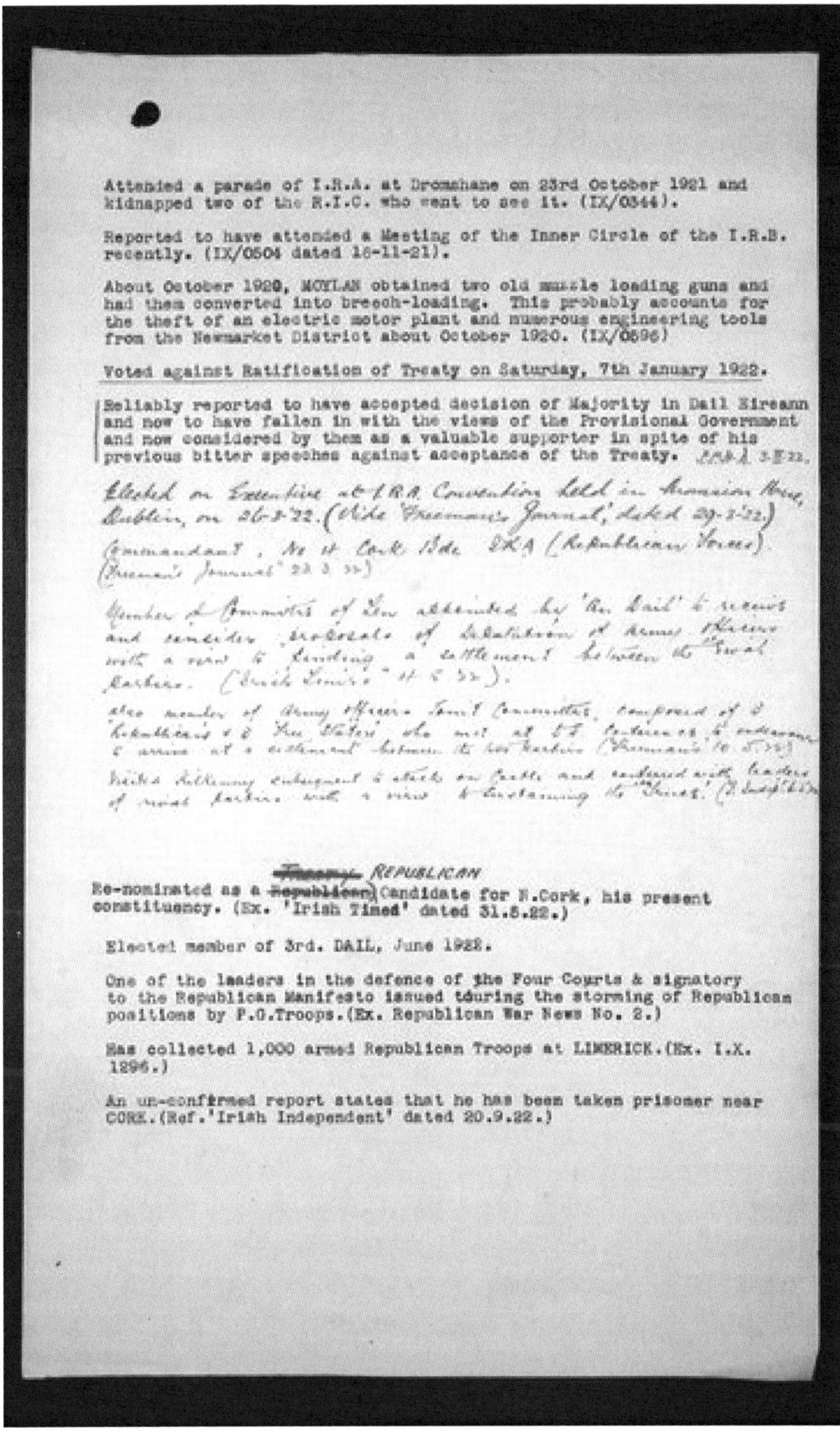

Attended a parade of I.R.A. at Dromahane on 23rd October 1921 and kidnapped two of the R.I.C. who went to see it. (IX/0344).

Reported to have attended a Meeting of the Inner Circle of the I.R.B. recently. (IX/0504 dated 16-11-21).

About October 1920, MOYLAN obtained two old muzzle loading guns and had them converted into breech-loading. This probably accounts for the theft of an electric motor plant and numerous engineering tools from the Newmarket District about October 1920. (IX/0596)

Voted against Ratification of Treaty on Saturday, 7th January 1922.

Reliably reported to have accepted decision of Majority in Dail Eireann and now to have fallen in with the views of the Provisional Government and now considered by them as a valuable supporter in spite of his previous bitter speeches against acceptance of the Treaty. [illegible] 3.2.22.

Elected on Executive at I.R.A. Convention held in Mansion House, Dublin, on 26-3-22. (Vide 'Freeman's Journal', dated 29-3-22.)

Commandant, No [illegible] Cork Bde. IRA (Republican Forces). ('Freeman's Journal' 23.3.22)

Member of Committee of Ten appointed by 'An Dail' to receive and consider proposals of [illegible] of Army Officers with a view to finding a settlement between the rival parties. ('Irish Times' [illegible]).

Also member of Army Officers Joint Committee composed of 5 'Republicans' & 5 'Free Staters' who met at [illegible] to endeavour to arrive at a settlement between the two parties ('Freeman's' [illegible])

[illegible] Kilkenny [illegible] to attack on Castle and conferred with leaders of rival parties with a view to sustaining the 'Truce'. ([illegible])

~~[illegible]~~ *REPUBLICAN*
Re-nominated as a ~~Republican~~ Candidate for N.Cork, his present constituency. (Ex. 'Irish Timed' dated 31.5.22.)

Elected member of 3rd. DAIL, June 1922.

One of the leaders in the defence of the Four Courts & signatory to the Republican Manifesto issued during the storming of Republican positions by P.G.Troops.(Ex. Republican War News No. 2.)

Has collected 1,000 armed Republican Troops at LIMERICK.(Ex. I.X. 1296.)

An un-confirmed report states that he has been taken prisoner near CORK.(Ref.'Irish Independent' dated 20.9.22.)

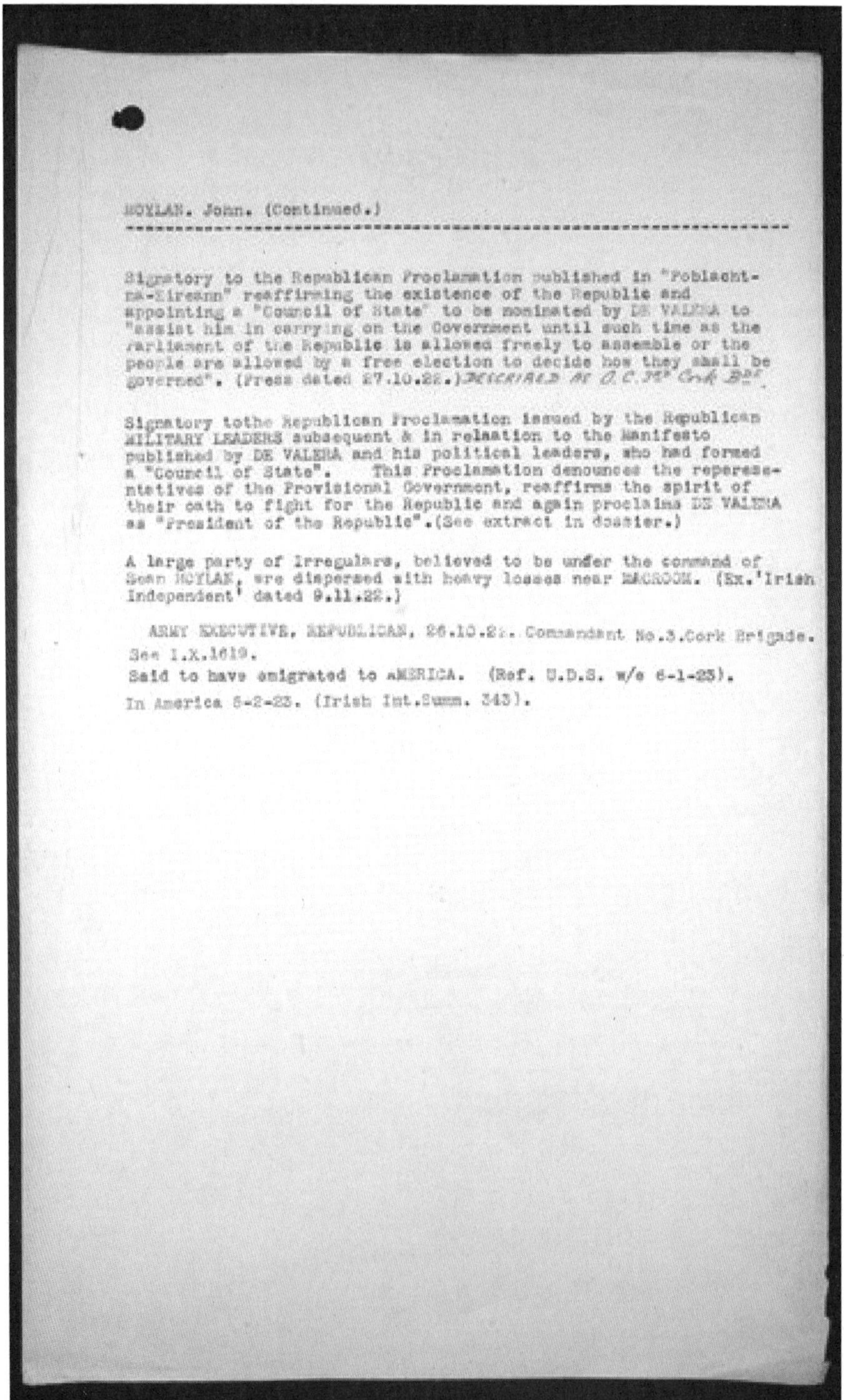

MOYLAN. John. (Continued.)

Signatory to the Republican Proclamation published in "Poblacht-na-Eireann" reaffirming the existence of the Republic and appointing a "Council of State" to be nominated by DE VALERA to "assist him in carrying on the Government until such time as the Parliament of the Republic is allowed freely to assemble or the people are allowed by a free election to decide how they shall be governed". (Press dated 27.10.22.) DESCRIBED AS O.C. 3rd Cork Bde.

Signatory tothe Republican Proclamation issued by the Republican MILITARY LEADERS subsequent & in relaation to the Manifesto published by DE VALERA and his political leaders, who had formed a "Council of State". This Proclamation denounces the reperese-ntatives of the Provisional Government, reaffirms the spirit of their oath to fight for the Republic and again proclaims DE VALERA as "President of the Republic". (See extract in dossier.)

A large party of Irregulars, believed to be under the command of Sean MOYLAN, are dispersed with heavy losses near MACROOM. (Ex. 'Irish Independent' dated 9.11.22.)

ARMY EXECUTIVE, REPUBLICAN, 26.10.22. Commandant No.3.Cork Brigade. See I.X.1619.
Said to have emigrated to AMERICA. (Ref. U.D.S. w/e 6-1-23).
In America 5-2-23. (Irish Int.Summ. 343).

References

Chapter 1

1. Brian Lenihan, Commemoration Speech at Kiskeam, *Irish Examiner*, 12 November 2007
2. Aideen Carroll, *Sean Moylan, Rebel Leader*, Mercier Press, 2006, p.20
3. Sean Moylan, Witness Statement No. 838, Bureau of Military History, p.14
4. Ibid., p.17
5. Carroll, p.24
6. Moylan W/S 838, p.23

Chapter 2

7. Moylan W/S 838, pp.65–66
8. Carroll, pp.30–32
9. Moylan W/S 838, p.72

Chapter 3

10. Moylan W/S 838, p.82
11. Ibid., p.82
12. Ibid., p.30

Chapter 4

13. Moylan W/S 838, p.88
14. Ibid., pp.88–89
15. Ibid., p.89
16. Ibid., pp.89–90
17. *The Irish Times*, 1 July 1920

18. *The Times* (London), 4 August 1920
19. Moylan W/S 838, p.94
20. Ibid., p.95
21. Ibid., p.98
22. Ibid., p.98

Chapter 5

23. Moylan W/S 838, p.101
24. Ibid., p.105
25. Shea, Patrick, *Voices and the Sound of Drums*, Blackstaff Press, Belfast, 1981, p.45
26. Moylan W/S 838, p.119
27. Paddy O'Brien, Witness Statement No. 764, Bureau of Military History

Chapter 6

28. Moylan W/S 838, p.136
29. Ibid., p.138
30. Ibid., p.147
31. Ibid.
32. Ibid.

Chapter 7

33. Moylan W/S 838, pp.156–157
34. Ibid., p.159
35. *The Irish Times*, 6 January 1921
36. Ibid.
37. Moylan W/S 838, p.161
38. Ibid., pp.162–164
39. Ibid., p.165
40. Ibid., pp.166–167
41. James Cashman, Witness Statement No. 1270, Bureau of Military History
42. Moylan W/S 838, p.170

Chapter 8

43. Moylan W/S 838, pp.178–179
44. Ibid., p.181
45. Ibid., p.183
46. Ibid., p.185
47. Ibid., p.187
48. Ibid., p.187

Chapter 9

49. Con Meany, Witness Statement No. 787, Bureau of Military History, No. 787
50. Moylan W/S 838, p.195
51. Carroll, p.100
52. Moylan W/S 838, p.197
53. Ibid., pp.198–199
54. Ibid., p.200
55. Strickland Papers 6th Division Record of the Rebellion, p.90
56. Moylan W/S 838, p.204

Chapter 10

57. Moylan W/S 838, p.208
58. Ibid., p.210
59. Ibid., pp.213–214
60. Ibid., p.214
61. Ibid., p.215
62. Ibid., pp.217–218
63. Ibid., p.219
64. Ibid., p.220

Chapter 11

65. Moylan W/S 838, pp.224–225
66. Tom Barry, *Guerrilla Days in Ireland*, Irish Press, 1949, p.157

67. Tom Barry, *The Reality of the Anglo-Irish War 1920–21 in West Cork. Refutations, Corrections and Comments on Liam Deasy's Towards Ireland Free*, Anvil Press, Tralee, 1974, p.43.
68. Moylan W/S 838, p.227
69. Ibid., pp.229–230

Chapter 12

70. Lieutenant R.M. Grazebrook, Diary, Soldiers of Gloucestershire Museum, p.15
71. Captain A.H. Richards, Memoir, Soldiers of Gloucestershire Museum, p.1
72. Moylan W/S 838, p.247
73. Ibid., p.237
74. Ibid., p.238
75. Ibid., p.241
76. Grazebrook, pp.30–31

Chapter 13

77. Moylan W/S 838, p.244
78. Ibid., pp.245–246
79. Ibid., p.246
80. Grazebrook, p.33
81. 6th Division Record of the Rebellion, Strickland Papers, p.107
82. Moylan W/S 838, pp.249–250
83. Ibid., p.250
84. Grazebrook, p.240
85. Moylan W/S 838, p.251
86. Ibid., pp.252–253
87. Ibid., p.253

Chapter 14

88. Moylan W/S 838, p.255
89. Carroll, p.141
90. Ibid.

91. Moylan W/S 838, p.257
92. Ibid., pp.258–259
93. Ibid., p.259
94. *Cork Examiner*, 31 May 1921
95. Carroll, p.147
96. *Cork Examiner*, 31 May 1921
97. Ibid.
98. Hansard H.C. Debates 1 June 1921, Vol. 142, Col. 1047–1048
99. Ibid., Col. 1223
100. *The Irish Times*, 6 June 1921

Chapter 15

101. Hansard H.C. Debates 21 June 1921, Vol. 143, Col. 1106
102. Moylan W/S 838, p.265
103. Ibid.
104. Ibid., pp.266–267
105. Ibid., pp.268–269
106. Carroll, p.164
107. Moylan W/S 838, pp.271–272

Chapter 16

108. Pro Cab/24/136, National Archives, Kew, 6 April 1922
109. Moylan W/S 838, pp.272–273
110. 6th Division Records of the Rebellion, Strickland Papers, p.130
111. Pro Cab/118/26/295, National Archives, Kew
112. Moylan W/S 838, p.274
113. Dáil Éireann Treaty Debates, 14 December 1921, Vol. T No. 2
114. Ibid.
115. Ibid.
116. Dáil Éireann Treaty Debates, 10 January 1922 Vol. T No. 17
117. Dáil Éireann Treaty Debates, 17 December 1921 Vol. T No. 5
118. Dáil Éireann Treaty Debates, 14 December 1921 Vol. T No. 2
119. Dáil Éireann Treaty Debates, 19 December 1921 Vol. T No. 6
120. Dáil Éireann Treaty Debates, 17 December 1921 Vol. T No. 5
121. Dáil Éireann Treaty Debates, 22 December 1921 Vol. T No. 9

Chapter 17

122. Eamonn Duggan, '1922 A Year of Uncertainty and Turmoil', *Ireland's Own*, 9 December 2022, p.4
123. Ibid.
124. Ibid., p.5
125. Carroll, p.175
126. Michael Hopkinson, *Green Against Green, The Civil War*, Gill Books, 2004, p.67
127. Ibid.
128. Dáil Éireann Treaty Debates, Vol. S2, Col. 340, 28 April 1922
129. Hopkinson, p.93
130. Ibid., p.94
131. Dáil Éireann Treaty Debates, Vol. S2, Col. 363, 3 May 1922, The National Situation

Chapter 18

132. Hopkinson, p.75
133. Ibid., p.123
134. Ibid.
135. Ibid., p.144
136. Ibid.
137. Ibid.
138. Ibid.
139. Ibid.
140. Ibid.
141. *New York Times*, 14 July 1922
142. *The Irish Times*, 9 November 1922
143. Eamonn Duggan, 'The Civil War. The American and British View', *Ireland's Own*, 7 April 2023
144. Ibid.
145. Ibid.
146. McGarrity Papers 17466/1, National Library of Ireland
147. Ibid.
148. Ibid.
149. Hopkinson, pp.257–258
150. Eamonn Duggan, 'Frank Aiken, The Freedom Fighter Who Delivered Peace', *Ireland's Own*, 5 May 2023

Chapter 19

151. McGarrity Papers 17466/1, National Library of Ireland
152. Carroll, p.220

Chapter 20

153. Carroll, p.234
154. Dáil Éireann Treaty Debates, 2 September 1939, The Emergency
155. Eamon de Valera, Speech to the League of Nations, July 1936, Documents on Irish Foreign Policy, Vol. 4, Doc. 347
156. *The Irish Times*, 28 August 1940
157. Dublin City Library and Archive, North Strand and Donore Road Bombing Records, CMD/1941/2
158. *The Irish Times*, 2 June 1941

Chapter 21

159. Carroll, p.252
160. Ibid.
161. Ibid., p.253
162. Dáil Éireann Treaty Debates, Vol. 145, Col. 947–951, 23 April 1954, Adjournment Debate, Punishment of Industrial Schoolboy
163. Carroll, p.260
164. Ibid., p.261
165. Ibid., p.262
166. Ibid., pp.262–263
167. Dublin City Library and Archive, 24 March 1957
168. Dáil Éireann Treaty Debates, Vol. 161, Col. 1500–1508, 16 May 1957
169. Carroll, p.264
170. *Kerryman*, 23 November 1957

Sources

Sean Moylan, Witness Statement No. 838, Bureau of Military History
Aideen Carroll, *Sean Moylan. Rebel Leader*, Mercier Press, 2010
Michael Hopkinson, *Green Against Green, The Civil War*, Gill Books, 2004
Tom Barry, *Guerrilla Days in Ireland*, Irish Press, 1949
Tom Barry, *The Reality of the Anglo-Irish War 1920–21 in West Cork Refutations, Corrections and Comments on Liam Deasy's Towards Ireland Free*, Anvil Press, Tralee, 1974
Irish Examiner, 12 November 2007
The Irish Times
The London Times
Paddy O'Brien, Witness Statement No. 764, Bureau of Military History
Con Meany, Witness Statement No. 787. p.18, Bureau of Military History
James Cashman, Witness Statement No. 1270, Bureau of Military History
Strickland Papers, 6th Division Record of the Rebellion
Soldiers of Gloucestershire Museum
Cork Examiner
Hansard House of Commons Debates
Dáil Éireann Treaty Debates
Eamonn Duggan, various articles, *Ireland's Own*
New York Times
McGarrity Papers 17466/1, National Library of Ireland
Eamon de Valera, Speech to the League of Nations, July 1936
Dublin City Library and Archive
Sunday Independent
Kerryman